The PM System
Preventive Medicine for Total Health

J.A. Muir Gray, MD, MRCGP, MRCP (Glas), FFCM, is a specialist in Community Medicine, based at the Radcliffe Infirmary in Oxford. In helping to promote preventive medicine in the community, he has served on Working Parties for the Royal College of General Practitioners, has published numerous articles and books, including 'Essentials of Preventive Medicine' and 'Cancer Risks and Cancer Preventions'. He is currently working with the Faculty of Community Medicine on a new Cervical Cancer screening programme, and is responsible for collating and organising the educational information necessary to implement the Forrest Report, instigator of Britain's first national breast screening project.

Marie Johnston, BSc, PhD, Dip Psych, FBPsS, is Senior Lecturer in Clinical Psychology at the Royal Free Hospital of Medicine and Chair of the Department of Psychology of the Royal Free Hospital and Hampstead Community, London. She has published widely in the field of Health Psychology, including publications on the work of a clinical psychologist in primary care. She is joint author of 'Psychological Problems in General Practice', and joint editor of 'Stress and Medical Procedures' and 'Health Psychology: Research and Reviews'. In 1986 she was elected as the first Chair of the Health Psychology Section of the British Psychological Society.

Susan Michie, BA, M Phil, D Phil, is Senior Clinical Psychologist and Honorary Lecturer at the Royal Free Hospital, London. She has published widely in the fields of developmental and clinical psychology, and is currently involved in research investigating psychological aspects of pregnancy and childbirth.

Anna Bradley, BA, is a project researcher and writer in the field of diet and health for a leading consumer organisation in London.

Alex Clarke, **Jo Willison**, **Robert Bor** and **Kate Ridout** contributed to the preventive programs and are all clinical psychologists working in the Department of Psychology at the Royal Free Hospital, London.

THE PM SYSTEM

Preventive Medicine
for Total Health

Dr J.A. Muir Gray
Consultant Editor

ARROW BOOKS

Arrow Books Limited
62-65 Chandos Place, London WC2N 4NW

An imprint of Century Hutchinson Limited

London Melbourne Sydney Auckland
Johannesburg and agencies throughout
the world

Conceived, edited, designed and produced by
Pilot Productions Limited
17 Munster Road, London SW6 4ER

First published in 1989

Acknowledgements
The Weight/Height chart, page 22, from *Treat Obesity Seriously*
by J. S. Garrow (Churchill Livingstone, 1981).
The Fibre questionnaire on page 37 from the August 1986
edition of *Which?* magazine, published by the Consumer
Association.
Many of the addresses, page 283 etc, from The Patients
Association, 18 Charing Cross Road, London, WC2H OHR.
Telephone 01 240 0671.

Typeset by Dorchester Typesetting Limited, Dorchester, Dorset
Printed and bound in Great Britain by
Hazell, Watson & Viney Limited, Aylesbury, Buckinghamshire

ISBN 0 09 959020 4

CONTENTS

How to Use the PM System

The PM System operates like a computerised 'expert' system. It uses self-diagnosis to pinpoint risk of ill-health inherent in a person's

genetic history
environment
occupation
personality
lifestyle
personal habits
behaviour
thinking
moods and feelings

Self-diagnosis then leads to preventive programs designed to reduce risk to serious physical and psychological illness.

1. If you suffer regularly from a symptom or group of symptoms – headache, tiredness, for example – and wish to prevent them in the future, turn to the Symptom Chart (page 7), locate your symptom(s) and turn to an appropriate Profile Scan. The Profile Scans will direct you to Preventive Programs designed to overcome the problems that are causing your symptom(s) to recur. If in doubt as to which scan to consult, work through them in the order listed against your symptom(s).

2. If you are simply interested in analysing the health properties of your personality, emotions, habits, lifestyle, etc, turn to the Profile Scan Index (page 21) and enter the PM System wherever you like.

3. If you do not suffer regularly from any of the symptoms listed in the Symptom Chart, but are concerned that you may be at risk to a particular physical or psychological illness, move directly to the Vulnerability Scans (Index, page 103) and thence to the Preventive Programs.

NOTES: All the scans are questionnaires. Some require you to tick YES or NO to the questions, others to produce a score from your YES/NO answers. The scores have no relevance other than as a means to direct you to appropriate preventive programs.

The Preventive Programs are referred to throughout by their labels **P1**, **P2**, etc. Use the Program Index (page 156) to locate the program you want. Before embarking on any program read the Program Introduction (page 153). If a program fails to help you, turn to **P1**, and then either return to the original program or to one suggested by **P1**.

The Symptom Chart

| SYMPTOM | WARNING SIGNS: CONSULT YOUR DOCTOR | PROFILE SCANS & INDEX |

Select a Profile Scan appropriate to your symptom by turning to the page number listed in column 3. In the few cases where 2 scans begin on the same page, they are referred to as a and b in the order they appear. If you are not sure which scan is appropriate to your symptom, work through them in the order listed.

Abdomen, distension of — Always consult a doctor.

heavy feeling, quick satiation at meals — Always consult a doctor.

pain in — Consult a doctor with any unexplained abdominal pain. In particular, if sudden, persistent or un-relieved by vomiting; if present in lower areas of abdomen or below ribs on right side; if experienced during pregnancy or cramp-like in lower abdomen after giving birth. — Habits & Lifestyle, **50** / Emotional Profile, **71, 89, 97**

Aches *see* **Pain**

Acne — Personality Profile, **62** / Physical Health, **31**

Anger *see also* **Irritability** — Personality Profile, **68, 59a, 59b** / Emotional Profile, **92, 71**

Anxiety — Emotional Profile, **89, 96** / Personality Profile, **68**

Apathy — Habits & Lifestyle, **49, 50** / Emotional Profile, **94, 71** / Fitness Profile, **22** / Environment & Occupation, **45**

SYMPTOM	WARNING SIGNS: CONSULT YOUR DOCTOR	PROFILE SCANS & INDEX
Appetite, loss of *see also* **Weight Loss**	If appetite loss is combined with nausea or vomiting or a heavy feeling in the stomach; if you are pregnant, or you feel pain below ribs on right side.	Emotional Profile, **89**, **94** Personality Profile, **67b**
Apprehension *see* **Fear, Confidence**		
Back Pain	If accompanied by weakness in legs, or difficulty passing water, or a dull ache/hard mass in testes.	Physical Health, **24b** Environment & Occupation, **45** Personality Profile, **59a** Emotional Profile, **97**
Balance, loss of *see* **Dizziness**		
Belching		Habits & Lifestyle, **48** Emotional Profile, **89**
Bleeding	Any unusual bleeding or discharge.	
Blurred Vision	If accompanied by nausea, vomiting, or pain in head or eye.	Physical Health, **41** Habits & Lifestyle, **49**, **50** Emotional Profile, **89**, **71**
Blushing		Personality Profile, **62** Emotional Profile, **89**, **71**
Boredom		Emotional Profile, **94**, **71** Fitness Profile, **24b**, **28**
Breast Pain	If you are breast-feeding, consult your health visitor. If part or all of one breast is inflamed, see your doctor, you may have a breast abscess.	Emotional Profile, **97**

SYMPTOM	WARNING SIGNS: CONSULT YOUR DOCTOR	PROFILE SCANS & INDEX
Breathing, problems with	If accompanied by chest pain, or if noticeably more breathless in last 3 months.	Habits & Lifestyle, **57** Fitness Profile, **22** Emotional Profile, **89**, **91**, **71** Physical Health, **38**
overbreathing		Emotional Profile, **89**, **91**, **71**
Butterflies in Stomach		Emotional Profile, **89**, **91** Personality Profile, **62**
Chest Pain	If it occurs with a cough, or when you exert yourself or are under emotional stress. If any chest pain fails to abate after resting.	
Chills	If accompanied by fever.	Emotional Profile, **96**
Concentration, lack of	If an event, illness or injury precipitated the condition.	Physical Health, **41** Emotional Profile, **89**, **92**, **94**, **71** Habits & Lifestyle, **49**, **50**
Conception, difficulties with		Relationships, Sex & Reproduction, **101**, **98**
Confidence, lack of		Personality Profile, **62** Emotional Profile, **89**, **91**, **94**
Constipation	If persistent, or if constipation alternates with diarrhoea.	Physical Health, **35b**
Cough	If it persists for more than 3 weeks, or is accompanied by phlegm.	Habits & Lifestyle, **57** Fitness Profile, **22** Environment & Occupation, **45**
Cramp *see* **Muscular Pain**		
Deafness *see* **Hearing Problems**		

SYMPTOM	WARNING SIGNS: CONSULT YOUR DOCTOR	PROFILE SCANS & INDEX
Depression	If you have recently had a baby. If you have ever had thoughts of suicide. If you lose control of actions or emotions.	Emotional Profile, **94, 71, 96** Relationships, Sex & Reproduction, **98** Habits & Lifestyle, **49, 50**
Diarrhoea	Frequently due to Gastro-enteritis virus or food poisoning. Go to bed; eat nothing but take sips of water. Call doctor if diarrhoea is persistent, if it alternates with constipation, or is bloody.	Emotional Profile, **89, 71** Habits & Lifestyle, **49** Physical Health, **38**
Discharge, vaginal	If there is any unusual discharge or bleeding. Most women have a slight mucous discharge, which may get heavier during pregnancy. Just before labour a 'show' is common.	
Dizziness	If accompanied by numbness or prickling on face, arms, legs, side (especially if on one side only).	Physical Health, **39** Habits & Lifestyle, **50** Emotional Profile, **89, 91, 71** Physical Health, **38**
Double Vision *see also* **Blurred Vision**	If momentary and unexplained.	Physical Health, **41** Habits & Lifestyle, **50** Emotional Profile, **89, 71**
Drowsiness *see* **Fatigue**		
Ear-ache	If persistent or recurring.	Physical Health, **39**
ringing in		Physical Health, **39** Emotional Profile, **71**
Ejaculation, premature		Relationships, Sex & Reproduction, **98**
pain during	Always consult a doctor.	

SYMPTOM	WARNING SIGNS: CONSULT YOUR DOCTOR	PROFILE SCANS & INDEX
Emotional Upset		Emotional Profile, **92, 96, 97**
Eye Pain	If persistent or accompanied by nausea, vomiting, or blurred vision.	Physical Health, **41** Emotional Profile, **89, 71**
Fatigue	If you recently suffered chronic blood loss, have heavy periods, are pregnant, or if you have just had a baby. If you are restless or irritable without apparent reason; if you notice a swelling in your neck; if fatigue is combined with excessive thirst, fever, severe abdominal pain, or with shortness of breath. In any case of sudden or increasing fatigue, if you are engaged in prolonged sports training, or if you have recently had an operation or a viral infection.	Fitness Profile, **22** Emotional Profile, **71, 94, 96** Environment & Occupation, **45** Habits & Lifestyle, **49, 50** Physical Health, **38**
Fear		Emotional Profile, **89, 96, 91, 71** Personality Profile, **67a**
Feelings, absence of		Relationships, Sex & Reproduction, **98** Emotional Profile, **94** Personality Profile, **59b**
of unreality		Emotional Profile, **94**
Fever	If accompanied by rise in temperature above 38°C (100°F) for more than 48 hours, or if temperature exceeds 40°C (104°F).	
Flashing Lights		Physical Health, **38**

SYMPTOM	WARNING SIGNS: CONSULT YOUR DOCTOR	PROFILE SCANS & INDEX
Flatulence		Habits & Lifestyle, **48** Emotional Profile, **89**
Flushes		Emotional Profile, **96, 89**
Forgetfulness *see* **Memory Loss**		
Frustration		Personality Profile, **64**
Giddiness *see* **Dizziness**		
Glands, swollen	Always consult a doctor.	
Guilt		Personality Profile, **66**
Hallucination	Always consult a doctor.	
Headache	If accompanied by vomiting or nausea, weakness or loss of feeling in any part of your body; if persistent after taking paracetamol/aspirin over a period of 12 hours.	Environment & Occupation, **45** Personality Profile, **59a** Emotional Profile, **89, 96, 97, 91, 71** Fitness Profile, **22** Habits & Lifestyle, **49, 50, 57** Physical Health, **38**
Hearing, problems with	If momentary and either partial or complete. If a result of a bang on the head. If you hear voices.	
Heartburn	If accompanied by distended abdomen, a heavy feeling in upper abdomen, or quick satiation at meals.	Habits & Lifestyle, **48** Emotional Profile, **89**
Hoarseness	If lasts for 3 weeks or more.	Habits & Lifestyle, **57**
Hyperactivity		Personality Profile, **68**
Hypochondria		Habits & Lifestyle, **55** Emotional Profile, **94**

SYMPTOM	WARNING SIGNS: CONSULT YOUR DOCTOR	PROFILE SCANS & INDEX
Impatience *see* **Irritability**		
Impotence		Relationships, Sex & Reproduction, **98** Habits & Lifestyle, **49, 50** Emotional Profile, **89, 71**
Indecisiveness		Personality Profile, **62** Emotional Profile, **89, 94, 71** Physical Health, **43**
Indigestion	If lasts for 3 weeks or more.	Habits & Lifestyle, **48** Emotional Profile, **89, 71** Personality Profile, **59a, 68** Habits & Lifestyle, **57, 49**
Infertility		Relationships, Sex & Reproduction, **101**
Insomnia		Personality Profile, **59a** Emotional Profile, **71, 96, 89, 94** Relationships, Sex & Reproduction, **98** Habits & Lifestyle, **49, 50**
Irritability	If you are restless or irritable without apparent reason and have a swelling in your neck.	Personality Profile, **59b, 68, 64** Emotional Profile, **92, 71, 96, 97** Physical Health, **38** Habits & Lifestyle, **49, 50**
Itching *see* **Skin Problems** *see* **Rectal Itching**		
Jealousy		Relationships, Sex & Reproduction, **98** Personality Profile, **67**
Joint Pain	If unrelated to exercise.	Physical Health, **24b**

SYMPTOM	WARNING SIGNS: CONSULT YOUR DOCTOR	PROFILE SCANS & INDEX
Lump	Any lump or thickening, anywhere in the body.	
Memory Loss	If you have ever been concussed or had a serious blow to the head. If there was a definite point at which the memory loss occurred (illness, injury, important event).	Physical Health, **43** Emotional Profile, **71** Habits & Lifestyle, **49, 50**
Mole or Wart	If it has changed appearance.	
Moodiness *see also* **Irritability**		Emotional Profile, **92, 94, 96, 97**
Motivation, lack of *see* **Fatigue**		
Mouth	If white patches or spots appear, or if any sore or spot does not heal.	
dry		Habits & Lifestyle, **50**
ulcers in		Emotional Profile, **71**
Muscular Pain	If accompanied by running nose or fever.	Physical Health, **24b** Emotional Profile, **89** Personality Profile, **59a** Emotional Profile, **71**
Nail-biting		Personality Profile, **59a**
Nasal Congestion		Habits & Lifestyle, **57** Physical Health, **38**
Nausea	If accompanied by severe unrelieved pain or headache, blurred vision or eye pain; or if blood or black granules like ground coffee appear in vomit. If you might be pregnant, have a pregnancy test.	Emotional Profile, **89, 91, 71, 96, 97** Habits & Lifestyle, **48, 49, 50** Physical Health, **39, 38**

SYMPTOM	WARNING SIGNS: CONSULT YOUR DOCTOR	PROFILE SCANS & INDEX
Nervousness		Emotional Profile, **89**, **97** Personality Profile, **59a**, **62**, **68**, **66**
Nosebleed	Nearly always the result of damage to the nose lining; also common in pregnancy due to increased supply of blood then. Go to your doctor if nosebleed is a result of a blow to the head, or if persistent.	
Numbness	If you experience numbness or prickling on face, arms, legs, side (especially if on one side only), or any sudden paralysis.	Emotional Profile, **89**, **71** Physical Health, **38**
Obesity		Fitness Profile, **22**
Obsessional Behaviour		Personality Profile, **67b**
Pallor	If you have suffered recent, chronic blood loss.	Fitness Profile, **22**
Palpitations	If you feel generally unwell or if they occur with chest pain.	Habits & Lifestyle, **57**, **50** Emotional Profile, **89**, **96**, **91**, **71**
Pain *see* **Abdomen, Back, Breast, Chest, Cramps, Ear, Ejaculation, Eye, Headache, Joint, Muscular, Testicles, Urination**		
Panic		Emotional Profile, **89**, **91**, **71**
Periods, irregular	Always consult a doctor.	

SYMPTOM	WARNING SIGNS: CONSULT YOUR DOCTOR	PROFILE SCANS & INDEX
Phlegm	Heavy phlegm is always a doctor issue, especially if combined with shortness of breath or fever.	
Prickling Feeling *see* **Numbness**		
Pulse, irregular	If it fails to settle after you have lain down.	Habits & Lifestyle, **57** Emotional Profile, **71**
racing	If it fails to settle after you have lain down.	Emotional Profile, **89**
Rectal Pain, Itching	If in pain and you do not have piles.	Physical Health, **35b**
Restlessness	If you have a neck swelling.	Personality Profile, **68, 64** Emotional Profile, **89**
Seeing Problems *see also* **Blurred Vision, Double Vision, Flashing Lights, Hallucination**		Physical Health, **41**
Self-consciousness		Personality Profile, **62** Emotional Profile, **89**
Self-esteem, low		Personality Profile, **62** Emotional Profile, **94**
Sexual Dissatisfaction		Relationships, Sex & Reproduction, **98**
Shaking		Habits & Lifestyle, **49** Emotional Profile, **89, 71**
Skin Problems *see also* **Acne**	If presented as pink or purple raised blotches, or red weals. Any sore that does not heal.	Emotional Profile, **89** Physical Health, **38** Emotional Profile, **96, 97**

SYMPTOM	WARNING SIGNS: CONSULT YOUR DOCTOR	PROFILE SCANS & INDEX
Sneezing *see also* **Cough**		Habits & Lifestyle, **50** Physical Health, **38**
Sore	If slow to heal.	
Speech Problems	If momentary and unexplained.	Emotional Profile, **89**
Submissiveness		Personality Profile, **62**
Suspiciousness		Personality Profile, **67a**
Swallowing, difficulties in	If accompanied by a feeling of pressure (however indistinct) beneath the breastbone, or by nausea, numbness, headache or double vision.	Emotional Profile, **89**
Sweating, increased	See Warning Signs for Fever. Also consult a doctor if in a cold sweat, soaking night sweat or if sweating is accompanied by unexplained weight loss.	Fitness Profile, **22** Habits & Lifestyle, **49** Emotional Profile, **96**, **89**, **91**
decreased		Habits & Lifestyle, **50**
Swelling	If unexplained. If you feel generally unwell. If you are pregnant and your ankles, feet or hands swell.	Habits & Lifestyle, **50** Physical Health, **38**
Tearfulness *see* **Unhappiness**		
Tension		Emotional Profile, **97** Personality Profile, **59a**, **68**, **64**, **66**
Testicles, pain in	Always consult a doctor.	
Thirst, excessive	If there is diabetes in the family go to your doctor for a blood test.	Physical Health, **38**

SYMPTOM	WARNING SIGNS: CONSULT YOUR DOCTOR	PROFILE SCANS & INDEX
Tongue, spots on	If white patches or spots appear.	
Understanding, difficulties in	If sudden and momentary.	Physical Health, **39** Habits & Lifestyle, **49, 50** Emotional Profile, **89, 71**
Unhappiness	If accompanied by chest pain. If you have recently had a baby. If you have ever contemplated suicide.	Emotional Profile, **71** etc. Personality Profile, **59** etc. Relationships, Sex & Reproduction, **98** Habits & Lifestyle, **49, 50**
Urination, difficulty in	Always a doctor issue, as it is if a man finds his urine dribbling when he tries to stop.	
increased frequency of	If there is diabetes in the family go to your doctor for a blood test.	Emotional Profile, **89, 71**
pain during	Always consult a doctor.	
blood during	Always consult a doctor.	
Vomiting see **Nausea**		
Wart or Mole	If it has changed in appearance.	
Weight Loss	In the event of sudden or inexplicable weight loss. If you weigh 10 or less in the Weight scan (p 22), or less than 20 and have lost more than 5kg in 3 months. If you have reduced by more than 5 kg in 3 months and did not wish to, or despite increasing your calorie intake. If it is combined with nausea, vomiting, excessive thirst, or increased hunger. If you are pregnant.	Fitness Profile, **24a** Emotional Profile, **89** Personality Profile, **67b**

CANCER: Early Warning Signs

1 Any unusual bleeding or discharge.

2 A lump or thickening anywhere on the body.

3 A sore that does not heal.

4 A persistent change in bowel habits; diarrhoea alternating with constipation.

5 Hoarseness or coughing lasting 3 weeks or more.

6 Indigestion or difficulty in swallowing lasting 3 weeks or more.

7 A change in the size, shape or appearance of a wart or mole.

8 An unexplained loss of weight.

9 Slight chest pain, mild cough/wheezing and shortness of breath.

10 A lump in a breast, a nipple that has retracted in a way that hasn't happened before, or bleeding or discharge from a nipple.

11 A difficulty in swallowing and a feeling of pressure (however indistinct) beneath the breastbone.

12 Heartburn and distended abdomen plus a heavy feeling in the upper abdomen and quick satiation at meals.

13 Pain with solid or hard mass in the testes.

The Profile Scan Index

Yes	No

FITNESS PROFILE

For an **overall Fitness score** (for use in other, related scans) add your scores together in the Exercise and Diet Scans (pp 24, 28). A score of less than 15 indicates that you are well-prepared physically to meet the stressful demands of the modern world. A good overall Fitness score will lower your risk to stress-related disease, even if your score in the Stress scan (p 71) is relatively high.

I WEIGHT
1   According to the Weight Chart, are you
   a overweight
   b very overweight
   c obese
   d below ideal weight
   e about right?

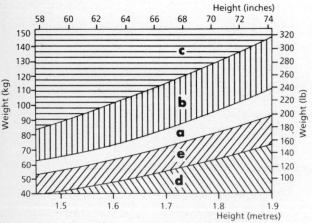

From the diagram you can judge how your own weight compares with the desirable range for your height. a = overweight; b = very overweight; c = obese; d = below ideal weight; e = about right.

Readers who have turned to this chart from the Underweight Scan, or 'Weight Loss' in the Symptom Chart, will need to calculate their height/weight ratio in figures. Do this by multiplying your height in metres by itself (H^2), and then dividing your weight in kilograms (W) by the answer. The formula is W/H^2. For example, for a person 1.7m tall, weighing 60kg, the calculation is $60 \div (1.7 \times 1.7) = \frac{60}{2.89} = 20.76$. If the result is below 10, see your doctor.

| ACTION ⟩ |

Yes to 1d   Go to Underweight Scan (p24).
Yes to 1e   Leave the Weight Scan.

Yes to 1a, b   For most people excess weight is a matter of having
or c   got the equation between energy intake and
                     energy output wrong, in other words eating more
                     calories (energy) than the body actually uses.
                     Logically, to put the equation right you need to
                     look both at your energy input (in the form of food
                     that you eat and liquid that you drink) and your
                     energy output (in the shape of the exercise that you
                     take). And, as in any action designed to change our
                     daily habits, there is the question of will power. Go
                     to question 2.

                     2   Have you tried unsuccessfully to diet before?

| YES ⟩ | **P9**, then **P5** and **P19**. |

| NO ⟩ | **P19** |

                     3   Do you take vigorous exercise at least once a
                         week?

| NO ⟩ | **P21**. Aerobic exercise (such as cycling, jogging, rowing, swimming, even brisk walking) uses up more energy than any other sort of exercise, because it employs the large muscles of the arms and legs. Aerobic exercise also produces a number of hormones which, in turn, release the body's fatty tissue as a source of energy to be expended during the exercise program. If YES to 1b or c or you suffer from joint or back pain, first complete the full Exercise scan, **P24**. |

                     4   Do you drink more than 35 units of alcohol a
                         week?*

                     *1 standard unit of alcohol is equivalent to:
                     ½ pint (280ml/10fl oz) normal strength beer; or
                     ½ gill (47ml/1.7fl oz) sherry/martini/fortified wine; or
                     ⅙ gill (23ml/0.9 fl oz) distilled spirits (40% alcohol); or
                     a small glass of wine (125ml/4.4 fl oz).

| YES ⟩ | **P5**. Alcohol is very high in calories. |

**Yes to 1a, b
or c**

ASSOCIATED RISK
Obesity is probably the single most common diet-related disorder in the West. It is known to be a contributory factor in the development of High Blood Pressure, Heart Disease, Diabetes, Gallstones, Arthritis and joint pain, even Cancer of the Womb and Gall Bladder, as well as a number of psychological problems. Being overweight also makes surgery and childbirth more risky, and it can cause back and joint pain and aggravate Arthritis and respiratory disorders. Consult the following Vulnerability Scans:

High Blood Pressure   Gallstones (p 117)
  (p 110)   Diabetes (p 118)
Heart Disease (p 113)   Cancer of the Uterus
Stroke (p 116)   (p 138)

Yes	No

UNDERWEIGHT SCAN
1   Did you measure 10 or less on the Chart (p 22)?

2   Have you lost more than 5 kg in the last 3 months?

3   If YES to 2, did you want to lose weight?

ACTION

Yes to 1   Consult your doctor.

Yes to 2   Consult your doctor if you have lost more than 5kg in the last 3 months, and were less than 20 on the chart to start with. See also Anorexia, p 151.

No to 3   Consult your doctor.

ASSOCIATED RISK
Rapid weight loss carries its own set of problems, see the Symptom Chart on p 8, and if you are concerned, consult your doctor.

Yes	No
3	
2	
1	

II EXERCISE
1   How many times a week do you take vigorous exercise?
    a less than once a week
    b once a week for at least 20 minutes
    c twice a week or more for at least 20 minutes?

Yes	No

2 How much exercise does your daily routine involve?

6   *Light* – sitting most of the day (eg sedentary office work, professional jobs, domestic work, driving, or sedentary industrial work)

3   *Moderate* – mostly standing, moving about a fair bit, but not strenuous activity (eg manual housework, teaching, being a student, non-manual industrial and agricultural work)

2   *Vigorous* – manual work (eg carpentry, car mechanics, gardening)

1   *Very vigorous* – on foot all day, strenuous activity (eg labouring, heavy industry, loading, army training, or sporting activity)

3 3 Do you avoid physical effort whenever possible (eg take lifts or escalators instead of walking up stairs, use electrical rather than manual equipment, always drive rather than walk, push or pull rather than carry)?

4 Which of these are true of you?

2   a My heart pounds when I take exercise like walking up a few flights of stairs.

2   b If I have to run 50 yards to catch a bus, it leaves me gasping for breath.

2   c It is an effort to bend down and tie up my shoe laces, pick something off the floor or bend down to get into the back of a two-door car.

2   d It is an effort to stretch up to the top shelf, I usually ask someone to do it for me.

2   e If I take more exercise than usual, for example, dig the garden, I am left aching all over and very tired.

2   f I am often very keyed up and find it difficult to relax, especially after a day at work.

SCORE

1-8   You are probably reasonably fit, especially if you answered YES to question 1c.

9-11   You probably need more exercise, but not necessarily in all aspects of fitness.

12+   You are badly in need of some exercise.

Yes	No	ACTION
		5 Are you over 60?
		6 Do you or any close relative suffer from Diabetes?
		7 Do you smoke?
		8 Do you suffer from High Blood Pressure?
		9 Have you ever suffered chest pain, tightness, discomfort, breathlessness or palpitations?
		10 Is there a history of Heart Attack in your family?
		11 Do you suffer from muscle cramp or joint pain?
		12 Do you suffer from back pain?

Yes to any of 5-10   You are advised to make an appointment with your doctor before embarking upon **P21**.

Score of 1-8   Fitness Test 2 in **P21**

Score of 9+   Fitness Test 1 in **P21**

Yes to 11 and score of 12+   If you are very overweight according to the Weight Profile you should go to **P19** and follow the 'Getting Fit to Get Fit' section of **P21**. Being overweight makes you more likely to stress joints, especially if your muscles are also weak or ill-developed. If you are not overweight, go to Fitness Test 1 of **P21** paying particular attention to the suppleness and strength exercises. Exercise of the sort prescribed there can also have a preventive effect against Osteoarthritis. Osteoarthritis affects 80 to 90% of people aged 60 years or over, and causes pain, stiffness and sometimes enlargement of joints. At each joint, two or more bones meet and are cushioned from one another by cartilage. The joint is lubricated to reduce friction and held together by muscles which can move it in various directions. The right kind of exercise keeps the muscles flexible (without it they can shrink and become stiff) and encourages the flow of lubricant, thus easing joint motion and helping protect joints against damage.

Yes to 11 and score of less than 12

Go to your doctor if the pain you experience is not due to exercise. Commonly, joint pain among people who do exercise regularly is due to a failure to warm up properly before embarking upon vigorous aerobic exercise. See **P21**.

Yes to 12 and score of less than 12

Back pain can be caused by too sudden and vigorous exercise. See 'Getting Fit to Get Fit' **P21**.

Yes to 12 and score of 12+

Exercise can help relieve some forms of back pain, especially in the lower back. The key is the strength of the trunk muscle. The back and abdominal muscles form a cylinder which holds the bones of the spine in the correct position. All the leg and arm muscles act against this central cylinder of muscle. If the tummy muscles are weak, postural problems and back pain can follow. If the back muscles themselves are weak, the vertebrae may pull out of line, resulting in Lumbago, Sciatica or Fibrositis.

If you score high in the scans for Tension (p 59), Stress (p 71) or Weight (p 22), follow their Action Advice, then go to Fitness Test 1 of **P21** and pay particular attention to the strength exercises.

Certain 'occupational' hazards are described in the Environment and Occupation scan (p 45).

ASSOCIATED RISK
Lack of exercise can lay you open to a whole host of psychological disorders, including Depression (see p 94). Consult the following scans to assess risk to physical disorders:

Common Infection (p104)

High Blood Pressure (p110)

Heart Disease (p113)
Stroke (p116)
Diabetes (p118)

Yes	No	
		III DIET: VITAMINS AND MINERALS
		1 How often do you use fresh or frozen, unprocessed ingredients in your cooking eg fish, meat, vegetables, pulses, cheese and eggs?
3		**a** occasionally
2		**b** 1-2 times a week
		c 3-4 times a week
		2 How often do you eat yellow, orange or dark green fruit and vegetables (particularly carrots and green cabbage)?
3		**a** occasionally
2		**b** 1-2 times a week
		c 3-4 times a week
		3 How often do you eat citrus fruits?
3		**a** occasionally
2		**b** 1-2 times a week
		c 3-4 times a week
	2	4 Do you eat liver at least once a month, or some other good source of iron more regularly (such as shellfish, certain fortified breakfast cereals, dried peas and beans, raisins, molasses, wholewheat bread, chocolate or green leafy vegetables)?
3		5 Do you have set daily menus?
3		6 If YES to 5, is the pattern continued over weeks or months?
		7 Do you generally cook your vegetables by
		a steaming
		b braising
2		**c** boiling
3		**d** frying?
		8 Do you eat your vegetables
3		**a** well done
2		**b** lightly cooked
		c raw?
		9 Do you eat your fruit
1		**a** cooked
		b raw?

Yes	No	
2		10 Are you a vegetarian?
	2	11 Do you eat wholewheat grains and cereals?
	2	12 Do you eat some meat or dairy produce such as cheese, daily?
3		13 Are you a vegan?
		14 Do you take
2		a the Pill
2		b regular courses of tetracycline-based antibiotics
2		c regular doses of aspirin
2		d any other regular course of drugs?
3		15 Do you slim regularly?
3		16 Are you pregnant?
3		17 Are you breast-feeding?
2		18 Are you aged 50 years or more?
5		19 Do you smoke 10 cigarettes or more a day, or inhale the smoke of 2 or more cigars?
5		20 Do you drink alcohol most days?
	2	21 Do you get out into the fresh air for at least an hour every day?

SCORE
A score over 30 suggests a possible deficiency of vitamins and minerals in your diet. 15 or more suggests that advice would be beneficial.

| ACTION |

Score of 15 or more
Consult **P22/5** for a list of vitamins and minerals, in what foods they can be obtained, and what levels you require. A vitamin or mineral deficiency can make you especially prone to infection, see p 104.

Yes to 5, 6
The more varied your diet, the more likely you are receiving a healthy balance of nutrients.

Yes to 14a	The contraceptive pill can reduce the availability of Vitamin C and some of the B vitamins.
Yes to 14b or 14c	These can also reduce the effect of Vitamin B and C. Indeed many drugs can increase your vitamin requirements, so if you are taking any drug for an extended period, be sure to balance its effect by referring to the tables in **P22/5**.
Yes to 15 or 18	Both elderly people and regular slimmers are likely to have low calorie intakes, which makes it all the more difficult to achieve healthy levels of vitamins and minerals.
Yes to 19	**P5**. Smoking destroys Vitamin B and C.
Yes to 20	Regular intake of alcohol can so irritate the stomach that vitamins and minerals in the food you eat cannot be absorbed into the blood stream. Excessive alcohol can cause deficiencies, especially of the B vitamins. (See Drinking Habits scan, p 49.)
No to 21	Most of the Vitamin D that we need is made by our own bodies in response to ultra-violet light, usually gained from natural sunlight.

ASSOCIATED RISK

A shortage of vitamins and minerals has been found to play an important part in the development of a number of disorders. If you score high in the Smoking Habits scan (p 57) or the Drinking Habits scan (p 49), and in this scan, complete the Peptic Ulcer scan (p 140).

Low levels of calcium increase the risk of developing a disease called Osteoporosis, which leaves the bones fragile and breakable, particularly in women who have passed through the menopause.

High intakes of Vitamin A and C have been associated with the prevention of certain forms of Cancer, and Vitamin C is known to inhibit the production of nitrosamines in the stomach (see the Cancer of the Stomach scan, p 136).

Vitamin A plays a part in regulating the growth of certain body cells and may have some controlling influence on early Cancer cells (see Cancer, p 125 following).

The body's immune system requires a healthy diet to serve you well, both against Infection (see scan p 104) and against the psychological effects of a stressful situation and lifestyle (see the Stress scan, p 71). Low levels of zinc in your diet have been linked with a heightened risk of psychological problems such as Depression (see scan, p 94).

DIET: FATS AND FIBRE

Yes	No	
		1 What milk do you usually use?
3		a Channel Island or gold top
2		b ordinary (silver/red top)
1		c semi-skimmed
		d skimmed
		e I never use milk
		2 How often do you use cream or evaporated milk?
3		a every day
2		b several times a week
1		c about once a week
		d less than once a week or never
		3 What do you usually use as a spread?
3		a butter or hard margarine
2		b soft margarine
2		c polyunsaturated margarine
1		d low fat spread
		e no spread
		4 How do you spread this fat on your bread?
3		a thickly
2		b medium
1		c a thin scrape
		5 What do you use for cooking and baking?
3		a solid fat (lard, dripping, butter or margarine)
2		b a mixed (or blended) vegetable oil
1		c a pure vegetable oil (corn, sunflower or olive oil)
		6 How often do you eat chips?
3		a 5 or more times a week
2		b 2-4 times a week
1		c once a week
		d very occasionally or never

Yes	No

7 What type of cheese do you eat most of?

a HIGH FAT (more than 25% fat): — **4**
   Cheddar type
   Cream cheese
   Danish blue type
   Stilton type

b MEDIUM FAT (less than 25% fat): — **3**
   Camembert type
   Cheese spread
   Edam type
   Low fat hard cheese

c LOW FAT (less than 1% fat): — **1**
   Cottage cheese
   Curd cheese

8 How often do you eat high fat or medium fat cheese?
a 6 or more times a week — **3**
b 3-5 times a week — **2**
c once or twice a week — **1**
d very occasionally or never

9 Do you usually eat
a all the fat on your meat — **4**
b some of the fat — **3**
c none of the fat?

10 How often do you eat sausages/meat pies/burgers?
a 6 times a week or more — **3**
b 3-5 times a week — **2**
c once or twice a week — **1**
d very occasionally or never

11 When cooking products like bacon or burgers do you
a fry — **3**
b grill with added oil or fat — **2**
c grill without adding fat? — **1**
d I very occasionally or never eat these

12 How many times a week do you eat a whole packet of nuts?

Yes	No
3	
2	
1	

a 6 or more
b 3-5 times
c once or twice
d very occasionally or never

13 How many times a week do you eat a whole packet of potato crisps?

Yes	No
3	
2	
1	

a 6 or more
b 3-5 times
c once or twice
d very occasionally or never

14 How many times a week do you eat cream cakes?

Yes	No
3	
2	
1	

a 6 or more
b 3-5 times
c once or twice
d very occasionally or never

15 How many times a week do you eat chocolate bars?

Yes	No
3	
2	
1	

a 6 or more
b 3-5 times
c once or twice
d very occasionally or never

SCORE
Add up your TOTAL A (questions 1 to 15) . . .

16 What bread or chapatis do you usually eat?

Yes	No
3	
2	
1	
2	

a wholemeal
b brown
c white
d a mixture

17 How many slices of bread, rolls or chapatis do you eat on a typical day?

Yes	No
6	
4	
2	

a 6 or more
b 3-5
c 1-2

18 How often do you eat boiled, mashed or jacket potatoes?

Yes	No
6	
4	
2	

a 6 or more times a week
b 3-5 times a week
c once or twice a week

Yes	No
6	
4	
2	
4	
3	
2	

19 How often do you eat rice or pasta (spaghetti, etc)?
   a 6 or more times a week
   b 3-5 times a week
   c once or twice a week
   d very occasionally or never

20 How many times a week do you eat a breakfast cereal?
   a 6 or more
   b 3-5 times
   c once or twice
   d very occasionally or never

SCORE
Add up your TOTAL B (questions 16 to 20) . . .

OVERALL FATS/FIBRE SCORE
If your Total A is about the same as Total B, you're probably eating a bit too much fat.

If your total A is greater than total B, then you will need to follow a more balanced dietary schedule. Follow ACTION below:

ACTION

P22/1 and **P22/2**.

ASSOCIATED RISK
A predominantly fatty diet is conducive to a number of health problems. Consult the following Vulnerability Scans:

High Blood Pressure (p 110)
Heart Disease (p 113)
Stroke (p 116)
Gallstones (p 117)
Cancer of the Breast (p 130)
Cancer of the Prostrate (p 133)
Diabetes (p 118)
Varicose Veins (p 119)

A diet with a markedly low fibre content also raises the risk of specific health problems. Consult the following scans:

Bowel Disorders (p 109)
Cancer of the Colon and Rectum (p 134)

DIET: SALT

Yes	No
2	
1	
2	
1	
2	
1	

1 Do you add salt to your food?
   a always
   b sometimes, depending on the taste
   c never or rarely

2 Do you add salt when cooking?
   a always
   b sometimes, depending on the taste
   c rarely if ever

3 How often do uou eat really salty foods such as peanuts, crisps, bacon, or smoked or pickled foods?
   a most days
   b 3-4 times a week
   c rarely or only occasionally

ACTION ⟩

Score of 3 or more   **P22/4**

ASSOCIATED RISK
A high salt (sodium chloride) diet contributes to the development of High Blood Pressure. High Blood Pressure is, in turn, a major cause of Stroke and a contributory cause of Coronary Heart Disease. A high salt diet has also been linked with Stomach Cancer. Consult the following scans:

Cancer of the Stomach (p 136)   Heart Disease (p 113)
High Blood Pressure (p 110)   Stroke (p 116)

BOWEL HABITS

Yes	No

1 How often do you move your bowels?
   a once a day
   b once every two days
   c less than once every two days

If YES to 1b or 1c, tick YES or NO to questions 2 and 3, and complete question 4.

Yes	No

2 Did you score 12 or more in the Exercise scan (p 24)?

3 Do you take laxatives regularly?

4 How often do you eat the foods in sections 1 to 4?
   a never or rarely
   b about once a fortnight
   c about once a week
   d 2 to 4 times a week
   e once a day
   f twice a day
   g 3 or more times a day

Give your answers the following values, section by section:

	Section 1	Section 2	Section 3	Section 4
a	0	0	0	0
b	5	3	2	1
c	9	5	3	2
d	27	15	10	5
e	63	35	22	11
f	126	70	45	21
g	189	125	77	36

Section 1
Dried apricots or figs
Bran-based breakfast cereal
Raw or boiled spinach
Baked beans
Peas (frozen, processed or canned)

Section 2
Wholemeal or rye bread
Baked potato eaten with skin
Kidney beans, butter beans, lentils or other pulses
Wholemeal pasta
Wheat flakes or biscuit breakfast cereal
Sweetcorn kernels

Section 3
Chipped potatoes or French fries
Brown rice
Fresh fruit

Yes	No

Soft fruits
Crisps
Nuts of any type
Wholemeal or fruit cake
Brown or malted wheatgrain bread
Muesli-type, oat crunchy breakfast cereals
Wholemeal or rye crispbread
Root vegetables
Green leafy vegetables

Section 4
White bread
White pasta or white rice
Digestive or bran biscuits
Puffed rice or corn breakfast cereal
Salad and other 'watery' vegetables (e.g. lettuce, cucumber, tomatoes, peppers)
Boiled or mashed potatoes

Question 4 less than 109

FIBRE SCORE
You need to increase the fibre content of your diet.

nearer 109 than 175

You need to be aware that your diet is barely adequate in terms of fibre.

ACTION

Yes to 2

P21. Weakness of anal muscles due to general unfitness is a common cause of constipation.

No to 2

If you scored 9 or less in the Exercise scan or take exercise in a hot country, your constipation may be due to excessive loss of body water through perspiration.

Yes to 3

P21 and **P22/2**. Regular use of laxatives may lead to dependence and their ineffectiveness.

Less than 109 for 4

P22/2. A high fibre diet results in softer, bulkier stools, which are pushed along by the muscular gut wall and passed easily through the body.

109-175 for 4

P22/2. Consider eating a little more fibre, especially if your score is nearer 109.

ASSOCIATED RISK

Constipation is a condition where the stools move through the colon very slowly and are passed in small hard lumps at irregular intervals. Constipation is associated with a whole range of secondary problems such as Piles, Varicose Veins and Inguinal Hernia. It is also linked with Diverticular Disease and Cancer of the Colon and Rectum.

Bowel Disorders (p 109)
Varicose Veins (p 119)
Cancer of the Colon and Rectum (p 134)

Yes	No

ALLERGY

1 Have you suffered an allergic reaction before?

2 Did you begin a new prescription of drugs shortly before experiencing the symptoms which have brought you to this scan?

3 Do your parents, brothers or sisters have any allergies?

4 Do you know that you were bottle-fed on a cow's milk formula or weaned onto high protein solids before the age of six months?

5 Does your shopping list include goods containing any of the following?

   a food colourings:
   E102, E104, 107, E110, E122, E123, E124, E127, E128, E131, E132, 133, E142, E151, 154, 155, E180.

   b food preservatives:
   E210 – 224, E226/7

   c antioxidants: E320/1 and E310-12

| ACTION |

All foods bar about 10 can theoretically cause an allergic reaction in human beings, yet none in themselves can be held responsible. They depend for their harmful effect upon the physical and psychological response of the individual involved. The same principle is true of drugs, alcohol, dust and other known allergy agents.

Because identifying the cause or trigger of a person's allergy can be difficult, you are advised in the first instance to complete other Profile Scans, related to your symptoms and listed in the Symptom Chart. If, then, you have answered YES to any question in this scan, go to **P2**.

The Allergy Preventive Program (**P2**) shows you how to analyse your own environment and intake of food and drugs and judge your personal reaction to these. Guidance is given as to which foods, additives, drugs, environmental factors and emotional reactions have caused allergic reaction in others.

Yes	No

HEARING

1   Do you experience persistent or recurring pain in the ear, even after a 12-hour course of aspirin or paracetamol?

2   Are your hearing difficulties
    a of a momentary sort, do they come and go suddenly without explanation?
    b progressively worse over the past weeks or months?

3   Have you recently suffered a blow to the head or concussion?

4   Did the onset of symptoms coincide with the beginning of a new prescription or purchase of drugs, or are you taking diuretics, medication for High Blood Pressure, or drugs for Anxiety?

5   Do you suffer dizziness, giddiness or loss of balance?

6   Is there a discharge of any kind from the ear?

7   Can you hear ringing in your ears or some other noise?

Yes	No

8 Do you have a blocked-up feeling in one or both ears?

9 Do you work in very noisy surroundings or have you recently been exposed to very loud music?

10 Do you have a long-term, medically diagnosed ear disorder?

Yes to 1   Consult your doctor. You probably have an infection.

Yes to 2a   Consult your doctor immediately.

Yes to 2b   Consult your doctor; this may be due to a wax blockage, but whatever the cause, have your ears examined.

Yes to 3 & 6   Consult your doctor.

Yes to 4   If the drugs are on prescription, consult your doctor; if not it is advisable to stop taking them.

Yes to 5   Consult your doctor, you may have a disorder of the inner ear. If upon examination, no such disorder is found, go to the following scans:

Anxiety (p 89)
Fears and Phobias (p 91)
Stress (p 71)
Drug Habits (p 50)
Allergy (p 38)

Yes to 7   Ringing in the ears is very often a side effect of an excessive intake of aspirin. If the problem persists having stopped the course, go to the Stress scan (p 71).

Yes to 8   Try swallowing repeatedly, or pinching your nostrils while attempting to blow air through your nose. The problem may well be due to a change in air pressure such as is caused by swimming in deep water or travelling in an aircraft. If it persists for more than 24 hours, consult your doctor.

Yes to 9   Much damage to ears is caused by the high level of noise in workplaces or at music concerts. Implicitly, prevention lies in avoiding environments that damage hearing. If difficulties persist, go to your doctor.

Yes to 10   Consult the Distress scan (p 149) if appropriate.

Yes	No

VISION

1   Have you suddenly lost all or part of the vision in one or both eyes?

2   Has your vision deteriorated over a period of weeks or months?

3   Have you suffered accident or injury to the eye, concussion or a severe blow to the head, or was there some other definite starting point to your sight problems?

4   Do you have blurred vision?

5   Is there a discharge from the eye of any kind?

6   Are you in pain?

7   Do you experience hallucination?

8   Do you see flashing lights and then suffer a severe headache?

9   Do you have a long-term, medically diagnosed eye disorder?

10 Do you have difficulty concentrating for any length of time?

11 If YES to 10, do you have problems sleeping?

| ACTION >

Yes to 1   Consult your doctor immediately.

Yes to 2   Consult an optician. If he finds your sight is not
                      impaired, go to the following Profile Scans:

                      Anxiety (p 89)
                      Stress (p 71)

Yes to 3   Consult your doctor. If a domestic bleach or
                      cleaning agent comes into contact with the eye,
                      immediately hold the eye open beneath a tap
                      running with cold water. After a couple of minutes,
                      sufficient to flood the chemical agent from the eye,
                      cover with a clean, soft pad and call the accident
                      department of your local hospital.

Yes to 4   Consult your doctor. If there is nothing physically
                      wrong, go to the following scans:

                      Anxiety (p 89)
                      Stress (p 71)
                      Drug Habits (p 50)
                      Drinking Habits (p 49)

Yes to 5   Consult your doctor.

Yes to 6   First, go to your doctor. If there is nothing physically
                      wrong, consult the following scans:

                      Tense Personality (p 59)
                      Anxiety (p 89)
                      Stress (p 71)
                      Allergy (p 38)

Yes to 7   Consult your doctor.

Yes to 8   **P2**

Yes to 9   Consult the Distress scan (p 149).

Yes to 11   **P15**

No to 11   Go to an optician and have your eyes tested. If the
                      problem persists, consult the following Profile
                      Scans:

                      Anxiety (p 89)   Drinking Habits (p 49)
                      Stress (p 71)   Drug Habits (p 50)
                      Exercise (p 24)   Depression (p 94)

Yes	No

MEMORY

1 Have you had a car accident in the last 6 months?

2 Are you less confident travelling than you used to be?

3 Do you have problems remembering the names of people you know?

4 Do you often lose things?

5 Do you often forget to do things?

6 Is it difficult to remember what you did yesterday?

7 Is it difficult to remember where you bought this book?

> ACTION

Yes to 3 or more

P10 and then **P18**.

Also answer the following questions:

8 Do you think that your loss of memory may be due to a stressful situation?

> YES   **P11**

9 Do you drink heavily or take other drugs?

> YES   **P5**

10 Do you suffer from this problem more often or strongly when you are anxious?

> YES   **P17**

11 Do you find it difficult to relax?

> YES   **P10**

Do you have difficulty concentrating?

> YES   **P11**

Yes	No

HEREDITARY TRAITS

1 Did either of your parents or your grandparents suffer from Varicose Veins?

2 If you are planning to give birth,

   a do you have any close relatives who have experienced serious psychological problems?

   b is there a history of genetic abnormality in your family?

3 Is there a history of any of the following diseases in your family?
   a Diabetes
   b Respiratory disorders, such as Bronchitis
   c Hypertension (High Blood Pressure)
   d Heart Disease
   e Cancer of the Mouth, Throat, Larynx
   f Cancer of the Lung
   g Cancer of the Breast
   h Cancer of the Uterus

4 Is there a history of digestive diseases in your family?

> **ACTION**

Consult the following Vulnerability Scans, as appropriate:

Yes to 1	Varicose Veins (p 119)
Yes to 2a	Motherhood Problems (p 145)
Yes to 2b	Birth Abnormalities (p 147)
Yes to 3a	Diabetes (p 118)
	Stroke (p 116)
Yes to 3b	Respiratory Disorders (p 123)
Yes to 3c	High Blood Pressure (p 110)
	Heart Disease (p 113)
Yes to 3d	Heart Disease (p 113)
Yes to 3e	Cancer of the Mouth and Throat (p 128)
Yes to 3f	Cancer of the Lung (p 125)
Yes to 3g	Cancer of the Breast (p 130)
Yes to 3h	Cancer of the Uterus (p 138)
Yes to 4	Cancer of the Colon and Rectum (p 134)

Yes	No

ENVIRONMENT AND OCCUPATION

1 Do you spend long periods each day standing with little movement, eg in bar or restaurant work, shopkeeping, factory line work, teaching?

2 Do you have to lift a lot of things as part of your job (including young babies or children)?

3 Does your job involve sitting for long periods?

4 Do you ride in a car, bus, train, or plane for substantial lengths of time in the course of a week?

5 Are the tables or work surfaces you regularly use at a comfortable height – ie elbow height – so that you can use them without leaning or bending over?

6 Does your job involve your working with any of the following chemicals or materials?
   a alpha- or beta-napthylamine
   b benzidine
   c ortho-tolidine
   d methylene-bis?
   e asbestos
   f arsenic
   g chrome
   h nickel
   i chlorenethyl
   j ethers
   k coal tar distillates
   l mustard gas
   m uranium

7 Do you work in a factory making paint, textiles, rubber, dyes or pigments?

8 Do you work on-machine in the print industry?

9 Are you a bus or truck driver?

10 Do you habitually have to retain urine due to your occupation (eg truck or taxi drivers, pilot etc)?

Yes	No

11 Are you a hot metal typsetter or compositor?

12 Are you a welder or painter?

13 Do you work in the nuclear power industry, or do you live in the vicinity of a chemical plant, refinery, nuclear plant or testing site?

14 If you are a woman, does your sexual partner come into contact with any of the following materials in his work?
a metal and machine tools
b leather

15 Do you work in a coal mine?

16 Does your work involve contact with soot, tars or mineral oils?

17 Are you involved in agricultural work?

18 Do you come into contact with pesticides?

19 Do you work in a smokey environment?

20 Do you work or live in a dusty or fumey environment?

21 Do you live or work in cold, crowded or damp conditions?

22 Do you live in an institution?

23 Do you live or work in an air-conditioned environment?

24 Do you live and/or work in a centrally heated, poorly ventilated environment?

25 Do you work under flickering lights or for more than an hour a day in front of a VDU?

26 Do you work in a newly carpeted modern office?

27 Is your home or workplace noisy or overcrowded?

Yes	No

28 Does your house require substantial building or decorative work?

29 Are your surroundings at home or at work messy or chaotic?

30 Do you live in a tower block?

31 Does your telephone constantly ring?

> **ACTION**

Yes to 1	Varicose Veins (p 119)
Yes to 2, 3, or 4, or No to 5	If you experience back pain, see Fitness Profile (Exercise, Action section, p 26).
Yes to 6a, b or c, 7, 8 or 9	Cancer of the Bladder, especially if male (p 129)
Yes to 6e-m or 13	Cancer of the Lung (p 125)
Yes to 10	If you are male, Enlarged Prostate (p 139)
Yes to 11, 12 or 13	If you are male, Cancer of the Prostate (p 133)
Yes to 13, 17 or 18	If you are male, Cancer of the Testicles (p 137)
Yes to 14	If you are female, Cancer of the Cervix (p 132)
Yes to 6e, 15 or 16	Cancer of the Colon and Rectum (p 134)
Yes to 6e or 15	Cancer of the Stomach (p 136)
Yes to any of 19-21	Respiratory Disorders (p 123)
Yes to any of 22-26	Common Infection (p 104)
Yes to any of 27-31	Stress (p 71)

EATING HABITS

Yes	No	
1		1 Do you leave the table feeling bloated?
1		2 Do you eat in a rush?
	1	3 Do you chew your food thoroughly?
1		4 Do you regularly eat rich or highly spiced food, cucumber, onion, garlic, unripe fruit, or raw meat?
2		5 Do you drink black coffee or alcohol on an empty stomach?
1		6 Do you chew gum?
2		7 Do you finish your meals more quickly than others?
2		8 Do you smoke immediately before, during, or after a meal?

ACTION ⟩

3 or more

Some of the 'eating habits' listed above are symptomatic of Stress and Anxiety. Consult the following scans:

Anxiety (p 89)
Type-A Personality (p 68)
Stress (p 71)

Yes to 4 or 5

Certain foods and food additives can aggravate the stomach and intestine, and produce more gastric juices than are healthy, and should not be eaten regularly. Spices, particularly hot curry spices, do this, as do alcohol and coffee, particularly if drunk on an empty stomach. Interestingly, it is not the caffeine in coffee that does the damage, because de-caffeinated coffee is, if anything, worse in this respect. Certain additives are also known to have this effect: E220-227, E239, E249-252, E310-312, 503, 508, 525, 621 and 924, though it takes quite large quantities to cause symptoms such as nausea. Adjust your diet accordingly. Consult the Peptic Ulcer scan (p 140).

Yes	No

DRINKING HABITS

1 How much alcohol do you drink in a week?*

Male

Yes	No	
3		a less than 20 units
5		b between 20 and 35 units
6		c between 35 and 50 units
7		d more than 50 units

Female

Yes	No	
3		a less than 13 units
5		b between 13 and 20 units
6		c between 20 and 35 units
7		d more than 35 units

*1 standard unit of alcohol is equivalent to:
½ pint (280ml/10fl oz) normal strength beer; or
½ gill (47ml/1.7fl oz) sherry/martini/fortified wine; or
⅙ gill (23ml/0.9 fl oz) distilled spirits (40% alcohol);
or a small glass of wine (125ml/4.4 fl oz).

2 How many days per week do you drink no alcohol at all?

Yes	No	
1		a 3 or more days
2		b 2 days
3		c 1 day
5		d you drink every day

3 What time of day do you tend to have a first drink?

Yes	No	
1		a evening
2		b midday/lunchtime
3		c morning

4 How fast do you drink?

Yes	No	
1		a about the same speed or slower than your friends/drinking companions
2		b faster than some and slower than others
3		c faster than most

ACTION ⟩

8 or more   **P5**

Yes to 2c or d   Some people develop alcohol disorders at very low levels of drinking. This is made more likely if you drink regularly. The liver has amazing powers of regeneration, so if you give it a break it can repair itself, sometimes in as little as 72 hours.

Yes to 3b or c   The body seems to be able to cope with alcohol in the evening rather better than first thing in the morning or at midday.

Yes to 4a, b or c   Your liver can process about one unit of alcohol an hour. If you drink at this rate, your liver will be kept busy but your blood alcohol level will remain low. If you drink too fast for your liver to process the alcohol, blood levels remain high and very dangerous.

ASSOCIATED RISK
Alcohol is capable of seriously injuring the health of anyone who drinks too much, too often. While the habit may often be rooted in Anxiety, boredom or Depression, alcohol itself is actually most efficient in causing these states. In general, it will lower your tolerance to stressful conditions, spoil relationships and sexual enjoyment, and, if you are a driver, make you prone to road accidents. Additionally, serious abuse makes you vulnerable to fatal disease. If you scored 12 or more, consult the following scans:

Liver and Kidney Disease (p 120)

Birth Abnormalities (p 147)

High Blood Pressure (p 110)

Cancer of the Mouth and Throat (p 128)

Heart Disease (p 113)

Stroke (p 116)

DRUG HABITS

Yes	No	
		1 Which of these statements best describes your attitude to medical drugs?
3		a I generally take some medicine when I feel run down or ill.
4		b I know what my body needs, and there are times when certain medicines are the best thing for me.

Yes	No	
2		**c** I only take medicine when I feel really bad.
1		**d** I only take medicine when the doctor prescribes it.
		e I rarely take medicine.

2 Which of these sentences most nearly describes your attitude to your doctor?

Yes	No	
4		**a** I generally tell my doctor what I think is wrong with me and ask for the medicine I want.
1		**b** I sometimes refuse a prescription if my doctor offers it, or just don't collect the medicine from the chemist.
3		**c** I generally expect my doctor to give me a prescription when I visit him or her.
		d none of these.
4		3 If YES to 1b and/or 2a, have you ever changed your doctor to one that will provide the medicines you feel you need?
	1	4 If you buy drugs from a chemist, do you tell him/her what other drugs you are taking?
3		5 Do you ever take other people's prescribed medicine (ie medicines not prescribed for you, personally)?
3		6 Do you ever feel uncertain about how much of a drug you should be taking, or how often you should take it and when you should start, after you have left the doctor's surgery or the chemist shop?

7 How many jars, boxes, packets, bottles of medicine do you keep in stock in the house?

Yes	No	
1		**a** less than 10
3		**b** between 10 and 20
4		**c** more than 20

Yes	No	
		8 How often do you visit a chemist shop for medical supplies?
1		**a** about once a month or less
2		**b** about once a week
3		**c** more than once a week
4		9 Do you take drugs for pleasure?
3		10 Do you take drugs
		a for stress
		b for anxiety
		c for insomnia
		d to boost your confidence
		e to help you relax
		f to enhance the excitement of life?
		11 If so, how often do you use them?
1		**a** once a month
2		**b** once a fortnight
3		**c** once a week
4		**d** several times a week
5		**e** most days
		12 Do you ever take
3		**a** marijuana
4		**b** cocaine
4		**c** amphetamines
5		**d** heroin
5		**e** glue or solvent
5		**f** LSD or other hallucinogens?
		13 If so, how often do you use them?
1		**a** once a month
2		**b** once a fortnight
4		**c** once a week
5		**d** several times a week
5		**e** most days
		14 Do you inject drugs into your veins?
		15 Are you pregnant?
		16 Do you suffer regularly from coughs and colds?
		17 Do you regularly take aspirin-based painkillers or non-steroidal anti-inflammatory drugs?

Yes	No

18 Do you experience any of the following side-effects during or after taking drugs of any kind?

Abdominal pain
Anxiety
Blurred vision
Concentration difficulties
Decreased sweating
Dizziness
Drowsiness
Dry mouth and throat
Fatigue
Headache
Impotence
Insomnia
Listlessness
Loss of libido
Moodiness
Memory loss
Nasal congestion
Palpitations
Understanding difficulties

19 Do you get migraines, skin rashes, swellings, bowel problems, feelings of nausea or bouts of sneezing?

SCORE

12 or more for questions 1-8
Your attitude to drugs is not healthy and may be putting your health at *serious* risk. Scores higher than 7 are a matter of concern. There is not a magic drug for every condition and often other action is preferable or safer.

7 or more for questions 9-13
Regular intake of any drug, either for pleasure or medical purposes, carries risk of physical and/or psychological side-effects.

Yes to 10 or 12
P5

Yes to 10a
P11

Yes to 10b   P17

Yes to 10c   P15

Yes to 10d   P7

Yes to 10e   P10

Yes to 10f   You may find **P4** helpful, if not try **P1**.

Yes to 18   The possible effects of drugs are numerous. At one
end of the scale they can produce short-term
secondary or side-effects which are different in type
to the purposes required of the drugs as prescribed.
For example, anti-histamines may be prescribed to
intervene in an allergic response but frequently
cause drowsiness; antibiotics taken to combat a
throat infection also attack the bacteria which are
naturally and healthily present in the female
vagina, and can increase a woman's risk to yeast-
like infections, such as Thrush. Again, some drugs
taken to control blood pressure, and certain anti-
depressants, can reduce sexual desire; tetracycline-
based antibiotics can cause listlessness and fatigue.
Consult your doctor if you believe the symptoms
you feel are caused by prescribed drugs. If they are
caused by drugs you have bought, treat any side-
effects as serious warning signs of drug abuse.

Yes to 19   **P2**. In some people, drugs provoke an allergic
reaction. For example, penicillin causes skin rash, a
swollen face or throat, fever or swollen joints in
some people. There is also a range of problematic
additives used in the flavouring and colouring of
medicines. For example, the orange colour in some
medicines comes from tartrazine (E102), which has
been clearly linked with allergy in some children.
Unfortunately, in Britain, ingredients do not have
to be listed on drug labels.

ASSOCIATED RISK

15 or more   Your liver or kidneys may be in danger of being
overall   damaged, consult the Liver and Kidney Disease Scan
(p 120).

High score in You are susceptible to the condition known as
questions 1-8   Hypochondria, consult the next scan.

No to 4   When obtaining drugs from your doctor or pharmacist, be sure to tell him/her about any other drugs you are taking. Sometimes one drug can stop another working efficiently; sometimes they create a new and harmful effect together.

Yes to 10 or 12   All the drugs referred to in these questions are potentially addictive, either physically or psychologically, and your answers suggest that you are at risk.

Yes to 14   Careless use of unsterilised needles can cause Hepatitis (p 108) and AIDS (p 107). Consult these scans to assess your risk.

Yes to 15   There are many drugs which have a potentially detrimental effect upon the developing foetus, and carry a particular risk during the first three months of pregnancy. Drugs can also find their way to a baby through a mother's breast milk. You are advised to consult the Birth Abnormalities scan (p 147).

Yes to 16   A careless or cavalier attitude to drugs will increase your susceptibility to infection. You may find it useful to consult the Common Infection scan (p 104).

Yes to 17   These can cause stomach irritation and bleeding, and may cause Acute Gastritis, especially if they are taken regularly. Gastritis usually occurs between 8 and 24 hours after taking the drug and, typically, carries symptoms of lower abdominal pain, nausea, vomiting and loss of appetite.

Yes	No

HYPOCHONDRIA

1 How many times have you visited a doctor in the last six months?
   a not at all or once
   b once or twice
   c between 2 and 5 times
   d 6 or more times

2 How often do you worry that there might be something serious, and as yet undiscovered, wrong with you?

Yes	No

a never
b occasionally
c several times a month
d several times a day

3 How often do you talk about your ailments to
   other people?
   a never
   b occasionally
   c several times a month
   d several times a day

4 When you experience bodily sensations, such as
   twinges of pain or feelings of fatigue, do you
   assume that they must mean that there is
   something wrong with you?
   a no
   b sometimes
   c usually
   d always

5 Do other people think you make more of a fuss
   about your ailments than need be?
   a no
   b sometimes
   c usually
   d always

6 How often do you worry that you are not getting
   the right kind of exercise or diet?
   a never
   b occasionally
   c several times a month
   d several times a day

ACTION

If you have answered YES to at least one "d" or "c",
or three "b's", complete **P1** and then complete **P7**
and **P11**.

SMOKING HABITS

Yes	No	

1 Do you smoke
   a cigarettes
   b pipe
   c cigars?

ACTION
If YES to **a** go to question 4
If YES to **b** or **c** go to question 2

2a Do you smoke pipe or cigars
   a occasionally — **1**
   b most days — **2**
   c every day — **5**
   d several times a day — **7**
   e most of the time? — **8**

2b Do you inhale the smoke? — **5**

3 Do you also smoke cigarettes?
   (If YES go to 4; if NO go to 7)

4a How many cigarettes do you smoke each day?
   a less than ten — **5**
   b less than 20 but more than 10 — **8**
   c more than 20 — **10**

4b Do you inhale the smoke? — **5**

5 Do you smoke
   a high tar cigarettes — **3**
   b medium tar cigarettes — **2**
   c low tar cigarettes? — **1**

6 Do you smoke
   a filtered cigarettes — **1**
   b unfiltered cigarettes? — **2**

7 At what age did you start to smoke regularly?
   a 15-19 — **3**
   b 20-24 — **2**
   c 25+ — **1**

Yes	No
1	
2	
3	
4	
5	
1	
2	
3	
4	
1	
1	
2	

8 How long have you been smoking?
   a less than 15 years
   b 15-29 years
   c 30-44 years
   d 45-59 years
   e 60+

9 Do you live in a house with
   a one smoker
   b two smokers
   c three smokers?

10 Do you regularly smoke cannabis?

11 Do you work in a smokey office or factory environment?

12 Do you live in
   a the country
   b the town
   c a heavily populated city?

> **ACTION**

The higher the score the more vulnerable you are to the many fatal or debilitating diseases known to be caused by smoking, and any positive score requires action. If you score 7 or more, see Associated Risk below.

7 or more   P9 then **P5**. If at first **P5** does not help, go to **P1**.

ASSOCIATED RISK
Smoke is responsible for between 15% and 20% of all deaths in Britain. If you scored 7 or more, you are advised to consult the following scans.

Respiratory Disorders (p 123)
Cancer of the Lung (p 125)
Cancer of the Mouth and Throat (p 128)
Peptic Ulcer (p 140)
High Blood Pressure (p 110)
Heart Disease (p 113)

Stroke (p 116)
Cancer of the Bladder (p 129)
Birth Abnormalities (p 147)
Cancer of the Cervix (p 132)
Cancer of the Stomach (p 136)

Yes	No

TENSE PERSONALITY

1   Do you spend much of the day fidgeting?

2   Do you find it difficult to 'switch off'?

3   Do you find it difficult to fall asleep?

4   Do you have any nervous habits, eg nail biting, tooth grinding, hair twiddling?

5   Are your muscles tense (eg clenched hand, jaw, furrowed or raised forehead, tense neck or shoulders)?

6   Do you lose your temper or snap for no particular reason?

7   Are you a woman?

ACTION ⟩

If you have answered YES to any of the questions 1 to 6, go to **P1** and then **P11** and **P17**.

Yes to 7   Your problem may be related to the menstrual cycle and we suggest you go to **P10**.

ASSOCIATED RISK
Tension can herald the development of psychological and physical disorders associated with Anxiety and Stress. Complete the Personal Profile Scans for Stress (p 71) and Anxiety (p 89), and you will be directed to Vulnerability Scans appropriate to your case.

Yes	No

AGGRESSIVE PERSONALITY

1   Are you easily provoked to temper?

2   Do you get irritated by people around you?

3   Do you often feel anger?

4   Do you harbour grudges and resentments?

Yes	No

5 Do most people around you tread warily in your presence?

6 Do you tend to make people cry?

7 Do your aggressive outbursts usually achieve what you want?

8 Do you think that you need to be aggressive to achieve the success you desire?

9 Do you enjoy the company of aggressive people?

10 Do you ever hit people?

SCORE

Yes to any   You exhibit the characteristics of this personality.

Yes	No

ACTION

Complete the questions below:

11 Have you always exhibited aggressive behaviour or has it only occurred since an accident or a significant event in your life?

12 Do you have difficulties communicating or expressing yourself?

13 Do you feel unable to control or change things in your life?

14 Are you unconfident or frightened?

15 Are you dissatisfied with what you are achieving in life?

16 Do you lack an enjoyable intimate relationship?

17 Have your relationships suffered as a result of your aggressive or irritable behaviour?

18 Has your social life suffered as a result of your aggressive or irritable behaviour?

Yes	No

19 Do you spend little time in enjoyable leisure pursuits (eg hobbies, sport, social activity)?

20 Do you seldom take physical exercise?

21 Do you set very high standards for yourself and/or other people?

22 Do you think that your aggressiveness may be in response to a stressful situation?

23 Do you often feel guilty about your behaviour to other people?

24 Do you have any ways of getting what you want other than by aggressive outbursts?

25 Are you sexually frustrated?

26 If you are a woman, do your angry feelings appear near or during your menstruation period?

27 Are you disabled or suffering from a long-term illness, disability or deformity?

28 Do you have problems sleeping?

29 Do you drink alcohol or take drugs?

ACTION

	P10 and **P13**
Yes to 11	**P11**
Yes to 12, 13 or **14**	**P3**
Yes to 15	**P3** and **P7**
Yes to 16-18 or **23-25**	**P8** and/or **P6**
Yes to 17, 18 or **24**	**P13**

Yes to 20	**P21**
Yes to 19	**P9**
Yes to 26	**P10**
Yes to 27	Consult the Distress scan (p 149).
Yes to 28	**P15**
Yes to 29	**P9** and then **P5**.

ASSOCIATED RISK
You may be vulnerable to physical problems
typically associated with this personality; consult
the following scans:

High Blood Pressure (p 110)
Heart Disease (p 113)
Stroke (p 116)

Yes	No

NON-ASSERTIVE PERSONALITY

Section A
1 Do you get on badly with people?

2 Do you find it difficult to go to parties or other
   social gatherings, meet new people, or make
   friends at work?

3 Do you have difficulty thinking of things to say?

4 Do you lack people around you who like you and
   are supportive towards you?

Section B
5 Do you think that what you have to say is
   unimportant or boring?

6 Are you ready to criticise or blame yourself for
   things that go wrong?

Yes	No

7   Do you often have negative thoughts about yourself?

8   Are you overly eager to please?

9   In general, do you think you are worth less than other people?

10 Do you have any physical features or skin blemishes that you are unhappy with?

11 Do you lack skills?

Section C
12 Do you feel undermined by people at home/ work?

13 Do you feel that when there are problems at work, at home or in family matters it tends to fall to you to sort them out?

Section D
14 Do you worry about the consequences of your decisions?

15 Do you have difficulty thinking clearly?

16 If YES to 15, is it worse when you are anxious?

17 Do you find it difficult to take decisions?

18 Does this difficulty interfere with your everyday activities?

Section E
19 Do you have any behaviour or mannerism that you are not happy with?

Section F
20 Are you disabled or do you suffer from a long-term illness?

21 Do you rarely laugh?

SCORE
If you have ticked YES to one or more questions in
each of Sections A to C, you display certain
characteristics of the Non-assertive Personality.

> **ACTION**

Yes to any of Section A	**P8**
Yes to any of Section B	**P7**
Yes to any of Section C	**P3**
Yes to 19	**P5**
Yes to 15, 17 or 18	Step 5/**P4**
Yes to 14 or 16	**P17**
Yes to 20	Consult the Distress scan (p 149).
Yes to 21	**P14**

ASSOCIATED RISK
By behaving assertively you can lower Stress. By
saying what you want to say or doing what you
want to do, you avoid building up resentment and
'bottling up' your feelings. Also, by expressing
yourself in a controlled way rather than in angry
outbursts, Stress is reduced. A high score in this scan
suggests that you are at risk to Stress-related
disorders, which are both psychological (see
especially Depression, p 94) and physical. To assess
your risk to Stress-related disorders, complete the
full Stress scan (p 71).

Yes	No

FRUSTRATED PERSONALITY

1 Do you find it difficult to express yourself in
   words?

Yes	No

2 Do you find it difficult to stand up for your rights?

3 Do you set very high standards for yourself and/or others?

4 Is your situation making it difficult to achieve what you want?

5 Do you expect things to go the way you want them to?

6 Do you often get upset when things are not as you would like them to be?

7 Do you often get impatient?

8 Do you often feel hindered from controlling or changing things in your life?

> **ACTION**

If you have ticked YES to one or more questions, complete **P10** and then either **P1** or move to programs appropriate to your specific responses as detailed below:

9 Are you disabled or do you suffer from a long-term, debilitating illness?

Yes to 9   Consult the Distress scan (p 149).

Yes to 1   **P8**

Yes to 2   **P3**

Yes to 3, 4   **P9**
or 5

Yes to 6   **P11** or **P14**

Yes to 7   **P10** and **P13**

ASSOCIATED RISK
If you answer YES to any one of the questions then feelings of frustration are probably not new to you.

The more frustrated your reactions are to your situation, the higher your risk to physical and psychological disorders typically associated with Anxiety and Stress. See especially the following scans:

Peptic Ulcer (p 140)
High Blood Pressure (p 110)
Heart Disease (p 113)
Stroke (p 116)

GUILT-LADEN PERSONALITY

Yes	No

1 Do you tend to blame youself when things go wrong?

2 Do other people often blame you for things that go wrong?

3 Do you have strong religious beliefs?

4 Do you feel responsible for the actions of others?

5 If something is bothering you, do you find it difficult to talk about it?

| ACTION ⟩ |

Yes to 2 or more

You display characteristics of this personality type. Complete the Non-assertive Personality scan (p 62).

Yes	No

7 Have you recently suffered a bereavement?

8 Have you caused someone injury in a road or other type of accident, or have you dealt someone a blow (physically or emotionally)?

Yes to 7 or 8

Consult **P14** (Depression Control) or **P11** Stress Management), as applicable.

ASSOCIATED RISK
Strongly held feelings of guilt can cause Depression (see p 94) and trigger disorders associated with Anxiety (p 89) and Stress (p 71).

Yes	No

SUSPICIOUS PERSONALITY

1   Do you often suspect people's motives?

2   Do you sometimes think that people are conspiring against you?

3   Do you have a sense that most people are after what they can get from you?

4   Do you feel that no one can be completely trusted?

5   Do you ever check up on the whereabouts of a friend, wife, husband or lover?

6   Do you become excited in anticipation that your suspicions may turn out well-founded?

Yes to 3 or more

SCORE
Your behaviour and thinking display the characteristics of this personality style.

| ACTION ⟩

P1, then **P17**, and **P6** (Partners), if applicable.

ASSOCIATED RISK
This personality is at risk to Anxiety-related disorders, see p 91.

Yes	No

OBSESSIONAL PERSONALITY

1   Do you get very upset if things aren't done properly?

2   Is it very important for you to be in control of everything in your life?

3   Do you frequently check or go over things that you have done?

4   Do you find thoughts coming into your head that you can't get rid of?

Yes	No

5 Are these thoughts present for more than a few minutes each day?

6 Do you think most people around you are untidy and haphazard in their behaviour?

7 Did you score 12 or more in the Anxiety scan (p 89)?

Yes to 2 or more

SCORE
You exhibit the characteristics of this personality type.

| ACTION > |

P10, and then **P17**.

ASSOCIATED RISK
This personality is at risk to Anxiety and Stress-related disorders (p 91 and p89, respectively).
   If you are pregnant, see the Vulnerability Scan for Motherhood Problems (p 145). If you are underweight according to the Weight chart on p 22, complete the Anorexia scan (p 151).

Yes	No

TYPE-A PERSONALITY

1 Do you take on more tasks than are possible to do in an orderly way?

2 Are you very competitive?

3 Do you have high ambitions for yourself?

4 Are you easily provoked to losing your temper?

5 Are you frequently irritated by the people around you?

6 Do you regularly feel angry?

7 Are you always in a hurry?

8 Do you get upset if you or others are late?

Yes	No

9 Do you feel pressured to get things done?

10 Do you get impatient quite often?

11 Do you often feel you are racing against time?

12 Do you talk rapidly?

13 Do you gesticulate more than most?

14 Do you take work home with you?

15 Do you work more than 10 hours a day or at weekends in addition to weekdays?

16 Do you put work before family life?

17 Do you regularly stay up late?

18 Do you spend little time on home life and take little part in domestic decisions?

19 Do you make snap decisions?

20 Do you display any nervous mannerisms, twitches or habits like nailbiting?

21 Are you keen to get promoted at work?

22 Are you keen to improve your financial position?

23 Are you keen to improve your social position?

24 Are you dissatisfied with your work performance?

25 Do you get restless?

26 Do you feel responsible for what you and others do?

27 Do you tend to interrupt people before they have finished speaking?

28 Do you find it difficult to wait patiently?

Yes	No

29 Do you try to get as much done as possible in any given period of time?

30 Do you take minimal holidays?

31 Do you push yourself to keep going, even when you are tired?

32 Do you try to ignore physical symptoms?

33 Do you visit a doctor less than once a year?

34 Do you find it difficult to switch off or have rests during the day?

35 Do you feel uneasy if you are not busy?

36 Do you finish your meals more quickly than other people?

37 Do you swallow your food without chewing it thoroughly?

38 Do you get upset if things are not done perfectly?

39 Do you feel a strong need to excel?

SCORE
If you ticked YES to more than 10 questions, you exhibit the characteristics of this personality type.

> **ACTION**

P4

ASSOCIATED RISK
By reacting more frequently and intensely to daily stresses and provocations, this racing, competitive personality is vulnerable to arterial disorders.
Complete the following scans:

High Blood Pressure (p110)
Heart Disease (p113)
Stroke (p116)

STRESS
For your **overall Stress score**, see page 89.

Yes	No

A. THE ENVIRONMENT

1 Are your living conditions inadequate?

2 Is your home or workplace noisy?

3 Do you lack a room of your own where you can get peace and quiet or a time in the day when you can be alone?

4 Does your house require substantial building or decorative work?

5 Are your surroundings at home or at work messy or chaotic?

6 Do you live in a tower block?

7 Are there too many people living in your home?

8 Is your neighbourhood crowded?

9 Do you lack access to a garden, park or the countryside?

10 Are robberies and muggings common in the neighbourhood?

11 Do you worry about your home being vandalised or broken into?

12 Do you have a poor relationship with your neighbours?

13 Does your telephone ring constantly?

14 Do you have financial worries?

15 Do you drive in heavy traffic every day?

16 Do you often get shouted at?

17 Are you often hit?

Yes	No

18 Have you lived in this country for less than 5 years?

19 Do you have worries about residency or citizenship of this country?

20 Do you suffer by reason of your race, sex or beliefs?

21 Do you live far from your family?

22 Is your environment or any of the above a conscious problem to you?

ACTION

If you ticked YES to five questions (or if you ticked YES to question 22), go to **P1** and **P11**.

Yes	No

B. YOUR LIFESTYLE

1 In the last 12 months have you been off work for health reasons on more than 3 occasions?

2 Are you unemployed?

3 If so, have you been unemployed for more than 6 months?

4 Have you changed your job more than twice in the last 5 years?

5 Do you skip meals and/or breaks?

6 Do you take medicines (including aspirins, cough sweets, etc.) more than once a week?

7 Did you visit your doctor more than 3 times last year?

8 Do you smoke?

9 Do you drink more than 35 units of alcohol a week?

*1 standard unit of alcohol is equivalent to:
½ pint (280ml/10fl oz) normal strength beer;
½ gill (47ml/1.7fl oz) sherry/martini/fortified wine;

⅙ gill (23ml/0.9 fl oz) distilled spirits (40% alcohol); a small glass of wine (125ml/4.4 fl oz).

Yes	No	
		10 Do you regularly stay up late?
		11 Do you take cocaine, heroin, or amphetamines?
		12 Is your life full of change and new events?
		13 Do you have extra-marital affairs?
		14 Do you have more than one affair at a time?
		15 Are you cheating on anyone in your work?
		16 Do you live on your own?
		17 Have you moved house more than twice in the past 5 years?
		18 Do you look after an elderly, sick or disabled relative?
		19 Are you responsible for looking after children during the day?
		20 Do you look after children under 5 years of age?
		21 Do you find looking after dependants a burden?
		22 Are you physically handicapped?

> ACTION

Yes to 5 questions +

P1 and then **P11** and **P4**.

Yes	No	
		23 Do you engage in non-competitive sports such as walking, swimming or cycling?
		24 Did you score between 1 and 8 in the Exercise scan (p 24)?
		25 Are you able to relax and unwind regularly?

No to 23 or 24   P21

No to 25   P10

Yes to 8, 9 or 11   P5

Yes	No	**C. YOUR WORK**
		1 Do you have to work very hard or fast?
		2 Do you find your job too demanding?
		3 Does your job lack challenge?
		4 Is your job boring, mechanical or repetitive?
		5 Are you engaged in shift work?
		6 Do you feel you have too many or too few responsibilities?
		7 Do you have to work to deadlines?
		8 Are you constantly having to make decisions?
		9 Do you feel you are excluded from making decisions?
		10 Do you feel that you are not consulted sufficiently about things?
		11 Is your work physically draining?
		12 Is your work mentally exhausting?
		13 Do you work at weekends?
		14 Do you work 10 hours a day or more?
		15 Do you take your work home with you?
		16 Do you dislike your work hours?
		17 Do you feel under too much pressure?

Yes	No

18 Do you often make mistakes?

19 Do you dislike your work?

20 Do you seldom receive praise for what you do?

21 Do you lack opportunities for promotion or advancement at work?

22 Do you want promotion badly?

23 Does it seem that your work is never finished?

24 Are you unclear about what you have to do at work?

25 Are you made to carry out tasks which you do not feel are part of your working brief?

26 Do you get on badly with people at work?

27 Is your boss unsupportive?

28 Do people ignore you at work?

29 Do you think that what you do is worthless?

30 Do you feel that your talents and abilities are insufficiently employed in your work?

31 Has your performance deteriorated?

32 Do you feel frustrated at work?

33 Do you worry about your performance?

| ACTION ⟩ |

Yes to 5 questions +   **P1**, and then **P11** and **P3**.

Yes	No

D. YOUR HOME LIFE
1   Do you feel uncomfortable with people you live with?

2   Are you taken for granted at home?

Yes	No

3 Do you and your partner both work full-time?

4 Are you alone responsible for household and child-care tasks?

5 Is your sleep interrupted by children?

6 Do you worry about your children?

7 Do you harbour feelings of resentment?

8 Do you feel trapped in your home life?

9 Do you have a strained relationship with your partner?

10 Do you spend too little time with your partner?

11 Is your relationship with him/her a volatile one?

12 Do you often have rows at home?

13 Are you disappointed by your marriage/relationship?

14 Do you often get upset by your partner's fauts?

15 Is sex a source of worry?

| ACTION |

Yes to 5 questions +	P1
Yes to 1 or 2	P3
Yes to 9 or any of 11-15	P6
Yes to 11, 12 or 14	P13
Yes to 7 or 8	P9

Yes	No
3	
3	

E. THINGS THAT HAPPEN TO YOU

1 Did you lose a close relative in childhood?

2 Have you experienced any of the following
   a in the past year
   b in the last 5 years
   c ever?

[Score 3 for **a** (ie in the past year), 2 for **b**, 1 for **c**]

Serious illness, injury, accident or operation

Serious illness, injury, accident or operation on a close relative or friend

The death of a close friend or relative

Any other major loss, a job perhaps

Mugging, robbery, rape, or similarly upsetting event

Major financial difficulty or improvement

Divorce, separation or break-up of an intimate relationship

Any other marital or family problem

Marriage or reconciliation

The birth of a child or other addition to the family

Retirement

Major trouble with the Law

An unplanned pregnancy

Sexual difficulties of any kind

Imprisonment

3 Have you taken out a large loan in the last few years?

ACTION

A score of 6 or more

There is a risk of Depression and, possibly, other Stress-related problems. Check the Emotional Profile Scans listed in the Profile Scan Index (p 21). If the index fails to suggest a scan that seems appropriate, consult **P11**.

Yes	No

F. YOUR SOCIAL LIFE

1 Do you have someone to trust and confide in?

2 Can you name 3 good friends?

3 Do you have a satisfying emotional relationship with someone?

4 Do you have people you can rely upon to help out when need be?

5 If you live alone, does someone visit you, socially, at least once a week?

6 Are you satisfied with your social life?

7 Do you belong to any clubs or organisations that meet fairly regularly?

8 Do you find it easy meeting new people?

9 Do you avoid people?

10 Are you a lonely person?

11 Can you count on someone comforting, holding you in their arms, when you are feeling down?

12 Do you have a satisfying sexual relationship with someone?

13 Do you see this person more than once a week?

14 Do you see any of your friends more than once a week?

15 Do you enjoy seeing family and friends?

Yes	No

16 Do you harbour feelings of resentment about being dependent upon people?

17 Do you feel people make excessive demands upon you?

18 Do you dislike social occasions?

> ACTION

No to any of 1-8   **P8**

Yes to 9 or 10   **P8**

No to 3, 11 or 12   **P6**

No to any of 13-15   **P3**

Yes to any of 16-18   **P3**

Yes	No

G. YOUR BEHAVIOUR

I. General

1 Do you have difficulty getting off to sleep?

2 Do you wake frequently during the night?

3 Do you wake in the early hours?

4 Do you wake in a panic?

5 Do you have nightmares?

6 Are you worried about your sexual performance?

7 Do you eat to console yourself?

8 Do you crave food other than at meal times?

9 Do you have no appetite at meal times?

Yes	No

10 Do you drink to unwind?

11 Do you smoke to calm your nerves?

12 Have you increased your drinking and smoking recently?

13 Do you find it difficult to sit still?

14 Do you bite your nails, twiddle your hair or have any similar habit?

15 Do you make little effort with your appearance?

16 Do you find it difficult to relax or laugh?

17 Are you always rushing?

18 Do you eat quickly and not chew thoroughly?

19 Do you take drugs to make things feel better?

20 Do you tend to take on too many things?

21 Are you uneasy if you are not busy?

22 Are you compulsive about tidying up or about any other activity?

23 Do you often have accidents?

24 Do you often find yourself trying to avoid situations that you find difficult?

25 Do you fail to make the most of opportunities that come your way?

26 If a problem arises, do you keep it to yourself rather than talking it over with someone?

27 Do you often get drunk?

28 Are you ever violent?

29 Do you delay doing things because you are worried about the consequences?

| ACTION ⟩

Yes to any of 1-5	**P15**
Yes to 6	**P6**
Yes to 7 or 8	**P5** and **P19**
Yes to 9	Complete the Profile Scans for Anxiety and Depression (pp 89, 94). Try also **P21**.
Yes to any of 10-14, 18, 19, 27	**P11** and **P5**
Yes to 15 or 25	**P7**
Yes to any of 18, 20-23	**P4**. Try also **P17**, if YES to 18 or 22.
Yes to 16	**P10**
Yes to 28	**P13**
Yes to 29	**P1** and try Step 5 of **P4**.

Yes	No	
		II. Social
		1 Do you find it difficult to speak your mind or show your emotions?
		2 Do you find it difficult to start or continue conversations?
		3 Do you find it difficult to refuse a request?
		4 Do you often get into arguments?
		5 Do you have difficulty standing up for yourself in difficult situations?
		6 Are you unable to contradict someone if you know that they are wrong?
		7 Do you fail to protest if you are 'done down'?

Yes	No	
		8 Do you often shout at people or lose your temper?
		9 Do you find it difficult to give or receive compliments?
		10 Do you find it difficult to put forward your point of view?
		11 Do you find it difficult to give or receive criticism?
		12 Are you bossy or domineering?
		13 Do you avoid looking people in the eye?
		14 Do you often stutter or get tongue-tied?
		15 Do you tend to mumble?
		16 Do you speak fast?
		17 Do you talk too much, or too little?

ACTION ⟩

Yes to any **P3.** In addition, if you have ticked YES to 2 or 10-17, complete **P8**, and if you have ticked YES to 4 or 8, complete **P13**.

Yes	No	**H YOUR FEELINGS**
		I. Physical
		1 Do you feel very tired?
		2 Do you frequently feel nauseous?
		3 Do you sweat or get flushed for no obvious reason?
		4 Do you blush easily?
		5 Do you ever faint or have dizzy spells?
		6 Do you feel breathless and tight-chested when not exerting yourself?

Yes	No

7 Does your heart pound or race when not exerting yourself?

8 Do you often feel tearful?

9 Do you suffer chronic pain?

10 Do you suffer from unexplained aches and pains?

11 Are you sexually frustrated?

| ACTION ⟩ |

Yes to any   P17

Yes to 1, 8 or 10   P14

Yes to 9   P12

Yes to 11   P1 and then, as appropriate, complete **P8** and **P6**.

Yes	No

II. Emotional

1 Do you feel guilty easily?

2 Do you often feel jealous?

3 Are you irritable without obvious cause?

4 Do you feel sad?

5 Do you feel no warmth and affection for those near to you?

6 Do you feel constantly under strain?

7 Do you fail to enjoy your day-to-day activities?

8 Do you get scared or panicky for no good reason?

9 Does your mood go up and down for no particular reason?

10 Do you feel harassed?

ACTION ⟩	
Yes to 1 or 2	**P1** and **P3**
Yes to 3, 6 or 10	**P11**
Yes to 4, 5, 7 or 9	**P14**
Yes to 8	**P17**

Yes	No	
		III. About yourself

1 Do you lack interest in life?

2 Do you often feel bored?

3 Do you feel helpless or unable to cope?

4 Do you feel unconfident and/or insecure?

5 Do you feel frustrated with your lot in life?

6 Are you dissatisfied with your life?

7 Do you often feel there is little meaning in life?

8 Do you feel overwhelmed by the demands in your life?

9 Do you often find things getting on top of you?

10 Do you ever feel that life is not worth living?

11 Do you feel rejected by other people?

12 Do you feel that something terrible is going to happen to you?

ACTION ⟩	
Yes to 1, 3, 7 or 10-12	**P14**
Yes to 8 or 9	**P11**
Yes to 2 or 4-6	**P1**

Yes	No

J YOUR THINKING

I. What You Think

1 Do you feel a strong need to excel at things?

2 Do you get upset if things are not done properly?

3 Do you feel pressed for time?

4 Are you dissatisfied with yourself?

5 Do you get upset when you have to wait for things?

6 Do you feel that other people dislike you?

7 Are you very self-critical?

8 Do you feel hard done by in life?

9 Do you feel a failure in any area of your life?

10 Do you dislike yourself physically?

11 Do you dislike your personality?

12 Do you feel that you're not playing a useful role?

13 Do you worry about illness or death?

14 Do you feel pessimistic about the future?

15 Do you think that you are good at nothing?

16 Do you worry a lot about trivial things?

17 Are you unfairly criticised?

18 Do you lack confidence in being able to overcome the difficulties in your life?

19 Do you tend to avoid facing up to your problems?

20 Do you lack control over what happens to you?

21 Do you find sudden changes difficult to handle?

Yes	No

22 Do you have unfulfilled ambitions?

23 Do you feel unable to change things in life?

24 Do you have a great need to be loved or admired by others?

25 Do you worry a lot about what people think?

26 Do you envy other people?

27 Do you feel guilty if you do things that you enjoy?

28 Are you a burden to those around you?

29 Are you bitter about the way you are treated at home or at work?

30 Do you worry a lot about your health?

31 Do you think you might have some serious disease?

32 Do you blame others for your shortcomings?

33 Do you get upset that other people are not better than they are?

34 Do you tend to think that things were always better in the past?

35 Do you have high standards that are difficult for you or others to attain?

36 Do you get upset when things are not as you want them to be?

37 Do you feel that you have not lived up to other people's expectations?

38 Do you feel a pressure to perform, or to be something you are not?

39 Do you tend to harbour grudges?

Yes	No

40 Do you blame yourself when things go wrong?

41 Do you feel a continual need to get things done?

42 Are you easily embarrassed?

43 Do you worry a lot about yourself and your behaviour?

44 Do you think worrying helps prevent problems?

45 Do you often feel inferior to those around you?

46 Do you think things will get out of control unless you try all the time to stay on top?

47 Do you thrive on stress and tension?

48 Do you always feel anxious to get going and finish whatever you have to do?

49 Do you feel a great need to control things?

50 Do you start worrying about things long before they happen?

51 Do you think that you could change the fact that you think these things?

ACTION >

No to 51	**P9**
Yes to 5, 41, or any of 1-3, 35 or 46-48	**P4**
Yes to any of 4, 6, 7, 9-12, 15, 24-28, 38, 42, 45	**P7**
Yes to any of 8, 18-20, 22, 23, 29, 32, 33, 36, 39	**P3**

| Yes to any of
13-17, 21, 30,
31, 34, 37, 40 | P14 |
| Yes to any of
43, 44, 49, 50 | P17 |

Yes	No	**II. How You Think**
		1 Do you think about work after working hours?
		2 Do you find it difficult to make up your mind or take decisions?
		3 Do you find it difficult to concentrate?
		4 Do you find planning and organising your work difficult?
		5 Do you find thinking clearly about your problems difficult?
		6 Do you often suppress your feelings?
		7 Do you find it difficult to switch off?
		8 Are you absent-minded or forgetful?
		9 Can you change your mind easily?
		10 Do you have repetitive and intrusive thoughts?
		11 Are you unable to attend to things for long periods of time?
		12 Do you ever feel mentally confused?
		13 Do you have odd thoughts or feelings, or feel unreal?
		14 Do you ever find your thoughts racing too quickly?
		15 Do you have periods when your mind goes blank against your will?
		16 Do you find any of the above a problem?

> **ACTION**

If YES to 16 or to two or more of 1-15, complete **P11**.

OVERALL STRESS SCORE
Score 1 for every YES or NO which required ACTION.

If you score more than 20 overall, go to **P1** and then **P11**. If your overall Fitness score (p 22) was more than 15, follow the appropriate Action advice there; fitness helps you bear stress. Your **overall Stress score** will be useful in completing other scans.

ASSOCIATED RISK
Stress can cause or contribute to a number of disorders (including Depression, see p 94). Consult the following:

Respiratory Disorders (p 123)
Diabetes (p 118)
Liver and Kidney Disease (p 120)
Cancers (p 125 etc)

Peptic Ulcer (p 140)
Infection (p 104)
High Blood Pressure (p 110)
Heart Disease (p 113)
Stroke (p 116)

ANXIETY

Yes	No	
1		1 Do you worry about or dread things before they happen?
1		2 If YES, how often? **a** less than once a week
2		**b** between once and 3 times a week
3		**c** most days
1		3 How much do you worry? **a** slightly
2		**b** moderately
3		**c** extremely
1		4 Do you have difficulty falling asleep and/or wake up feeling your sleep was unsatisfactory? **a** occasionally
2		**b** sometimes
3		**c** frequently

Yes	No
1	
2	
3	
2	
3	
4	
1	
2	
3	
1	
2	
3	

5 Do you worry that something terrible might happen?
   a occasionally
   b sometimes
   c frequently

6 Do you worry about worrying?
   a occasionally
   b sometimes
   c frequently

7 How many times a week do you experience the symptoms that directed you to this scan?
   a less than once
   b between once and 5 times
   c more often than 5 times

8 When you experience these symptoms, how severe are they?
   a slight
   b moderate
   c severe
   d very severe

| ACTION ⟩

If you score 12 or more, go to **P17**. Also answer the following questions.

Yes	No

9 Are you worried about some physical feature of your appearance?

10 Do you have problems sleeping?

11 Have you recently given up taking or cut down on your consumption of alcohol or addictive drugs?

12 Did you score 12+ in the Exercise scan (p 24)?

13 Do you think your anxiety is due to your stressful situation?

14 Do you lack confidence or try to cope by avoiding things?

15 Are you forever in a rush?

Yes	No

16 Do you lack confidence in meeting people?

17 Are you frightened of particular things or situations?

Yes to 9   P7

Yes to 10   P15

Yes to 11   P5

Yes to 12   Fitness Test 1, **P21**.

Yes to 13   P11

Yes to 14   P7

Yes to 15   P4

Yes to 16   P8

Yes to 17   Complete the Fears and Phobias scan (p 91).

ASSOCIATED RISK
Anxiety can render you vulnerable to a number of physical and psychological problems and disorders (including Depression, see p 94). Consult the following scans:

Peptic Ulcer (p 140)   Stroke (p 116)
High Blood Pressure   Anorexia (p 151)
   (p 110)
Heart Disease (p 113)

Yes	No

FEARS AND PHOBIAS

This scan is for people who are frightened of specific things or situations, rather than for people who are generally anxious.

1 How frightened do the following make you? [Score on a scale of **1** to **3** where **1** indicates 'not at all' and **3** indicates 'very much'.]

Drinking or eating in public
Speaking in public

Yes	No

Social situations, eg parties, 'get togethers'
Cinemas, theatres, pubs or restaurants
Hospitals, doctors or dentists
Animals or insects
Arguments and confrontation
Flying

2 To what extent do you try to avoid the following situations because they make you feel uncomfortable? [Score on a scale of **1** to **3** where **1** indicates 'occasionally' and **3** indicates 'frequently'.]

Going out alone
Travelling in cars, buses or trains
Being away from home
Being in lifts
Enclosed spaces
Crowded shops or other crowds
Becoming ill or panicky out of doors

ACTION ⟩

A score of **more than 2** **for question 1**	**P16**
more than 2 **for question 2**	**P7**
less than 3 for **question 2**	**P16**

Yes	No

EMOTIONAL UPSET

1 Do you cry easily?

2 Do your moods swing from high to low?

3 Do your moods sometimes change in unintelligible or unpredictable ways?

4 Do you sometimes lose control of your emotions?

5 Are you sensitive to criticism?

Yes	No

6 Do your moods stop you doing the things you want to do in life?

7 Are your moods difficult to control?

8 If YES, does this frighten you?

9 Do you ever worry that you might be 'going mad'?

10 Do you worry frequently?

SCORE

Yes to 4 questions or more
Clearly you are experiencing emotional difficulties, which may lead to Depression (see p 94). Read carefully the Action Advice below.

| ACTION ⟩

P10, **P3** and **P7** may well be helpful, but if you feel you are reacting normally to an extremely stressful situation, complete **P11**. Should you fail to find answers, **P1** may help you to analyse your problem in more detail.

If you are physically fit and eat a healthy diet you are more able to cope with life's stresses. Go to Fitness Test 1 in **P21**, and to **P22/5** paying particular attention to the recommended daily intake of zinc.

Yes	No

If you are a woman, answer the questions below.

11 Are you pregnant or have you recently had a baby?

12 Are you a woman between her late 30s and 50?

13 If you are a woman, do your moods change before or around the time of your menstrual period?

Yes to 11
Complete the Motherhood Problems scan (pp 142/144).

Yes to 12
Complete the Hormone Profile I scan (p 96).

Yes to 13   Complete the Hormone Profile II scan (p 97). If your mood changes also occur at other times, follow the general Action advice above (p 93).

ASSOCIATED RISK
Complete the Depression scan (p 94) and, if directed to them, the associated Vulnerability Scans.

DEPRESSION

Yes	No	
		1 How often do you think that life is not worth living? **a** never
1		**b** sometimes
2		**c** frequently
1		2 Have you lost your appetite?
1		3 Have you lost interest in sex?
1		4 Do you have fitful and disturbed sleep, waking frequently in the night?
1		5 Do you tend to wake up with gloomy thoughts?
1		6 Do you find it an effort to do things?
1		7 Do you find it difficult to think clearly and take decisions?
1		8 Do you often find your mind goes blank?
		9 How often do you cry? **a** a few times a month
1		**b** a few times a week
2		**c** daily
1		10 Do you rarely engage in enjoyable activities?
1		11 Do you rarely laugh?
1		12 Do you feel that you make no difference to what happens around you?
1		13 Are you often criticised at home or at work?

Yes	No
1	
1	
2	
1	
2	
1	

14 Do you have periods of being 'high' between depressed times?

15 Do you consider that you are worthless?
  a no
  b sometimes
  c frequently

16 Do you feel 'empty' or 'numb' inside?
  a no
  b sometimes
  c frequently

17 Do you rarely have warm feelings towards people?

> ACTION

P14 will be helpful if you scored 3 or more. If you feel that your depression is in response to a particularly stressful situation you should also read through **P11**.

If you are physically fit and eat a healthy diet you are more able to cope with life's stresses. Go to Fitness Test 1 in **P21** and **P22/5** paying particular attention to the recommended daily intake of zinc.

More personalised advice may be possible if you first answer the following questions:

Yes	No

18 Are you disabled, or suffering from disease or pain?

19 Are you a woman between her late 30s and 50?

20 Is being overweight part of the problem?

21 Do you find it difficult to assert yourself?

Yes to 18   Complete the Distress scan (p 149).

Yes to 19   Complete the Hormone Profile scan (p 96).

Yes to 20   **P19**

Yes to 21   Complete the Non-assertive scan (p 62).

HORMONE PROFILE I

Yes	No

1 Are you a woman and aged between your late 30s and 50?

2 Have your periods begun to change?

3 Do you regularly experience any of the following symptoms?

   Hot flushes
   Tingling sensations
   Chills
   Sweating
   Headache
   Fatigue
   Palpitations
   Insomnia
   Nausea
   Irritability
   Depression
   Anxiety
   Fears
   Mood swings

No to 1

Go to Hormone Profile II; if unhelpful, consult the Symptom Chart (p 8) for other references to the symptoms listed in question 3 above.

Yes to 1, 2 and/or 3

You are experiencing the menopause, go to **P1**. Also answer question 4 and following:

Yes	No

4 Do you smoke?

5 Are you underweight (see page 24)?

6 Did you score 30 or more in the Vitamins and Minerals scan (p 28)?

7 Did you score 12 or more in the Exercise scan (p 24)?

Yes to any two of 4-7

SCORE
You may be vulnerable to Osteoporosis, a disorder which leaves the bones fragile and breakable, particularly in post-menopausal women.

ACTION ⟩

Yes to 4   **P5**

Yes to 5 or 6   **P22/5**. Take special note of the Calcium table.

Yes to 7   **P21**

Yes	No

HORMONE PROFILE II

1 Do you experience any of the following
   symptoms just before or during a period?

   a Irritability
   b Nervousness
   c Mild to severe headaches
   d Emotional changes
   e Breast or back pain
   f Pain in the tummy
   g Mood Swings

ACTION ⟩

Yes to any of   **P17**
a-d, or g

Yes to any of   **P12**
e-f

You are also advised to follow a plan of action:

1. **P22/5**. Try to maintain a well-balanced diet and a
   regular eating pattern.

2. Avoid alcohol at menstruation time.

3. Organise menstruation week to be free of
   stressful activities.

4. Learn the relaxation techniques in **P10**.

5. **P22/4**. Salt can encourage retention of water in
   the body's tissues. It may be that your pain is
   eased if you exclude salt from your diet one week
   before menstruation.

Yes	No

RELATIONSHIP PROFILE
AND SEX PROBLEMS

1　Are you pregnant?

2　Have you recently had a baby?

3　Is your desire to conceive interfering with your enjoyment of sex?

4　Do you feel a pressure to perform well sexually?

5　Do you feel unskilled in lovemaking?

6　Was your overall Stress score (p 71) 20 or more?

7　Do you lack sexual feelings towards your partner or need sex less than him/her?

8　Do you resent or feel anger towards your sexual partner?

9　Are you anxious about getting AIDS or other sexually transmitted diseases?

10 Do you find it difficult to talk to your partner about what he/she enjoys sexually?

11 Do you feel that sex is dirty or something not to talk about?

12 Do you have religious or moral beliefs that inhibit your enjoyment of sex?

13 Do you no longer feel love or affection towards your partner?

14 Do you sleep less than 7 hours a night?

15 Are you worried about an unwanted pregnancy?

Yes	No

16 Do you find it difficult to relax and 'let go' during sex?

17 Has sex become routine and boring?

18 Do you feel anxious before and/or during sex?

19 Do you have enjoyable physical contact with your partner that does not lead to full intercourse?

20 Do you think it is important for both partners to have an orgasm every time you make love?

21 Do you pretend to have orgasms?

22 Do you take tranquilisers or antidepressants?

23 Do you have High Blood Pressure for which you regularly take drugs?

24 Did you score 8 or more for questions 1 to 4 in the Drinking Habits scan (p 49)?

25 Was your overall Fitness score (p 24) 15 or more?

26 Do you feel that you and your wants should be your partner's first concern?

27 Do you feel possessive?

28 If somebody you love, likes other people as much as yourself, does this make you feel

    a that she/he must like you less
    b that you are less sexually attractive
    c that you may lose her/his friendship
    d that you are made to look foolish in the eyes of other people?

29 Do you think it is wrong for a person who is part

Yes	No

of a couple to enjoy the company and close friendship of other people?

30 Do your feelings or behaviour harm your relationships?

> **ACTION** ⟩

Yes to 1

Pregnancy affects sexuality in different ways: some people find their sex drive increases while others lose interest and seek an outlet for emotional tenderness in being close to their partners rather than in physical sex. There is no evidence that either sexual intercourse or semen can in itself damage the unborn baby in the womb.

Yes to 2

Most women lose their libido for at least a month after childbirth and sometimes for very much longer; fathers may lose interest too and be unable to obtain or sustain an erection. Tiredness and becoming 'baby-centred' are common reasons for this very natural phenomenon. Feeling good about yourself and sexual desire generally go together, so at this stage, you may find **P7** a useful program. There is no rule about when couples resume sex after the baby is born; every couple is different. Talk about this with your partner, and if you find this difficult, see **P6**.

Yes to 3 or 16   **P10**

Yes to 4 or 5   **P10** and **P7**

Yes to 6   **P10**

Yes to any of 7, 8, 10-13, 19-21, 26-30   **P6**

Yes to 9   **P20**

Yes to 14   **P15**

Yes to 15 Consult your doctor about the best form of contraception for you. Talk this out with your partner. If you find this difficult for any reason, complete **P6**. If you have just had a baby, remember that even if menstruation has not yet recommenced, you may be fertile.

Yes to 18 **P1** and/or **P17**. If ever in doubt about which program is right for you, go first to **P1**.

Yes to 22 or 23 Some drugs can cause loss of sexual desire and affect sexual function for the duration of the prescription (eg drugs taken to control blood pressure and certain anti-depressants). Talk to your doctor if you are concerned.

Yes to 24 **P5**. Drinking alcohol can affect the level of sex hormones that circulate round your body. This can cause a loss of sexual drive, sometimes even impotence.

Yes to 25 **P21**. Physical fitness can improve your sex drive.

FERTILITY PROFILE

Scan for Men and Women

Yes	No	
		1 For how long have you been trying to conceive?
1		**a** 1 year
2		**b** 1-5 years
		2 What is your average frequency of sexual intercourse?
3		**a** several times a week
2		**b** several times a month
1		**c** once a month or less
		3 Do you drink alcohol?
		4 Do you take hard drugs?

| ACTION ⟩

Yes to 2c Complete the Relationship Profile and Sex Problems scan (p 98), even if you are not sure that this is relevant.

Yes to 3   Complete the Drinking Habits scan, to check whether your level of alcohol intake is harmless (p 49).

Yes to 4   Complete the Drug Habits scan (p 50).

If you scored more than 3 for questions 1 and 2, complete the rest of the scan with your partner.

Yes	No	
1		**Scan for Women**
2		1 How old are you?
3		**a** under 25 years
		b between 25 and 35 years
		c over 35 years
	3	2 Is your menstrual cycle regular?
	2	3 Are you aware of the most fertile times of the month?

> ACTION

If you scored more than 3, or are otherwise concerned, speak to your doctor.

If you answered YES to 1c or NO to 2, complete the Hormone Profile I scan (p 90).

Yes	No	
		Scan for Men
		1 Have you suffered from any of the following problems?
		Undescended Testicles
		Diabetes
		Kidney Failure
		Venereal Disease

> ACTION

Yes to any   Arrange through your doctor to have your sperm
part of 1   count checked.

The Vulnerability Scan Index

COMMON INFECTION
Feeling under the Weather

Fatigue*
Coughs* and colds
Drowsiness
Lethargy
Headache*
Apathy
Boredom
Feeling of being 'run-down'
Lack of motivation

*See WARNING SIGNS, Symptom Chart, page 8.

Yes	No	
5		1 Did you score 15 or more in the Diet: Vitamins and Minerals scan (p28)?
5		2 Did you score 12 or more in the Exercise scan (p24)?
5		3 Do you take any drugs (prescribed or otherwise) regularly?
	3	4 Are you having enough sleep (for most people this is 7 hours a night)?
2		5 Do you have children at school?
2		6 Do you travel on public transport at rush hour?
2		7 Do you have contact with a large number of people each day?
2		8 Do you spend much time in crowded situations of any sort?
	2	9 Do you get out into the fresh air for at least an hour every day?
2		10 Do you live in an institution?
2		11 Do you live or work in an air-conditioned environment?
2		12 Do you live and/or work in a centrally heated, poorly ventilated environment?

Yes	No
1	
1	
5	
5	

13 Do you work under flickering lights or for more than an hour a day in front of a VDU?

14 Do you work in a newly carpeted modern office?

15 Did you score more than 20 in the Stress scan (p 71)?

16 Did you score 2 or more in the Depression scan (p 94)?

SCORE

More than 5 You are especially prone to common infections, and the symptoms listed above which so affect our physical and psychological well-being generally.

Yes to 1   P22/5

Yes to 2   P21

Yes to 3   Go to the Drug Habits scan (p 50) and follow the Action Advice appropriate to your case.

No to 4   P15

Yes to any of 5-8   There may be little you can or wish to do to change all these situations, which nevertheless clearly increase your vulnerability to infection. But a healthy diet (**P22/5**) and exercise (**P21**) will bolster your immune system to help cope with them.

No to 9   Most of the Vitamin D that we need is made by our own bodies in response to ultra-violet light, usually gained from natural sunlight

Yes to any of 10-14   The Department of the Environment has launched a research programme into what has been called 'sick-building syndrome'. Some modern office buildings and institutions may be at the root of some people's symptoms of headache, dry skin and lethargy, and certainly if you spend a large part of the day in an artificial environment of this sort it is important at least to balance its effects by making a point of spending at least an hour a day in the open air, and taking some form of regular exercise (see **P21**).

Yes to 15   **P11**

Yes to 16   Follow the Action Advice for this Profile Scan.

HERPES

Blisters around corners of mouth
Blisters on penis or inside vagina and/or cervix

1 Have you or has a close friend or sexual partner ever suffered from a cold sore or genital herpes?

If YES, you are at risk.

1 Wash hands after touching cold sores or applying medication to them.

2 Avoid touching your eyes; be especially careful when applying and removing make-up.

3 Avoid breaking the blisters and picking the scabs.

4 If sunlight triggers your attacks, wear a wide-rimmed hat or use a total sunblock cream/stick.

5 **P22/5**. Maintain a healthy diet.

6 Prepare for an upcoming event (holiday or special occasion) by taking one soluble aspirin, with food, for a few days before and during the time.

7 Try to avoid getting too tired or stressed. Go to **P10** and **P11**. Initially you may find **P9** useful.

8 In case of genital herpes, if male wear cotton underpants and avoid tight-fitting trousers, if female substitute stockings for tights. Bathe genital area with cool water.

Yes	No

AIDS
Acquired Immune Deficiency Syndrome

Unexplained fever, chills and soaking night sweats*
Swollen glands lasting several weeks*
Unexplained and increasing fatigue*
Sudden and persistent weight loss*
Persistent diarrhoea*
White patches or spots on the tongue or mouth*
Persistent dry cough*
Pink or purple flat or raised skin blotches that go
    away*

*See WARNING SIGNS, Symptom Chart, page 8.

1 Do you participate in any of the following sexual
    practices?
    a anal or vaginal intercourse without a condom
    b inserting any other part of your body into that
      of your partner
    c cunnilingus or fellatio
    d urinating as part of the sexual act
    e oral-anal contact

3 Do you ever use a needle for hypodermic
    injection that has been used by someone else?

4 Do you ever use enema or douching equipment
    or sex toys that have been used by someone else?

5 Do you ever use equipment for ear-piercing,
    tattooing or acupuncture that has been used by
    someone else?

6 Are you a health-care professional who has
    contact with body fluid?

7 Were you born to an HIV-infected mother?

8 Were you a recipient of blood or blood product
    before 1985?

SCORE
Whether you are homosexual, bisexual or
heterosexual, you are vulnerable to HIV (Human
Immunodeficiency Syndrome – the infection that
leads to AIDS) if you answered YES to any of the

above questions. Whether you will actually become infected by the virus depends upon

a whether the sexual practices detailed in questions 2a-d are carried out with an infected person;

b whether the virus is present on the equipment or in the fluid mentioned in questions 3-6 and 8, and

c whether, in the case of 6 alone, you have a lesion (cut, abrasion, chapped hands, needlestick or some other work-related injury) which admits the virus into your bloodstream.

The virus is found in most body fluids; it seems that it is mainly transmitted through blood, semen and vaginal secretions, but it has also been found in saliva. This means that there is also risk associated with French (wet) kissing, though it has yet to be proven that kissing has actually spread the disease.

P20

HEPATITIS B

Fatigue*
Headache*
Muscular ache*
Fever*
Loss of appetite*
Pain below ribs on right side*
Red weals*

*See WARNING SIGNS, Symptom Chart, page 8.

Yes	No	
		1 Have you recently been tatooed?
		2 Do you regularly inject yourself?
		3 Are you male and gay?
		4 Do you regularly handle blood or give injections or are you in danger of being bitten?

SCORE
YES to any question suggests some risk to
Hepatitis B.

| ACTION ⟩

If YES to any and the symptoms show, go to your
doctor. The virulent disease is often contracted
from unsterile needles. If YES to 4, go to your doctor
and ask about Hepatitis immunisation.

Yes	No

BOWEL DISORDERS

Piles
External Piles: Rectal itching
Internal Piles: Rectal pain and bleeding*

Inguinal Hernia
Lump in area of pubic hair*
Pain in area of groin (and possibly testicles) when
  exercising*

Diverticular Disease (a disease of the colon)
Pain in lower left of abdomen*
Distention of abdomen*
Nausea*
Chills*
Fever*

*See WARNING SIGNS, Symptom Chart, page 8.

1 Are you regularly constipated?

2 Do you strain on the lavatory?

3 Are you 40 years old or more?

4 Are you a woman?

5 Does your job involve lifting heavy weights or
   packages?

6 Do you have a chronic cough?

SCORE
Yes to 1 or 2   You are at risk to Piles (haemorrhoids).

Yes to 1 and 2, or 5, or 6, and No to 4

You are at risk to an Inguinal Hernia, a particularly male disease, though not unheard of in women. A weakness, either congenital or caused by the activites described in the questions creates an opening in the tissues or muscles of the lower abdomen and the intestines protrude.

Yes to 1 and 3

There is some risk of Diverticular Disease. Although this tends to be a disease affecting people of middle years on, you are in theory vulnerable whatever your age if you are regularly constipated and have been so for some time.

Yes	No	ACTION
		7 Did you score less than 109 in question 4 of the Bowel Habits scan (p 35)?
		8 Did you score 12+ in the Exercise scan (p 24)?

Yes to 7   **P22/2**

Yes to 8   **P21**, Fitness Test 1.

Yes to 1 but No to 7 or 8

Go to the following scans:

Anxiety (p 89)   Allergy (p 38)
Stress (p 71)   Drug Habits (p 50)

HIGH BLOOD PRESSURE
Hypertension

Yes	No	
2		1 Is there a history of Hypertension in your family?
2		2 Are you overweight according to the Weight scan (p 22)?
2		3 Do you smoke?
2		4 Does your consumption of alcohol, according to the Drinking Habits scan (p 49), put you at risk to Hypertension?
2		5 Do you take cocaine, amphetamines, benzedrine, cortisone, epinephrine or privine?

Yes	No	
2		6 Do you add salt to your food?
1		a always
		b sometimes, depending on the taste
		c never or rarely
		7 Do you add salt when cooking?
2		a always
1		b sometimes, depending on the taste
		c rarely if ever
		8 How often do uou eat really salty foods such as peanuts, crisps, bacon, or smoked or pickled foods, for example?
2		a most days
1		b 3-4 times a week
		c rarely or only occasionally
2		9 Did you score 20 or more in the Stress scan (p 71)?
2		10 Do you take the Pill?
	2	11 Do you take regular aerobic exercise (eg 2 or 3, 20-minute sessions a week, swimming, running or walking)?
2		12 Do you have a history of Heart Disease or suffer from a kidney disorder?

SCORE

10 or more
You are vulnerable to Hypertension, and your vulnerability increases with the size of your score. High Blood Pressure is, in turn, a major cause of Stroke, and Kidney failure, and a contributory cause of Coronary Heart Disease. Consult the following Vulnerability Scans.

Heart Disease (p 113)
Stroke (p 116)
Kidney Disease (p 120)

ACTION

If you have not had your blood pressure checked by your doctor within the past year, make an appointment now. Doctors like to keep regular blood pressure records of all their patients.

Yes to 2   Follow the Action Advice in the Weight scan (p 22).

Yes to 3 or 4   **P5**. Both these activites raise blood pressure.

Yes to 5   All these drugs raise blood pressure, even though
                    some are useful in treating other health problems.
                    Consult your doctor if you are concerned about a
                    prescription. Go to **P5** if you take drugs for pleasure.

Yes to any of   **P22/4**. A high salt (sodium chloride) diet contributes
6, 7 or 8   to the development of High Blood Pressure. More
                    precisely, it is the level of sodium that has this
                    effect. Some evidence suggests that the story is
                    rather more complicated than this, with not just
                    sodium implicated, but also calcium and potassium:
                    sodium and potassium are jointly responsible for
                    controlling the amount of fluid in the body; the
                    calcium/sodium balance is known to be important in
                    maintaining normal blood pressure.

Yes to 9   Follow the Action advice in the Stress scan (p 71).

Yes to 10   If otherwise vulnerable to Hypertension
                    (particularly if you smoke or are overweight or have
                    a history of Heart Disease), talk to your doctor
                    about alternative contraception. In any event, if you
                    intend taking the Pill continuously over a period of
                    time, arrange with your doctor to have regular
                    blood pressure checks.

No to 11   Go to **P21** Fitness Test 1, and then move to the
                    aerobic exercise plan. Aerobic exercise is repetitive
                    activity employing the large muscles of the arms
                    and legs. When they work hard, these large muscles
                    put an increased demand on the body for oxygen.
                    Your heart rate increases as it pumps oxygen-rich
                    blood around the body and your lungs work harder
                    to keep up with the heart's demand for oxygen. The
                    process trains your circulatory system to operate
                    more efficiently at all times (and with less strain on
                    the heart itself).

HEART DISEASE

Angina (chest pain*, usually appearing after
   exertion or emotional upset)
Shortness of breath*
Palpitations*
Nausea*
Cold Sweat*

*See WARNING SIGNS, Symptom Chart, page 8.

Yes	No	
3		1 In the Diet: Fats & Fibre scan (p 31) was your Total A more than your Total B?
		2 In the Weight scan (p 22) were you
1		**a** overweight
2		**b** very overweight
3		**c** obese
		d below ideal weight
		e about right?
3		3 Did you score 12 or more in the Exercise scan (p 24)?
3		4 Do you use cocaine regularly?
3		5 Did you score 12 or more in the Drinking Habits scan (p 49)?
3		6 Did you score 7 or more in the Smoking Habits scan (p 57)?
3		7 Did you score more than 20 in the Stress scan (p 71)?
4		8 Do you suffer from Angina (chest pain when you exert yourself or work hard, or when you are under emotional stress)?
2		9 Is there a history of Heart Disease in your family?
1		10 Have you taken the contraceptive pill for more than 5 years continuously?
1		11 Have you moved to live in another country within the past five years?

Yes	No
		12 How old are you?
		a under 35
1		**b** 35-64
2		**c** 65+
3		13 Do you have a heart abnormality?
3		14 Do you have High Blood Pressure?
1		15 Is there a history of High Blood Pressure in your family?
1		16 Do you suffer or have members of your family suffered Diabetes?
3		17 Have you ever had a heart attack?

SCORE

6 or more

You are vulnerable to Heart Disease, and increasingly so as your score builds. See also the following scans:

High Blood Pressure (p 110)
Stroke (p 116)

ACTION

Yes to 1

P22/1. Heart Disease is linked with high fat intakes and especially with intakes of saturated or animal fats which circulate high levels of cholesterol through the blood stream. Fish oil (as is found in mackerel and herring particularly), poly-unsaturated fats (as are found in vegetable margarine), and fibre (see **P22/2** for a list of foods containing fibre) have been shown in tests to help control the amount of cholesterol that circulates in the blood stream.

Yes to 2a, b or c

P19. Obesity puts excessive demands upon your heart, and overweight people generally eat higher levels of saturated and animal fats (see above).

Yes to 3

P21. Aerobic exercise, sometimes known as stamina or cardiovascular exercise – repetitive exercise involving the large muscles of the arms and legs (as in swimming, running, even walking) reduces the risk of heart attack. Besides making your blood circulatory system more efficient (see the High Blood Pressure scan, p 110) and reducing the strain which your heart is under, aerobic exercise also reduces cholesterol levels in the blood.

There are caveats about taking exercise if you already suffer from Heart Disease, Hypertension or Diabetes, or if you are elderly; these are clearly expressed in **P21**.

Yes to 4   **P5**

Yes to 5 or 6   **P5.** Years of heavy drinking can lead to weakening of the heart muscle (Alcoholic Cardiomyopathy), which can result in heart failure. Cigarette smoke releases adrenalin which increases heart rate and at the same time causes the blood vessels to narrow, thus raising blood pressure. It speeds the build-up of material (plaques) on the blood vessel walls and promotes the collection of fat around these plaques, thus disturbing the flow of blood to the heart and making it more likely for any blood clot present in the blood to form a fatal blockage. Carbon monoxide in cigarette smoke reduces the number of red blood cells available to transport oxygen around the body, impeding the blood supply to the heart. Perhaps in response to this effect of carbon monoxide, a compensatory production of red blood cells makes the blood stickier than usual. This increases the likelihood of a fatal blood clot developing in the first place.

Yes to 7   **P11.** Every time we are exposed to stress, changes occur in our bodies (such as changes in breathing, hormones and heart rate). If this occurs repeatedly, strain is put on the heart which increases risk of Heart Disease.

Yes to 8   Go to your doctor.

Yes to 10   Long-term use of the Pill has been linked with an increased risk of arterial disease, but you are much less susceptible if your answers were NO to questions 1, 2 and 6.

STROKE

Yes	No

Hearing Loss*
Nausea*
Numbness or prickling sensation in face, arms, legs, side*
Swallowing difficulties*
Understanding difficulties*
Memory loss*
Headache*
Double vision*
Paralysis*
Dizziness*

*See WARNING SIGNS, Symptom Chart, page 8.

Yes	No	
2		1 Are you overweight according to the Weight scan (p 22)?
2		2 Was your Total A more than your Total B in the Diet: Fats and Fibre scan (p 31)?
2		3 Did you score more than 7 in the High Blood Pressure scan (p 110)?
5		4 Do you have a history of High Blood Pressure?
5		5 Do you have a history of Heart Disease?
3		6 Do you suffer from Diabetes?

SCORE
Most people who suffer a stroke have a pre-history of High Blood Pressure and have some form of Heart Disease. Around 10% have already suffered a heart attack. Particularly susceptible are those who retain high cholesterol levels in their diets, smoke or drink too much alcohol, and are overweight (see High Blood Pressure and Heart Disease scans, pp 110, 113). A score of 5 demonstrates vulnerability, increasing with the score. People who score high and are 55 years old or more are especially vulnerable.

> ACTION

Yes to 1   P19

| Yes to 2 | P22/1 |

| Yes to 3 | See sections of the Action advice in the Hypertension scan which are relevant to you. |

| Yes to 4, 5 or 6 | Ensure that your doctor is aware of these conditions. |

GALLSTONES

Flatulence
Belching
Indigestion*

*See WARNING SIGNS, Symptom Chart, page 8.

Yes	No	
3		1 Was your Total A greater than Total B in the Diet: Fats & Fibre scan (p 31)?
2		2 Are you 40 years of age or more?
2		3 Are you overweight according to the Weight scan (p 22)?

SCORE

5 or more   You are at risk. The problem is more common among women, and Caucasians, though it is not exclusive to them.

| ACTION ⟩ |

P22/2. The most common type of gallstone is formed from crystallized cholesterol, probably the result of excess cholesterol circulating in the blood. Fibre is helpful in reducing the quantity of excess cholesterol.

P22/3. Sugar intake, particularly in the form of sucrose or cane sugar has also been linked with the development of gallstones. Insulin is known to encourage the body to make more of its own cholesterol, and the more sugar you eat, the more insulin the body needs to produce.

| Yes to 3 | P19 |

DIABETES

Yes	No

Excessive thirst*
Increased frequency of urination*
Excessive hunger yet weight loss*
Weariness
Blurred vision*
Numbness*
Cramps
Dry mouth
Impotence

*See WARNING SIGNS, Symptom Chart, page 8.

5 　 1 Have other members of your family suffered from Diabetes?

2 　 2 Are you overweight according to the Weight scan (p 22)?

2 　 3 Did you have a high fats/low fibre score in the Diet: Fats & Fibre scan (p 31)?

2 　 4 Do you take packet sugar in tea or coffee?

5 How often do you take soft drinks such as squash, lemonade, tonic water and cola?
3 　 a about once a day
2 　 b twice or more a day
1 　 c three or more times a week

2 　 6 Do you eat any of the following foods more than once a week: sweets and chocolates, cakes, biscuits, sugary puddings, jams, canned fruits in syrup, baked beans?

SCORE
If you answered YES to 1 and scored 9 or more you are at risk to Adult Onset Diabetes.

| ACTION 　 〉

Yes to 1 　 Diabetes frequently re-occurs in the same family. Go to your doctor and have a simple blood test to measure your blood sugar levels. If diabetes is in your family, also follow the Action points below:

Yes to 2	**P19** and **P21**. Obesity is present in more than half the cases of diabetes. Apart from helping you to burn off unwanted fat, aerobic exercise can improve blood sugar control. In diabetes, glucose (the body's major source of energy) collects in the blood, either because there is insufficient insulin to help the glucose get into the muscles, or because the muscle cells themselves are too insensitive to insulin. Aerobic exercise can help the latter problem. However, if you or a close relative suffer from diabetes, you should consult your doctor before embarking upon the program.
Yes to 3	**P22/2**. Adult Onset Diabetes has been linked to a diet that is low in fibre, and can often be controlled with a change to a higher fibre diet.
Score of 4 or more to questions 4-6	**P22/3**. The amount of sugar circulating in the blood is controlled by a delicate hormonal system involving insulin. It seems that a high sugar, low fibre diet can put so much strain on this controlling mechanism that in some people it will literally give up, causing Adult Onset Diabetes.

VARICOSE VEINS

Yes	No

Prominent bluish leg veins
Sometimes soreness
Leg fatigue

1 Are you pregnant?

2 Do either of your parents, or did your grandparents suffer from Varicose Veins?

3 Are you overweight on the Weight scan (p 22)?

4 Do you suffer from constipation and/or piles?

5 Do you follow a predominantly fatty diet, according to the Diet: Fats & Fibre scan (p 31)?

6 Does your job involve long periods of standing with little movement, eg bar or restaurant work, shopkeeping, factory line work, teaching?

Yes	No

7 Did you score 12 or more in the Exercise scan (p 24)?

Yes to 1 or 2

SCORE
You are at risk to Varicose Veins and increasingly vulnerable according to the number of questions 3 to 7 to which you answered YES. Varicose veins may develop at any stage during pregnancy and are often the result of excessive weight gain.

| ACTION |

Yes to 1
A proper diet is essential. Go to **P22/1, 2**. Exercise is also recommended (see **P21**, Fitness Test 1), although its hereditary nature means that this problem will almost certainly show during pregnancy if YES to 2. **P12** may be useful to those who suffer Varicose Veins and additional relief may come from avoiding tight underwear and sitting down as often as you can with your feet on a stool.

Yes to 3   **P19**

Yes to 4   **P22/2** and **P21** (Fitness Test 1)

Yes to 5   **P22/1**

Yes to 6 or 7   **P21**

LIVER AND KIDNEY DISEASE

Alcoholic Hepatitis
Cirrhosis of the Liver
Cancer of the Liver
Kidney Disease

Nausea*
Vomiting*
Swelling in feet or legs*
Flatulence
Loss of Weight*

*See WARNING SIGNS: Symptom Chart, page 8.

See also CANCER: EARLY WARNING SIGNS, page 20.

Yes	No	
5		1 Did you score 15 or more overall in the Drug Habits scan (p 50)?
5		2 Did you score 12 or more in the Drinking Habits scan (p 49)?
3		3 Do you take any drug regularly?
		4 Do you regularly take
1		**a** anti-depressants
1		**b** analgesics (pain killers)
1		**c** digitalis-type drugs
1		**d** antibiotics
1		**e** drugs for hypertension
		5 Do you take any drug for a long-lasting condition?
		6 Are you aged over 55?
		7 Do you inject drugs into your body?
		8 Have you suffered a liver disorder in the past?
		9 Do you suffer from High Blood Pressure?

SCORE

7 or more
You are prone to disorders of the liver, which include Alcoholic Hepatitis, Cirrhosis and Cancer. The risk increases with your score.

Yes to 2
The liver is responsible for breaking down alcohol into harmless products. The more alcohol the liver has to process, the harder and longer it has to work. Over-strain the liver and it could develop fatty deposits (Fatty Liver) and it may also become inflamed and tender (Alcoholic Hepatitis). After four years or so of heavy drinking, small areas of the liver may die (Cirrhosis). As the liver becomes less efficient it may simply cease to function (Liver Failure), or it may develop Cancer.

Yes to 1, 3 or 5
Many people take drugs as a part of their daily lives. Taking a drug for years puts you at risk. Once you have taken a drug, your body concentrates on

getting rid of it. First the drug is absorbed into the blood stream. Once in circulation, the body's objective is to purify the blood and excrete the drug. The kidneys are generally responsible for this process, but sometimes the liver plays a role. Long-term use of any drug heightens the risk of damage to kidneys and/or liver and possibly to other parts of the body.

Yes to any of 4a-e

Analgesics (pain killers), digitalis-type drugs, drugs for High Blood Pressure and some anti-depressants and antibiotics can have ill-effects on the liver and kidney, particularly if you have a history of liver or kidney disorders or take these drugs regularly over a long period. Antibiotics taken regularly to combat one infection can reduce your body's normal resistance to other infections.

Yes to 6

As you get older your metabolism tends to slow down and liver and kidneys become less efficient at clearing drugs or alcohol from the body system, which may result in a dangerous build-up. On average, older people take about twice as many drugs as the rest of the population, which obviously means that their average risk of suffering common side-effects is greater. In addition, the older you are the more slowly the gut is likely to move, and the slower the movement, the more of a drug is likely to be absorbed. This means that older people should, generally, require smaller dosages of medicine.

Yes to 7

Drugs, like heroin, injected immediately into the bloodstream put an appalling strain on liver and kidneys. There is also the major problem of infection from an unsterilised needle whatever kind of drug is injected in this way. Consult the Vulnerability Scans for Hepatitis (p 108) and AIDS (p 107).

ACTION

Yes to 1, 2 or 3   P5

RESPIRATORY DISORDERS

Bronchitis
Head cold
Running nose
Fever*
Chills*
Muscle ache*
Cough, initially dry and later with heavy phlegm*
Fatigue*

Emphysema
Shortness of breath*
Cough with heavy phlegm*
Fatigue*

*See WARNING SIGNS, Symptom Chart, page 8.

Yes	No		
3		1	Have other members of your family suffered from respiratory problems in the past?
4		2	Do you smoke?
		3	If NO to 2, have you smoked cigarettes in the past?
			If YES, go to 7.
		4	If YES to 2, do you smoke **a** cigarettes **b** pipe or cigars?
5		5	If YES to 4a, did you score 17 or more in the Smoking Habits scan (p 57)?
5		6	If YES to 4b, did you score more than 9 in the Smoking Habits scan (p 57)?
		7	Do you live in a house with –
1			**a** one smoker?
2			**b** two smokers?
3			**c** three smokers?
			d no smokers?
4		8	Do you regularly smoke cannabis?
5		9	Was your overall Fitness score 15 or more (p 22)?

Yes	No
3	
2	
3	
2	
2	
3	
3	
3	
4	
3	

10 Do you work in a smokey office or factory environment?

11 Do you live in –
a the country
b the town
c a heavily populated city?

12 Do you work or live in a dusty or fumey environment?

13 Do you live in cold, crowded or damp conditions?

14 Do you have a history of chest complaints as a child or more recently?

15 Are you exposed to others with respiratory disorders?

16 Turn to the Weight scan (p 22) and fill in the height/weight chart
a Are you a desirable weight?
b Are you overweight?
c Are you very overweight?
d Are you obese?
e Are you below ideal weight?

SCORE

12 or more

You are vulnerable to respiratory disorders such as Bronchitis and Emphysema, and Lung Cancer; your vulnerability increases to a maximum score of 44.

Nine out of every 10 lung disease deaths in Britain are caused by smoking. Smoking 25 or more cigarettes a day increases the risk of death from Chronic Bronchitis by 20 times that of a non-smoker. But if you stop smoking, the risk gradually disappears, symptoms subside and eventually you return to the standard risk for your age group. Environmental factors in these diseases multiply the harmful effects of smoking. If you are not in a position to change these factors, you should consider removing yourself from them for your health's sake.

Yes to any of 2-6 or 8	**P9** and then **P5**.
Yes to 9	Follow the Action Advice in the Fitness scan.
Yes to 16 b-d	**P19**

Yes	No	
		CANCER OF THE LUNG
		See CANCER: Early Warning Signs, page 20.
3		1 Did you tick YES to one or more questions in each of Sections A to C of the Non-assertive Personality scan (p 62)?
3		2 Do you feel that when there have been problems at home or in the family, it has fallen to you to sort them out?
7		3 Did you score 7 or more in the Smoking Habits scan (p 57)?
3		4 Is there a history of Lung Cancer in your family?
2		5 Does your job involve your working with any of the following chemicals? asbestos arsenic chrome nickel chlorenethyl ethers coal tar distillates mustard gas uranium
2		6 Have you lived or worked near a nuclear power facility: eg station, submarine, ship, train or testing site?
1		7 Did you score more than 30 in the Diet Vitamins and Minerals scan (p 28)?
2		8 Was your overall Stress score 20 or more (p 71)?

SCORE
Only a tiny proportion of Lung Cancer cases arise among non-smokers, susceptibility arises mainly out of a positive answer to 3. Between a score of 7 and 23 your vulnerability to contracting the disease rises accordingly. Experts don't know exactly how or why smoking has this effect, but the tar which smokers inhale and retain in the lung contains a number of chemicals that are known to cause Cancer. Giving up smoking soon reduces the risk of a number of Cancers, and the longer it is since you gave up the more the risk has been reduced.

The other questions relate to factors which have been seen to be associated with Lung Cancer victims, and although they cannot be said to be main causes they are certainly precipitative.

ACTION ⟩

Yes to 1	**P3**
Yes to 2 or 8	**P11**
Yes to 3	**P9** and then **P5**
Yes to 7	**P22/5**

DENTAL CARIES AND GUM DISORDERS

Pain
Tooth decay
Bad breath

Yes	No	
		1 Do you brush your teeth
4		**a** occasionally
3		**b** only when you get up
1		**c** after breakfast and last thing at night
		d after meals
1		**e** at least twice a day?
		2 Do you brush outer and inner surfaces of your teeth
		a with equal care
2		**b** more on outer than inner?

Yes	No	
		3 Do you always brush your teeth and gums
2		**a** in an 'up and down' motion
3		**b** in a horizontal motion
3		**c** no particular way
		d in a circular motion?
	3	4 Do you believe that brushing teeth helps to prevent dental caries?
2		5 Do you brush your teeth hard, to get them white?
		6 Do you floss your teeth or use dental sticks
		a every day
1		**b** occasionally
2		**c** on rare occasions
4		**d** never?
	2	9 Is it important to you that you should never lose your teeth and wear false ones?
2		10 Do you regularly eat processed foods?
		11 Do you add sugar to
5		**a** your tea
5		**b** your coffee?
		12 How often do you eat sweets/chocolate?
6		**a** most days
5		**b** 3-4 times a week
4		**c** occasionally
		13 How often do you eat sugary desserts?
6		**a** most days
5		**b** 3-4 times a week
1		**c** rarely
2		14 Do you eat between meals?
4		15 If YES to 14, do you tend to eat sweet things then?
3		16 Are you pregnant?

SCORE

18 or more You are at risk to dental caries and toothache, and risk increases with your score.

Yes to 3b   You risk loss of tooth substance where teeth meet gums.

ACTION $\rangle$

1 It is most important to brush teeth before going to bed; ideally after every meal.

2 Both inner and outer surfaces of teeth must of course be cleaned, softly and in a circular motion to help prevent gum disease.

3 Dental floss, and especially dental sticks remove trapped food very effectively, often where brushes fail to reach.

4 Tooth decay is caused by acid eating away at the tooth enamel. Eventually, if the enamel is breached, bacteria are free to enter the soft inner part of the tooth, causing infection, pain and possibly tooth loss. Bacteria (which live naturally in the mouth) use sugar sticking to teeth to produce the harmful acid. Diet is thus an essential aspect of dental hygiene. Go to **P22/3**.

5 Fluoride helps to strengthen tooth enamel and so protects against tooth decay, particularly among children. Fluoride drops or tablets can be given where water is not fluoridated.

CANCER OF THE MOUTH AND THROAT also CANCER OF THE LARYNX

See CANCER: Early Warning Signs, page 20.

Yes	No	
		1 Is there a history of Cancer in your family?
		2 Did you score 7 or more in the Smoking Habits scan (p 57)?
		3 Did you score 12 or more in the Drinking Habits scan (p 49)?
		4 Do you chew tobacco or betel nuts?
		5 Do you visit a dentist at least once a year?

Yes to 2 and 3   You are certainly at risk, and increasingly so if you answered YES to other questions. Drinkers who also smoke run many times the risk of developing these cancers; one study suggests that heavy drinkers who also smoke attract 40 times the normal risk.

Yes to 4   Risk has also been attached to these habits.

> **ACTION**

Yes to 2, 3 or 4   **P5**

Yes to 5   Oral hygiene is important, especially as you get older.

No to 5   Detection of early symptoms (such as whitish patches on the inside of the mouth) can catch the disease and avert fatality.

Yes	No	**CANCER OF THE BLADDER**
		See CANCER: Early Warning Signs, page 20.

4		1 Are you
		  a male
		  b female?

1
2
		2 Are you aged
		  a under 50 years
		  b between 50 and 70
		  c over 70?

2		3 Did you score 7 or more in the Smoking Habits scan (p 57)?
1		4 In your work are you ever exposed to these chemicals: alpha- or beta-napthylamine, benzidine, ortho-tolidine, or methylene-bis?
1		5 Do you work in a factory making paint, textiles, rubber, dyes or pigments?
1		6 Do you work on-machine in the print industry?
1		7 Do you drive a bus or truck as an occupation?

7 or more

SCORE
This disease is four times more common in men than women, and incidents rise when a man is aged 70. Long-term smoking and environmental problems connected with questions 5 to 7 add significantly to your vulnerability. Beta-napthylamine is also present in cigarette smoke (in industrial use it is massively carcinogencic). Carcinogens from tobacco smoke are carried by the blood stream to the bladder, where they wait to be excreted. The occupational risk among bus and truck drivers is thought to be from exposure to diesel fumes.

| ACTION ⟩ |

Yes to 3   P5

Yes to any of 5-7   Ask your occupational doctor or nurse or trade union if screening is offered.

CANCER OF THE BREAST

See CANCER: Early Warning Signs, page 20.

Yes	No	
1		1 Are you a woman aged 40 years or more?
2		2 Are you a close relative – mother, daughter, sister – of a person who developed Breast Cancer before she was 50?
1		3 Are you a close relative of a person who developed Breast Cancer after the age of 50?
	2	4 Do you have children?
1		5 Were you over 30 when you had your first baby?
1		6 Are you going through, or have you gone through the menopause?
1		7 Did you begin menstruating at 11 years or less?
2		8 In the Diet: Fats & Fibre Scan (p 31), was your Total A more than your Total B?
1		9 Are you on the Pill?

Yes	No
2	

10 Did you start using the Pill at 18 years or earlier?

SCORE
There is an increasing vulnerability to Breast Cancer with the number of your score. The maximum score is 14.

There appears to be a strong hereditary risk. Dr. Joan Slack a clinical geneticist at the Royal Free Hospital in London has collected statistics which show that close female relatives of women who have Breast Cancer before the menopause have a 1 in 4 chance of developing the disease compared to the average risk of 1 in 14, and that the risk is 1 in 8 for women with a close relative affected after the age of 50.

Question 7, which relates to the level of fat in your diet, appears because the risk of developing Breast Cancer is higher in those countries where there is, generally, a high fat diet. This could be because Breast Cancer is related to levels of male and female hormones present, and fat is known to have an effect on the levels of hormones produced in the body. The Cancer Prevention Society writes: 'Breast Cancer is more common in women who have not had children and also started using oral contraceptives at an early age. The hormone oestrogen is thought to be involved. Dietary fat may be a major factor causing Breast Cancer; this is very strongly suggested by statistical evidence.'

ACTION ⟩

Prevention resides mainly in early detection, in other words your vigilance. If you notice a lump in a breast or discharge from the nipple, go to your doctor. Take advantage of the national breast screening programme when it is available to you.

Yes to 8   P22/1

Yes to 9 or 10   You are advised to change your method of contraception.

CANCER OF THE CERVIX

Vaginal discharge*
Irregular menstruation*

*See WARNING SIGNS, Symptom Chart, page 8.

Yes	No	
		1 Are you a virgin?
		2 Have you had a hysterectomy?
3		3 Have you now or in the past had a number of different sexual partners?
		4 If YES to 3 did your sexual partners have multiple sexual partners too?
3		a yes
		b no
2		c don't know
		5 When did you first begin to have sex?
3		a under 15 years
2		b between 15 and 20 years
1		c between 20 and 25 years
3		6 Do you have three or more children born to you before the age of 25?
1		7 Have you been in contact with Genital Wart Virus?
1		8 Does your sexual partner come into contact with any of the following materials in his work? a metal and machine tools b leather
2		9 Did you score 7 or more in the Smoking Habits scan (p 57)?
	2	10 Are both you and your sexual partner careful about genital hygiene?
2		11 Have you taken the contraceptive pill for more than 5 years?

SCORE

Yes to 1 or 2   You are not at risk.

No to 3	You are unlikely to contract the disease.
7 or more for questions 3-6	Case histories show that you are susceptible, but it should be stressed that Cervical Cancer is preventable if caught early, so it is imperative that you have a regular smear test (see ACTION), and even if the disease is underway, it reacts very well to treatment (among Cancers it has one of the lowest death rates). Susceptibility increases with your score in the other questions.

ACTION ⟩

Early signs can be detected easily and at that stage the Cancer is readily treatable. Ensure a smear test at least once every 3 years.

Yes to 9	**P5**
No to 10	Personal hygiene is very important, and soap and water is preferable to special preparations.
Yes to 11	If you are more than 25 years old and have not had a smear test at all or within the last 3 years, or if a test was abnormal and you have not been to a follow-up check, go to your doctor.

CANCER OF THE PROSTATE

See CANCER: Early Warning Signs, page 20.

Yes	No	
		1 Are you male and over 50 years?
		2 Are you a hot metal typesetter or compositor?
		3 Are you a welder or painter?
		4 Do you work in the nuclear power industry?
		5 In the Diet: Fats & Fibre scan (p 31) was your Total A more than your Total B?

ACTION ⟩

Yes to 1 and either 2 or 4	An annual rectal examination is advisable. The Cancer Prevention Society writes: 'There is a distinct

occupational risk of this Cancer, especially for compositors and typesetters, welders and painters, but also for employees in the nuclear power industry, where exposure to low levels of background radiation has been implicated in Cancer of the Prostate. Diet may well play a part in some cases – an increase in fatty foods and cholesterol leading to slight obesity is a high risk factor for the disease.'

Yes to 5   **P22/1**

Yes	No

CANCER OF THE COLON AND RECTUM

See CANCER: Early Warning Signs, page 20.

1 Is there a family history of digestive diseases?

2 Do you eat red meat 3 times or more a week?

3 Did you score less than 109 in question 4 of the Bowel Habits scan (p 35)?

4 Was your Total A more than your Total B in the Diet: Fats & Fibre scan (p 31)?

5 Do you work in the asbestos industry?

6 Does your work involve contact with soot, tars or mineral oils?

7 If you scored more than 12 in the Drinking Habits scan (p 49), do you drink mainly beer?

SCORE
Your risk increases with the number of positive answers. Incidence of Rectal Cancer has been linked to family history, diet and certain environmental factors. A low fibre and high fat diet is suspected as heightening vulnerability, though as yet research is inconclusive. The dietary trigger may be explained as follows: a low fibre diet means that waste matter spends more time in the colon than necessary, giving bacteria, which naturally inhabit

the gut, longer to act upon the stools. We know that these bacteria produce chemicals as they interact with waste, some of which are known to produce Cancer in laboratory conditions. A high fat diet provides the bacteria with the right sort of waste matter from which to produce Cancer inducing chemicals.

As to environmental factors, the Cancer Prevention Society writes: 'There is an occupational risk, mainly in the asbestos industry and those industries involving soot, tars and mineral oils.'

| ACTION ⟩

If there is a family susceptibility (1), avoid risks implicit in the other questions. If YES to 3, go to **P22/2**; if YES to 4, go to **P22/1**.

CANCER OF THE SKIN

See CANCER: Early Warning Signs, page 20.

Yes	No	
1		1 Do you spend time in tropical or sub-tropical countries?
1		2 Are you Caucasian?
3		3 Do you expose your skin, without any kind of protection; to ultra-violet light?
3		4 Do you sunbathe between the hours of 11 am and 3 pm for more than half an hour continuously?
1		5 Are you aged 50 years or more?
1		6 Are you red-headed or blond?
1		7 Are you an albino?

SCORE

4 or more   You are at risk. The Cancer Prevention Society writes: 'Skin cancer is increasingly caused by careless over-exposure to the sun. Red-headed and blond people are at a slightly higher risk. Albinos are a very high-risk group. There is an occupational risk from chemical exposure: Squamous Cell Cancer caused by exposure to arsenic, tar, pitch, bitumen, mineral oil and soot, has been a Prescribed Industrial Disease in Britain since 1921.

> ACTION

Prevention subsists in the avoidance of excessive (see questions 3 and 4) exposure to ultra-violet light, in addition to caution in the presence of the materials listed above.

CANCER OF THE STOMACH

See CANCER: Early Warning Signs, page 20.

Yes	No	
2		1 Are you male?
2		2 Do you work in a coal mine or come into contact with asbestos?
2		3 Are you Blood Group A?
2		4 Do you suffer from pernicious anaemia?
2		5 Are you aged 50 years or over?
		6 Do you eat cured, smoked or pickled foods
		a less than once a week
1		b around 3 times a week
2		c most days?
	1	7 Do you eat yellow, orange or dark green fruit and vegetables at least 3 times a week?
	1	8 Do you eat citrus fruits at least 3 times a week?
1		9 Do you smoke?

SCORE
Risk increases with your score up to a maximum

score of 15. It is twice as common in men as women, and occurs mainly in later years.

The Cancer Prevention Society writes: 'Stomach cancer is associated with occupational exposure to various dusts – coal mining or asbestos work. People of Blood Group A, and pernicious anaemics, are at a high risk. Studies of smoking in connection with Stomach Cancer have had conflicting results, but since tobacco smoke is definitely co-carcinogenic in some cases, it may very well play a part.'

Diet is also thought to be significant. A high salt diet has been linked to incidents of Stomach Cancer, but while it is advisable to consult the Diet: Salt scan (p 35), the link is most marked in those countries where much of the salt is gained through the presence of cured, smoked and pickled foods in the diet. These also contain a high number of chemicals called nitrites, preservatives that are important in protecting against certain forms of food poisoning. Bacteria which naturally inhabit the stomach and intestine can transform nitrites into substances called nitrosamines, and these are capable of producing Cancer in animals, although we do not know for sure that they do in humans. High intakes of Vitamins A and C have been associated with Cancer prevention. Vitamin C is known to inhibit the production of nitrosamines.

> ACTION

Consider the advice above. See **P22/4** for further advice about the salt content of food, and **P22/5** about vitamin sources. For help in giving up smoking, see **P5**.

Yes	No
2	

CANCER OF THE TESTICLES

See CANCER: Early Warnings Signs, page 20.

1 Are you a male and aged between 20 and 35 years?

Yes	No
1	
2	
2	
1	

2 Are your testicles undescended?

3 Are you involved in agricultural work?

4 Do you come into contact with pesticides?

5 Do you live in the vicinity of a chemical plant, refinery, or nuclear plant?

SCORE

If you answered YES to 2 and your score is 4 or more, there is a measure of risk. Although Cancer of the Testicles represents a small proportion of Cancers in men, it accounts for a large percentage of Cancers in men in the early to middle years. It is not clear whether undescended testicles cause the Cancer or whether both are the result of the same hormonal trigger. It does appear, however, that environmental issues are important. The Cancer Prevention Society writes: 'Precise causes unknown but there are definite links with agricultural work (six-fold incidence), possibly through pesticide use. There is also a possible connection with residence near a chemical plant, refinery or nuclear power plant (greater than two-fold).'

> **ACTION**

Prevention subsists in avoiding sick environments of the sort listed.

CANCER OF THE UTERUS

See CANCER: Early Warning Signs, page 20.

Yes	No
2	
2	
1	
1	
	1

1 Have you been through the menopause?

2 Are you overweight according to the Weight scan (p 22)?

3 Have you received oestrogen therapy?

4 Are you a diabetic?

5 Do you have any children?

Yes	No
1	
1	
1	

6   Do you suffer from High Blood Pressure?

7   Have you undergone X-ray or radiation treatment?

8   Is there a family history of the disease?

SCORE

4 or more   Suggests some risk which increases with your score. The Cancer Prevention Society writes: 'Uterine Cancer is strongly associated with certain factors. It generally appears in women who are post-menopausal, diabetic, childless, hypertensive and above all obese. Women about 10-20 kilos overweight have 3 times the average risk; those more than 23 kilos overweight have a 10-fold risk.'

| ACTION ⟩

Detectable early and curable. Vaginal hygiene is important in its prevention, and a regular smear test is essential.

Yes to 2   **P19**

Yes to 6   Follow the Action Advice in the High Blood Pressure scan (p 109).

Yes	No
2	
1	
2	

ENLARGED PROSTATE

Pain in prostate region
Pain in urination or ejaculation*
Rise in blood pressure

*See WARNING SIGNS, Symptom Chart, page 8.

1   Are you
    a male
    b female?

2   Are you aged
    a over 50
    b over 60?

Yes	No
2	
1	

3 Are you using diuretic drugs, at a level higher than prescribed?

4 Do you habitually have to retain urine due to your occupation (truck/taxi driver, pilots etc)?

5 or more

SCORE
You may be vulnerable to developing an enlarged prostate, a very common condition in men over 60 years of age.

ACTION ⟩

Talk to your doctor.

PEPTIC ULCER

Yes	No

Steady abdominal pain*
Cramp in the abdomen between breastbone and navel
Heartburn*
Vomiting*
Blood in stools or in vomit*

*See WARNING SIGNS, Symptom Chart, page 8.

Yes	No
1	
1	
1	
1	
1	
1	
1	

1 Did you answer YES to question 4 or 5 in the Eating Habits scan (p 48)?

2 Do you sometimes go without a meal?

3 Did you score 12 or more in the Drinking Habits scan (p 49)?

4 Do you smoke cigarettes?

5 Do you suffer from constipation?

6 Did you score 12 or more in the Anxiety scan (p 98)?

7 Was your overall Stress score 20 or more (p 71)?

Yes	No
1	
1	
1	
1	

8 Is it very important for you to be in control of everything in your life?

9 Do you have high standards for yourself and/or others?

10 Was your overall Fitness score more than 15 (p 22)?

11 Do you have problems sleeping?

SCORE
Dyspepsia (indigestion) is nature's response to habits and lifestyles fuelled by the stresses and anxieties all too common in the modern world. Peptic ulcers are the end result expressed as sores in the stomach (Gastric Ulcers) or duodenum (Duodenal Ulcers).

6 or more You are likely to suffer a Peptic Ulcer.

| ACTION |

Yes to 1 Follow the Action advice for the Eating Habits scan.

Yes to 2, 8 or 9 P4

Yes to 3 Follow the Action Advice in the Drinking Habits scan.

Yes to 4 Men who smoke run twice the risk of developing ulcers as men who do not, and their ulcers are likely to take longer to heal. Normally the pancreas neutralises acid produced in the stomach and duodenum for digestive purposes, but smoking reduces pancreatic secretion and so acid in the stomach and duodenum remains for longer than usual. Follow the Action Advice in the Smoking Habits scan (p 57).

Yes to 5 Consult the Bowel Habits scan (p 35).

Yes to 6 P17

Yes to 7 P11

| Yes to 10 | Follow the Action Advice regarding diet (P22/5) and exercise (P21) in the Fitness scan. |

| Yes to 11 | P15 |

Yes	No	**MOTHERHOOD PROBLEMS**
		Ante-natal: Common Symptoms of Pregnancy
		Anxiety
		Fear
		Mood swing
		Heartburn
		Nausea
		Fatigue*
		Constipation
		Loss of libido
		Depression*
		Insomnia
		Backache
		Breathing problems
		Abdominal pain*
		Varicose veins
		Swelling of ankles, feet and/or hands*
		Vaginal discharge*
		Increased frequency of urination
		*See WARNING SIGNS, Symptom Chart, page 8.
	1	1 Do you eat regular meals?
1		2 Do you eat rich, acidic or highly spiced food?
1		3 Did you score 109 or less in question 4 of the Bowel Habits scan (p 35)?
	1	4 Are you attending ante-natal classes?
	1	5 Are you attending an ante-natal clinic regularly?
	1	6 Will you give birth in hospital?
	1	7 Are you taking exercise suggested at the ante-natal classes, regularly during your pregnancy?
	1	8 Do you know how to recognise when labour has begun?

Yes	No
	1
1	
1	
1	
1	
	1

9 Have you arranged for a companion to be with you during the birth, and for someone to help at home for the first week or so after the birth?

10 Are you upset about your increasing weight and changing physical appearance?

11 Have you previously had an abortion?

12 Did you score 12 or more in the Anxiety scan (p 89)?

13 Did you answer YES to 4 or more in the Emotional Upset Scan (p 92)?

14 Do you have a happy relationship with your partner?

Heartburn, morning sickness, constipation, insomnia, backache, shortness of breath, pelvic discomfort and varicose veins, and feelings of anxiety and depression are all fairly common symptoms of pregnancy, as are feelings of enormous well-being and happiness. The higher your score, out of a maximum 14, the more vulnerable you are to problems of pregnancy which are capable of being minimised, if not prevented altogether.

> ACTION

No to 1 or Yes to 2

Take frequent small meals and avoid acidic or highly spiced food to minimise morning sickness. A glass of milk or magnesia mixture may help prevent the heartburn typical of early pregnancy.

Yes to 3, No to 7 or Yes to 10

A proper fibre balanced diet and exercise can prevent constipation, varicose veins, and excessive weight gain. See **P22/2** and follow the exercise schedule suggested at your ante-natal classes, and if you are still depressed about your changing shape, go to **P7**. Shortness of breath is most common towards the end of pregnancy, the result of the expanding uterus which forces your diaphragm upwards into the chest. It may be helped by lying in bed propped up with pillows. Mention it to your doctor, but it is unlikely to be symptomatic of serious problems. Backache can be alleviated by paying particular attention to posture and taking rest with the whole length of your spine in contact with a flat surface, and also by massage.

No to any of 4-9

It is essential to follow the advice of your ante-natal clinic and attend ante-natal classes to prepare for a safe and happy birth. Consult your doctor. It is not essential to have your baby in a hospital, but the risk attached to having a baby at home depends upon the availability of emergency services in your area. Your doctor will advise you.

Yes to any of 11-13

Research undertaken by a London Teaching Hospital shows that groups who answer YES to these questions are most vulnerable to incidence of anxiety and depression in pregnancy. However the portrait of the pregnant woman as radiantly happy all of the time is now a well-laid myth. Some emotional upset in pregnancy is usual. **P10** and **P17** may be useful programs to help minimise this.

No to 14

P6. Your partner's support and understanding of your problems is key to emotional health during pregnancy and after the birth. In terms of sex drive, pregnancy affects different women in different ways, and one woman's sexual drive may be quite different from one pregnancy to the next. Normal sexual activity during pregnancy is not harmful.

Post-natal: Common Post-natal Symptoms
Mood swing
Tearfulness, unhappiness
Fatigue
Absence of feelings for the baby
Fears
Tension, anxiety
Irritability*
Loss of libido
Depression*
Stomach cramps
Vaginal discharge*
Soreness
Breast pain and tenderness, cracked nipples

*See WARNING SIGNS, Symptom Chart, page 8.

Cramps in the lower abdomen, similar to a contraction, should disappear soon, if they occur at all; consult your doctor if they persist.

For breast pain and tenderness see your doctor, you may have a breast abcess. Cracked nipples can be treated with protective sprays, creams, even breast shields if they help; vaginal soreness by soaking in a bath for half an hour.

Yes	No

1 Do you lack someone nearby during the day, a good friend or relative, with whom you can talk about your feelings and who is prepared to help in the day-to-day chores of the first weeks of motherhood?

2 Have you given up a demanding and fulfilling job in order to devote yourself full-time to motherhood?

3 Was your score 2 or more on the Obsessional Personality scan (p 67)?

4 Did you score on the Non-assertive Personality scan (p 62)?

5 Do you harbour regrets about the method of delivery you opted for?

6 Do you lack a happy, intimate relationship with your partner?

7 In the Stress scan (p 71) was your score in Section A more than 20?

8 Will you have recently moved house when the baby is born, or do you plan to do so shortly afterwards?

9 Do you have relatives who have experienced serious psychological problems in the past?

It is perfectly normal to experience mood swing and tearfulness along with the fatigue that birth and early motherhood often brings. The sheer physical effort and hormonal changes of childbirth account for a large part of every mother's vulnerability to post-natal emotional upset, which can tip over into loss of self-confidence. There is no one cause of post-natal Depression, but in any one case, some of the problems associated with the above questions are likely to be involved.

> ACTION

Yes to any of above questions

P10. Just as there is no single cause, there is no single preventive measure to anticipate the problem. All reactions to childbirth – from easy acceptance to the 'Baby Blues' to post-natal Depression – can be seen as varying degrees of reaction to a stressful event, and the same general preventive principles apply to all degrees of reaction. If you show some of the symptoms listed and the 10-point plan below is not, in your case, adequate, consult with your Health Visitor or Doctor.

1 Organise post-natal support: enlist your partner's support around the time of the birth, at ante-natal classes (at least once); involve him in the process.

2 Get to know your health visitor.

3 Remember that whatever you feel, you are not alone in your feelings; seek out other mothers-to-be before the birth and, later, at post-natal groups; share your experiences with these and friends who have seen it all before.

4 Enlist the help of dependable friends or relatives to rely upon after the birth, and find out what they can be relied upon to do (eg visiting you in the maternity ward, buying any last minute items, looking after your other children while you are in hospital, helping out with chores after the birth).

5 Make a list of 'panic' numbers for help with post-natal problems ranging from baby-sitters to getting advice when your baby brings you to the end of your tether.

6 Learn to delegate and adopt the idle woman's attitude to housework after the birth. If you answered YES to question 3, follow the Action advice on page 68.

7 Make mother-care activities a priority. Get some time on your own each day. Read **P10** and get some sleep whenever possible during the hectic day.

8 Arrange matters to minimise stress in the first few months of the baby's life (eg refuse any urge to move house or act as hostess to well-meaning friends or relatives).

9 Read **P7**.

10 If you answered YES to question 6, see **P6**.

BIRTH ABNORMALITIES

Yes	No
3	
3	
3	
3	
2	
2	
3	
2	
1	

1 Do you smoke?

2 Did you score 12 or more in the Drinking Habits scan (p 49)?

3 Are you taking drugs for pleasure?

4 Are you taking any drugs or being subjected to X-rays, without the knowledge of your ante-natal clinic?

5 Is there a history of genetic abnormality in your family?

6 Do you suffer from Diabetes or High Blood Pressure?

7 Have you been in contact with German Measles?

8 Are you over 35 years of age?

9 Did you score 12 or more in the Exercise scan (p 24)?

SCORE
A score of 3 suggests that your baby may be at risk;

a score of 5 or more suggests the possibility of serious complications.

Yes to 1   Nicotine and carbon monoxide are transferred from a smoking mother to her baby and these poisons impair heart and brain function in the foetus. Women who smoke during pregnancy, especially during the last five months or so, are more likely to have small babies. They also face twice the normal risk of miscarriage.

Yes to 2   When a pregnant woman drinks, her baby drinks too. Drinking during pregnancy is associated with an increased risk of miscarriage and stillbirth. Babies may be smaller, have mental handicaps, co-ordination problems and distinctive facial characteristics.

Yes to 3 or 4   Many drugs are potentially detrimental to the developing child and the risk is especially high during the first 3 months of pregnancy when the foetus is going through the very early and intricate stages of development. Drugs will also find their way to the baby after the birth, if the baby is breast-feeding.

Yes to 9   Athletes have fewer miscarriages, a lower incidence of blood pressure problems during pregnancy and a shorter second stage of labour than other women. Women who exercise also tend to have heavier babies. Low-birth-weight babies are at slightly higher risk in all respects.

> **ACTION**

Minimising risk means being frank at your ante-natal clinic.

Yes to 1, 2 or 3   **P9** and then **P5**.

Yes to 9   Pregnancy is not a good time to embark upon a vigorous exercise program, but aerobic activities such as swimming and walking are useful, as are ante-natal relaxation and suppleness exercises (**P10**, **P21**).

Yes	No

PSYCHOLOGICAL DISTRESS

from **Disability**
Deformity
Pain
Disease

Depression*
Emotional upset
Self-consciousness
Shyness
Lack of confidence
Low self-esteem
Unhappiness
Tearfulness
Boredom
Moodiness
Frustration
Impatience
Guilt
Tension
Communication difficulties
Pain*

*See WARNING SIGNS, Symptom Chart, page 8.

1 Are you sure that the medical cause of your
    problem has been diagnosed?

    If NO go to your doctor

    If YES, are you sure that nothing further can be
    done to cure the cause of your problem?

    If NO, see the list of addresses and get a second
    opinion.

    If YES, read on:

2 Tick which of the following areas are
    unsatisfactory, as a result of your problem.

    a self-image
    b your image of other people and your
        surroundings
    c your ability to learn new things
    d talking, listening or understanding speech

Yes	No

e activities that require seeing

f writing

g personal care, eg bathing, dressing, feeding yourself

h walking, running, climbing stairs, lifting, etc

i domestic duties eg shopping, housework, cooking, etc

j controlling your environment, eg moving things, opening windows, using gadgets, etc

k dependence on special care, eg special diets, equipment, aids, etc

l your relationships with and ability to cope with family members

m your social life

n involvement in work or recreational activities

o your tolerance of noise, bright lights, temperature extremes, work stresses, etc

p any other skills

q your sex life

3 Do you think your problem/disorder is unattractive?

4 Does it stop you doing things you would like to do?

5 Do you think about it frequently?

6 Do you think other people are conscious of it?

7 Do you think other people think less of you because of your problem?

8 Do you feel sexually unattractive?

9 Does the problem frighten you?

10 Are you frightened you might die?

11 Did you score 2 or more in the Depression scan (p 94)?

12 Do you have difficulty convincing others of the emotional or physical pain you are suffering?

13 Do you resent others for not better understanding your predicament?

Yes	No

14 If YES to 13, does this make you feel angry or upset?

15 Do you feel that you are a burden to others?

16 Do you feel guilty or ashamed at not being able to cope with your problem better?

17 Do you have physical pain associated with your problem that you cannot control?

18 Do you notice that the level of physical or emotional pain varies with your mood?

Add up your YES answers to questions 3 to 18.

Yes to 5 or more (3-18) — **P1** (using your answers to question 2 as a guide to the problems you might wish to analyse in **P1**), and then **P14**.

Yes to question 2a — **P7**

Yes to 2b, l, m or q — **P8** (Social Skills) and/or **P6** ('Partners') as appropriate.

Yes to 14 — **P13**

Yes to 17 — **P12**

ANOREXIA NERVOSA

Weight loss*
Appetite loss*
Deliberate vomiting
Perfectionism

*See WARNING SIGNS, Symptom Chart, page 8.

First, complete the following Profile Scans:
Weight Profile (p 22)
Obsessional Personality Profile (p 67)
Complete this scan if you were advised to:

Yes	No	
5		1 Did you score more than 2 on the Obsessional Personality scan?
		2 How often do you refrain from eating when you are hungry?
1		**a** never
2		**b** sometimes
3		**c** frequently
1		3 Do you feel disgusting or disgusted with yourself after eating a big meal?
1		4 Do you vomit if you have eaten too much?
1		5 Do you feel fat?
		6 Do other people think you are too fat?
		a yes
1		**b** no
		c don't know
1		7 Do other people comment about you being thin?
1		8 Do you wear clothes that hide the shape of your figure?
1		9 Do you think most people are too fat?
		10 How often do you weigh yourself?
3		**a** more than once a day
2		**b** most days
1		**c** frequently
		d rarely
1		11 Do you notice the loss or gain of a pound or two?
1		12 Are you fussy about what you eat?
1		13 Was food an issue in your family when you were a child?
1		14 Do you prefer to eat by yourself?

> ACTION

5 or more   **P1** and then **P10** and **P17**.

Introduction to Preventive Programs

These programs cannot guarantee instant cure. However, they will show you how to analyse the things that you want to change and how to plan activities to bring about the changes you would like. This requires work on your part – the more you put in, the more you get out. There are usually no quick or easy solutions – the treatment is not magic. But we think that you will be surprised how quite simple and straightforward methods can lead to dramatic improvements.

Become Your Own Psychologist

These methods include watching your own behaviour, keeping records and diaries, thinking about ways of changing yourself or your situation and acting on it. 'Practice makes perfect' has some truth; the more you follow our programs and practise the advice, the easier and more successful they will become. 'Persistence' and 'consistency' are also important. By persistence, we mean keeping going for the recommended periods of time and not stopping and starting in between. By consistency, we mean sticking closely to your plan of action and not changing what you are doing half way through.

In time, you will learn a scientific method of tackling your problems and managing your everyday life so that new problems are less likely to arise. In short, you will become your own psychologist.

Where to Start

We advise strongly that anyone wishing to benefit from the PM System of Health first completes P1 (Analysing and Managing Your Problem, page 157).

The first step is to decide which problem you want to tackle first. People often make the mistake of trying to do too much too quickly. Take one thing that you would like to change, and stick to that until you have achieved improvement. Then move on to the next thing. What to start with? Tackle easy things first and work up through successes to the more difficult ones.

Finding the Real Problem

Step 1 of P1 on page 157, shows you how to define a problem to solve, to be specific rather than general in your definition, to be concrete rather than abstract. This is as true of the more obvious problems such as drinking, smoking, and obesity as it is of problems of communication or depression. For example, you will more readily solve a drinking problem if you are able to define it as 'I drink too much when I am bored' or 'I drink too much when at parties with people I don't know' than, simply, 'I drink too much'. Again, 'I find it difficult to talk to people of the opposite sex' is a more useful definition than 'I'm bad at relating to people'. Every problem has a context or situation.

In solving habit problems and problems of stress, for example, the programs encourage you to look behind the general problem to what is actually keeping it going for you. If a program fails to solve your problem, it may be that you are not looking at the right problem. Go back to P1, paying particular attention to Step 1 (Definition) and Step 7 (Related Problems). Perhaps your smoking problem owes much to lack of confidence, social anxiety, or tension; there are programs designed to tackle these, and they should be completed before returning to Habit Control (P5) if that has failed you once. Again, perhaps P5 or, say, the Weight Reduction program (P19) failed you because you were not sufficiently committed to change. If so, try P9 (Deciding to Change), before returning to P19. Much of this 'sorting out' should have been achieved by the Profile Scans, but if a scan has directed you to a program which has not been successful, and P1 or P9 does not put you on the right lines, read the Program Index carefully and consider where the answer to your problem may lie.

Describing Your Problem

Having decided on the problem, you'll need to be able to describe it – what exactly does it look like or feel like? For example, if you are anxious, how do you know this? Probably you have some physical symptoms – perspiration, blushing, trembling, pounding heart or 'butterflies' in the stomach. You may notice that you are behaving anxiously: avoiding situations or talking too much or not enough. You may also have some thoughts that race through your mind - about how awful the situation is, about how terrible it is to feel anxious or about how badly you are coping.

Write these down – these are the things that you are aiming to change. Again, you can practise this in P1.

Self-monitoring: How Big is Your Problem?

Once you have described your problem clearly, the next step will be to decide how to measure it. Measures are a good way of keeping a record of how you are getting on. Instead of descriptions that are difficult to compare with each other, you simply write down the numbers that best describe what is happening. This makes recording both quicker and more precise.

We can measure things in different ways. The main ways we measure behaviours are by 'rating scales' and by 'frequency counts'. These are short-hand summaries of the size of your problem. 'Rating scales' give a number from, say, 0 to 4 with 0 being no problem to 4 being as bad as you can imagine. You decide what label to give each number and then decide which number best describes your problem at that time.

'Frequency counts' refer to the number of times the problem occurs in a given space of time. You use rating scales if the problem is one of amount: the strength of anxiety you feel, the loudness of your voice or how strongly you believe negative things about yourself. If the problem is more to do with how many times you do something or something happens, then frequency counts are more appropriate measures. Examples of this might be the number of cigarettes you smoke each day, the number of times you avoid something or how often you daydream.

Again, P1 will give you practice in devising and using measures.

Self-monitoring: Keeping Records
Before you start to change anything, you must have a good record of what things are really like at the moment. For this you will need to buy a notebook.

The first step will be to decide when you are going to record the problem. Initially, we recommend recording four times a day – when you first get up, the middle of the day, the end of the day and the end of the evening. P1 will show you how to make and fill in a chart, recording at the same time each day. This will give you an idea of the level and pattern of your problem during the day and day-by-day.

Since we all have good days and bad days, we recommend that you keep your chart for at least one week to give you an adequate picture of what is going on. You can then compare this record (your 'baseline') with your records as you try to change things. Sometimes you will see that things are improving even though you might not yet feel that things are getting better.

Psychologists ask their clients to keep records and have found that keeping records is sometimes sufficient to change things. You may find that, as a result of keeping records, your problem gets better before you have to do anything about it. This is probably because your records have made you think objectively and scientifically about yourself and your situation.

Equally, keeping records may redirect you to the real cause of your problem, what is in fact keeping the problem going, and thus direct you to the best program for you.

'Ups and Downs'

Improvement is rarely smooth and steady. It is usually a series of 'ups and downs' with the 'ups' lasting longer or being bigger than the 'downs'. This is normal. A lot of good work can be undone if you become despondent or panicky about the 'downs'. Such relapses do not necessarily mean that the program is not working for you. They are part of the process of change. Use the 'downs' to your benefit. Make them part of your continuing record; let them enlighten you as to what is keeping the problem going.

Every 'down' is an opportunity to learn how to cope with the problem. In fact, when you feel like you are succeeding, we suggest that you challenge yourself by creating one of the situations that have previously caused the problem. Then you can be sure that you have really beaten it.

Now, before you choose a problem or program, work through Analysing and Managing Your Problem (P1), which will give you the basic tools necessary for getting the most out of the other programs.

The Preventive Program Index

ANALYSING AND MANAGING YOUR PROBLEM   P1

STEP 1	Define the Problem

Do you know which problem you want to change? Write it down, using the following points:

1. Be precise rather than vague, specific rather than general. For example:

General: 'I drink too much.'
Specific: 'I drink too much when at parties with people I don't know.'

2. Be concrete rather than abstract. For example:

Abstract: 'I'm bad at relating to people.'
Concrete: 'I don't have anything to say to people of the opposite sex.'

Choose a problem that fits one or more of the following categories:

1. You can think reasonably clearly about it.
2. It has limits – it isn't confused with other problems.
3. You are keen to get rid of it – you can see obvious advantages in solving it.
4. It is not the major problem in your life. (It is easier to start with something relatively manageable.)

Now describe this problem as outlined above. Write it down.

STEP 2	Measure the Frequency of the Problem

Before deciding how you would like to change, find out exactly what things are like now. Measure the problem you have chosen.

Is it the sort of problem you can count?

YES | NO: STEP 3 ⟩

	M	T	W	T	F	S	S
Situations that make me anxious	0	0	3	2	0	1	0

	8-12pm	12pm-4pm	4pm-8pm	8pm-12am
Losing my temper	1	3	1	0
Number of cigarettes	12	15	10	9

In each case consider:

1. What you are counting. Be precise enough to know whether or not the problem has occurred.

2. How often the problem occurs.

3. Depending on your answers to 1 and 2, decide how often and for how long you should measure the problem. If the problem – say a nervous mannerism – is very frequent, monitor occurrences within a short (say 20-minute) period at particular times during the day:

	9.30am	12pm	4.15pm	8pm	10.50pm
Mannerisms during 20-minute period monitored at	1	0	2	2	1

Go to STEP 4.

STEP 3	Measure the Level of the Problem

Measure your problem according to a rating scale. According to the severity of the problem so the number increases. Use a rating scale of five points, where 0=no problem and 4=the worst case. For example:

FEELING ANXIOUS:

0	1	2	3	4
no anxiety	mild worry	definite worry	anxious	fear

FEELING ANGRY:

0	1	2	3	4
no anger	slight irritation	annoyed	heated	furious

In each case consider:

1. What you are rating. Be precise enough to know definitely whether your problem has got bigger or smaller.

2. What level each number represents. 0 should mark the absence of the problem, and 4 the worst occurrence. 2 should mark the average level.

As in STEP 2, note the time or period of time (day by day) at which the problem occurred, and be sure to include those times or periods when the problem was experienced at its worst.

If you are recording periods of time (rather than particular moments) and you are unsure what rating to give the problem because things were fine for most of the period when suddenly there was a bad occurrence, note two ratings; the first would describe the 'peak level', the second would describe the 'general level'.

STEP 4	Keep Records

You should now be clear about how to measure your problem. The next step is to draw up charts in which you collate your records. For example:

Date: Monday 11th March   8am   1pm   6pm   11pm
Trembling voice
Feeling anxious

For each 'time' enter one or more numbers; either the 'frequency' of the problem (as defined in STEP 2), or the 'general level' or 'peak level' ratings (as defined in STEP 3). For the sake of accuracy, make up your records as soon after the occurrence as possible.

Keep your records for a week, then go to STEP 5, unless your problem has already abated. Sometimes the keeping of records alone can solve a problem. If so, continue keeping weekly records for a while, and if the problem does not re-occur, leave the program.

STEP 5	Draw a Graph

You now have a numerical record of your problem. To obtain a clearer picture, convert these entries into a graph.

The graph depicts a problem measured in terms of its 'level', but the same method can be used for one measured in terms of 'frequency'.

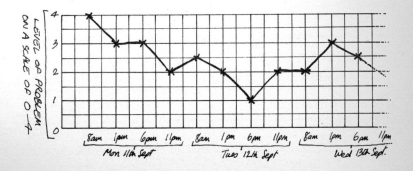

The scale on the vertical axis should be for the numbers which measure your problem. The scale on the horizontal axis is for the times it occurred.

Enter your records with a cross at the appropriate intersection of the two axis. Then draw a line through all the crosses. The graph shows whether the problem is increasing or decreasing, and whether a pattern has emerged – whether the problem tends to occur at particular times of the day or the week.

STEP 6	Establish a Pattern to the Problem

Can you see a pattern emerging?

NO	YES: STEP 8

Keep a further week's record of your behaviour, noting the following:

1. The situation in which the problem occurred. When it was, who was involved, what you were doing.

2. What had happened just before – these are 'early warning signs'.

3. What happened just after – these are the consequences.

DATE/TIME/PLACE/ PEOPLE	SITUATION	EARLY WARNING SIGNS	CONSEQUENCES

From this new record you should start to see a pattern. If the problem still seems to be random, persevere with your records for another week. If a pattern still fails to emerge, go to STEP 7.

STEP 7	Consider Related Problems

Consider whether your problem would be helped by working through one of the other programs. Is your problem related, in general, to:

1. **Stress** (for example, you find yourself sweating a lot, your heart racing)?

> P11 or P4

2. **Mood** (for example, you find yourself losing your temper, or feeling tired)?

> P10, P14, or P13:

3. **Social anxiety** (for example, you avoid meeting people)?

> P8

4. **Self-confidence** (for example, you avoid difficult situations, lack the will to do things)?

> P7

5. **Your relationships** (for example, you argue with your partner, feel unwanted)?

> P6 or P3

6. **Your situation** (for example, your daily routine makes you feel depressed)?

> P9

7. **A particular habit** (for example, you eat, drink, smoke, take drugs to excess)?

> P5

STEP 8	Change Your Problem

You are now ready to try to change your problem. Decide what you are aiming to achieve, what aspect of your problem you want to change. Write down your goal, and bear in mind the following points:

1. Describe your goal in terms of specific actions. It makes your task easier and allows you to establish when you have fulfilled your goal. For example, rather than aim to be 'less depressed', seek to spend more time doing things that you enjoy.

2. Choose a realistic goal which you feel able to achieve. For example,

if you feel depressed most of the time, aim for an hour of pleasurable activity rather than eight hours a day.

3. Build on success.

You have, through self-monitoring, successfully analysed your problem into a form in which it can be dealt with. You also have a clearly expressed goal. Look at your records and decide to change something that you have picked out as being related to your problem. Choose something that can be changed relatively easily, perhaps something that tends to happen before or during or after the problem; alternatively, dangerous times or situations which you have identified in your records and which could be readily avoided. Choose one thing only. Keep your records for another week and then go to STEP 9.

STEP 9	See the Difference

Has your attempt to change made any difference? Draw up another graph from your new information. To make any alteration easy to see, make the graph a continuation of your previous one.

If there is a marked improvement congratulate yourself. Reward yourself in some way. Decide upon another change, and keep a record. Go to STEP 10.

If there is no change, you have not changed what is keeping the problem going. Go back to STEP 6 and/or 7 to identify another possible course of action.

STEP 10	Setbacks

Keep recording until you experience a setback. Use the setback to make a big effort to put your plan for change into practice. Then you will see that setbacks are temporary, necessary stages in exercising control over your behaviour.

ALLERGY PROGRAM   P2

There are two types of abnormal reaction to food and drink; the first is what might be called a 'true allergy', the second an 'intolerance'.

True allergy is far easier to diagnose than intolerance, because the reaction tends to be immediate – you eat the food and, for example, within minutes your lips swell. In such cases it is relatively easy to identify a suspect product, and a doctor will be able to confirm your suspicion by conducting a simple test.

The cause of an intolerance is more difficult to spot because the reaction can develop some hours after you have eaten the food, and there are no reliable medical tests. In such cases, the process of detection is by trial and error: Do your symptoms cease when you stop eating certain foods? Do they reappear when you reintroduce these foods into your diet?

STEP 1	Should You Consult a Doctor?

Check the Symptom Chart to reassure yourself that the symptoms of your reaction do not indicate a serious medical complaint.

STEP 2	Make a Food Record

1. Record the time and date of every reaction you suffer; list all the foods you have eaten in the previous two hours, paying special attention to those foods which are most commonly associated with allergies: milk, wheat, cereal grains, tea, coffee, chocolate, pork, nuts, eggs, fish and shellfish. For example:

Date: 2nd March
Reaction: Sneezing
Time: One hour after eating
Products: Tea, sugar, milk, wheat flakes, cod in batter, bread, butter and marmalade.

2. Record every occasion on which you eat any food listed above, but when you did NOT suffer a reaction. For example:

Date: 7th March
Reaction: None
Time: Three hours after eating
Products: Sugar, milk, tea, cod, bread, butter and marmalade.

STEP 3	Isolate the Suspect Foods

Carry on recording and listing in this way, until you have recorded at least ten occasions on which the symptoms occurred. Now make a third list of foods that appear on your first list on at least three occasions, but which do *not* appear on your second list.

This third list of foods should include only foods that you ate two hours before having an attack of symptoms and which, on at least three separate occasions, appear to have provoked an attack of symptoms. This is your list of Suspect Foods.

Sometimes the suspect foods will be easily identifiable, (eg simple foods like eggs and milk), but occasionally, as in the example above of wheat flakes and batter, you'll need to identify harmful ingredients (in that case, both contain wheat).

STEP 4	Go To Your Doctor

Take your list of suspect foods to your doctor. He or she will be able to organise an allergy test to see if your suspicions are correct and whether you have an allergy. A positive allergy test means that you can be fairly certain of being able to avoid your allergic symptoms from now on, simply by not eating the problem foods. If the test is negative, all is not lost. You may not have an allergy, but you might have an intolerance. Discuss the next step (STEP 5) with your doctor.

STEP 5	Reintroduce the Suspect Foods

Cut out the suspect foods for two weeks or so. Then try eating a small amount of one suspect food. Re-introduce the suspect foods one at a time. If you are right about a particular item you won't get the symptoms at all during the first two weeks, but they should appear when you eat the food again.

Sometimes people develop more violent reactions to culprit foods after a period during which they haven't eaten them, so it is best for your doctor to know what you are doing and when. Also, the elimination procedure can create a deficiency in your nutritional requirements. This is a particular risk if you are planning to cut out several different foods from your diet, at once. Your doctor may, at this stage, refer you to a dietician to advise you.

If you find that you develop symptoms even though you are not eating the suspect food, or that you don't develop the symptoms when you eat the suspect food again, it's back to the drawing board. Proceed with STEP 6.

STEP 6	Make a Fuller Record

You now need to keep a diary of everything that goes into your system – what you eat and drink, any drugs you take and anything that you smoke. You also need to carry on noting each occasion on which your symptoms develop until you have at least ten or more instances. You should also record the recipes you use and keep the labels from any packaged and processed foods, so that you can refer to them later and record what they contained.

Analyse your record as before (STEP 3) and look especially at the processed foods that you eat. Do the attacks follow occasions on which you ate processed food? If so, list the ingredients/additives of any processed foods eaten within 24 hours of an attack and make a second list, of ingredients/additives you consumed without developing any symptoms. As before, cross out any items that appear in both lists. For example, you might find that E102 (Tartrazine) was in processed food you had eaten on 8 of the 10 occasions on which you developed symptoms. Now, you are ready to return to STEP 4 above, and take your findings to your doctor.

Many of the classic allergic reactions, such as asthma, sneezing and migraine, are commonly caused by stress. Suffering from stress doesn't mean that you have to feel hyped up, and you certainly don't have to be a high flying careerist or be in dire circumstances to be under pressure. Different people react to any one set of circumstances in very different ways, and almost any set of circumstances is likely to cause at least some individuals a degree of stress. Go to the Stress scan (p 71).

Typical Allergy Triggers
People who treat Migraine, Asthma and Eczema recognise triggers common to many who suffer from them. The following lists and points at the end) are designed to help sufferers identify their triggers, avoid commonly harmful environments and to allay some of the common psychological triggers.

Migraine
Do you notice that any of the following trigger your Migraine attacks?

1. Emotions
Anger
Worry
Shock
Excitement
Depression

2. Physical stress
Over-exertion
Travelling
Rising late from bed
Bending or stooping
Changes of routine

3. Diet
Alcohol (especially red wine, sherry or beer)
Chocolate, cheese, citrus fruit or fried food
Fasting or dieting
Irregular eating

4. Environment
Bright lights
Flickering or flashing lights
Noise
Smells
Climatic change
Stuffy atmosphere (smokey, centrally heated, etc)
Cold or very hot baths

5. Hormones
Menstruation/pre-menstrual tension
The contraceptive pill
Menopause

6. Other Triggers
Sleeping tablets
High blood pressure
Dental pain
Eye strain
Congested nose
Neck pain

Asthma
Is your Asthma an allergy? Could you be sensitive to any of the following or do you notice a connection between the onset of an asthmatic attack and being in their presence:

1. Pollen (especially grass pollen)

2. Animals, particularly those with hair or feathers. Cats (especially Siamese or Burmese) are probably the commonest trigger, but dogs (especially short haired ones), caged birds and horses have all been known to bring on an attack.

3. Horsehair mattresses, furniture upholstery, underfelts

4. House dust

5. Particular drugs you have been prescribed

6. Colophony resin in solder flux

7. Fruits, milk, cheese and alcoholic drink

8. Aspirin

9. A smokey atmosphere

10. Anxiety, anger, depression, stress

Eczema
Is your Eczema an allergy? Could you be sensitive to any of the following?

1. Perfume, shaving cream, skin cream, deodrant, talc, or aftershave

2. Nail enamel

3. Shampoo, hair creams or baby products

4. Hair bleach or dye (do you have your hair permed or straightened?)

5. Biological or low temperature laundry powders or liquids

6. Perfumed fabric conditioners

7. A centrally heated, stuffy or overheated environment

8. Water softener

9. Aerosols

ACTION
Try to isolate your personal trigger and adjust your environment or personal habits accordingly. Just being aware of what might trigger an attack is a significant first step in overcoming the problem. Even if you do not think that your allergy is food related, read through the step-by-step elimination process above. STEPS 2 to 4 are a useful identification procedure whether or not food is your problem.

Note especially the RELAXATION PROGRAM (P10). If you really work at the skills taught there you will soon be in a position to cope in the face of what was inordinately stressful. Any trigger which presupposes a habit which you find difficult to break (eg alcohol) can be tackled by turning to P5. And there are also programs designed to tackle anger (P13), anxiety (P17), depression (P14), and stress (P11).

Environmental Action
1. When buying any brand you are used to and know is safe, watch

out for NEW or IMPROVED signs, which can indicate a change which may not suit the Eczema sufferer.

2. Floor covering: wood, linoleum, ceramic or terrazzo tiles are best for you. Fitted carpets harbour dust, and the house dust mite can cause Eczema or aggravate Asthma.

3. Stuffy atmosphere: consider using an electric humidifier to increase the moisture in the atmosphere of the room in which you spend most of your time. A small bowl of water positioned near a heat source will moisturise the atmosphere as the water evaporates. Pay special attention to ventilation, which besides alleviating the stuffiness of the atmosphere also reduces the risk of condensation and mould.

4. Eczema sufferers can benefit from bathing frequently, using emollients. Ask your doctor for some to try.

5. If you suffer from Eczema, do you always wear PVC gloves with cotton inners before immersing your hands in detergents, soaps, powders and bleaches for household cleaning?

6. Is your home environment regularly cleaned? (Some Asthma and Eczema sufferers require it to be damp-dusted and wiped dry.)

ASSERTIVENESS PROGRAM   P3

The ability to assert yourself helps you in many different ways. In your dealings with other people it enables you to communicate clearly and directly, making it more likely that you will achieve your goals. It strengthens your relationships and keeps you calm and in control. You are more able to solve problems and make the most of opportunities.

Assertiveness is the art of sticking up for your own rights but without violating the rights of other people. It puts you in the best position for getting your own way, without offending or upsetting others. It lets other people know what you want without having to guess. The key to being assertive is to communicate in a direct, honest manner, appropriate to the situation – it does not mean being pushy or selfish.

By behaving assertively you can lower stress. By saying what you want to say and doing what you want to do, you avoid storing up resentment and bottling up your feelings. Also, by expressing yourself in a controlled yet decisive manner, there is no need for the angry outbursts that raise blood pressure and heighten stress.

No one is born assertive — assertiveness can only be acquired. Some people manage to be assertive in some situations but not in others, such as at home but not at work. This program will show you what skills are necessary in order to be assertive.

STEP 1	Recognizing Non-Assertive Behaviour

How many times have you come away from a difficult situation and thought "if only I'd said that . . ."? There are three types of non-assertive behaviour. Look at the descriptions below and think of examples from your own experience. Write them down.

1. *Aggressive behaviour.* It is important to realise that this is NOT assertive behaviour. You behave in an angry, hostile or sarcastic manner which others find unpleasant. In the long run this leads to guilt and frustration in yourself and hostility from others.

2. *Passive behaviour.* You agree readily, take the line of least resistance and don't speak up even when you have something to say. You don't complain or put forward your point of view, and never stick up for your rights. You do whatever is expected of you, even if you resent it. As a result you feel depressed and helpless.

3. *Manipulative behaviour.* You try and get what you want by making other people feel guilty. You may use emotional blackmail or other kinds of pressure, manoeuvring or underhand tactics. This kind of behaviour undermines friendships and is not good for your own self-image and confidence.

If you find it difficult to decide which category most applies to you, try the following exercises.
a) You are asked to carry out a task at work which you don't think is part of your job.

b) You are asked to do something at home which you don't consider to be your responsibility.

In each case what do you say?
1. If you refuse angrily, making the other person feel bad, this is a sign of aggressive behaviour.

2. If you agree, without intending to do it, this is a sign of passive behaviour.

3. If you agree, but then try to find ways to get round doing it, this is a sign of manipulative behaviour.

Your task is to notice when you are behaving unassertively –
aggressively, passively, manipulatively – and then transform this into
assertive behaviour.

When you next catch yourself acting unassertively, write down what
happened, what you said and did. This will give you a test case. Work
through the rest of this program, bearing in mind this one incident,
and at every stage decide what an alternative, assertive response
would be. Write this down and practise it in real life.

STEP 2	Establishing and Valuing Your Rights

In every situation, you have the following rights:

1. To be the judge of yourself and not to allow yourself to be unduly
influenced by what others think.

2. To be heard and to have your needs taken into account.

3. To have feelings and to show them.

4. To say no or to change your mind or to make mistakes.

5. To not have to justify your behaviour.

6. To refuse a request without having to feel guilty or selfish.

7. To value your own needs on a level with those of others.

In your test situation, what were your rights? List them and see
whether they occurred to you at the time. Probably they didn't. From
now on remember these seven points whenever you are confronted
with a decision. They provide the general context of an assertive
response.

STEP 3	Convince Yourself

Do you feel confident about the rights you have listed?

| YES | NO: P7 and then STEP 4 ⟩

STEP 4	Thinking Assertively

Only by thinking assertively will you appear and act assertively.
Consider your test case. In one column list your unassertive thoughts
and in another list alternative assertive thoughts, remembering the
list of rights in STEP 2. If that seems difficult, try the following

exercise and then go back to your test case. Write down the following non-assertive thoughts in your notebook under the heading Non-assertive Thoughts. Then under another column, headed Assertive Thoughts, list alternative assertive thoughts. Then compare them with our assertive thoughts below. If your assertive thoughts are different to ours, that's acceptable provided they reflect your rights and do not fall into the Aggressive, Passive or Manipulative categories described in STEP 1. The important thing is that you use thoughts which you find most helpful. You may need to try them out in real situations to find out which suit you best.

Non-assertive Thoughts
1. If I don't say yes, he'll think I am mean and won't like me, and that would be awful.

2. Who am I to disagree? He knows so much that I can't possibly be right. I'd better keep quiet.

3. I can't complain. There would have been an awful fuss and I would seem to be a trouble maker, and then I'd feel terrible.

Assertive Thoughts
1. I have the right to say no. If he doesn't like it, that's unfortunate, but not my fault that he takes it that way.

2. What I've got to say is important. Even if it is a small point it doesn't mean it's unimportant. I have a right to disagree with his opinion.

3. It was disgraceful to be treated like that. I should have complained to prevent other people being similarly treated in the future.

Build assertive thinking into your everyday life. Look out for and interrupt any non-assertive thoughts which you have. Replace them with assertive thoughts and say them to yourself over and over again. The more you practise this, the sooner they will become spontaneous.

STEP 5	Speaking Assertively

What you say, and how you deliver what you want to say – your 'message' – is very important. Your tone of voice, manner of delivery, the very choice of words, will all convey it more, or less, assertively. Using your test case, consider the following points and whether they might have been applicable.

1. Deliver your 'message' immediately. Don't wait until hours later when the situation will have changed and it will have less impact.

2. Decide on your main point and don't get side-tracked onto other less relevant issues. Keep returning to this main point, reiterating the same statement if necessary.

3. Be as brief and concise as possible so that you do not dilute the message. A flood of words, including apologies, explanations, justifications, will weaken the impact.

4. Be as concrete and specific as possible. Say exactly how you feel and what you want. Don't be vague.

5. When criticising others, concern yourself with what people *do* rather than what they *are*. People find it easier to change their actions than their personalities.

6. Say how the other person is making you feel, rather than simply blaming or praising them. Again, this helps them to change if change is desirable.

Using your test case, write a 'script' of what you should have said – an assertive 'message'. Although this situation may not arise again, writing down what you want to say can make you aware of all the non-assertions, the embellishments, the confusing asides that litter speech. This technique of 'scripting' can be applied to future situations. After several weeks of using this scripting technique you will find yourself speaking assertively without having to rehearse the 'message' in advance.

STEP 6	Acting Assertively

As well as knowing *what* you want to say, you should also know *how* you want to say it. Awkwardness will undermine the most clearly reasoned argument. Both how you sound and look are vital to being assertive. For an example, you can undermine the impact of a clear assertive message by mumbling and staring at the floor.

1. *How you sound*. Your voice should sound clear, firm and purposeful, with the right level of volume and speed of delivery. If it is too soft you will seem uncertain and timid. If it is too loud you will sound aggressive or angry. If it is too quick, you will sound nervous or agitated. Avoid all hesitations and stammers, 'ums' and 'ers'. A scripted argument may be a help. To develop these skills, use a tape recorder and listen to yourself. Try out different ways of speaking assertively until you are happy with the way you sound.

2. *How you look*. Look at the person with whom you are talking. If you find it difficult to look someone in the eye, choose another part

of their face. It may be easier to look at their cheek or nose, and it will look to them as if you are looking them in the eye. As you get more relaxed, you can gradually look nearer their eyes.

— The expression on your face should match the message you are giving. If you smile when you are trying to show disapproval, you will undermine your message. Practise in front of a mirror.

— Your physical posture and gestures are also important. You should stand or sit up straight and keep as still as possible. Fidgeting and slouching will reduce the impact of your message. Stand between 4 and 12 feet from the other person. Further away, you will seem diffident or fearful, and nearer will be seen as aggressive.

Practise these skills by 'role-play'. Get a friend to re-enact your test case situation with you and give their opinion about what in your behaviour needs changing.

STEP 7	Being Assertive in All Situations

You will have worked through this program in terms of your test case. However you will have to be able to maintain this level of assertive behaviour in real situations.

List those situations in which you would like to be assertive. Starting with the least difficult, describe it in as much detail as you can. Who, what, when, where etc. Then go back through STEP 2 to 6 using this situation as your new test case.

Now you must look for the opportunity to put this situation to the test. Perhaps you could even arrange for the situation to happen — this will itself be a measure of your assertiveness.

When you find yourself in the situation remember to think, speak and act assertively. Afterwards, examine your performance. What still needs working at? What did you do well? Can you follow it up with another attempt?

Congratulate yourself on your success and make a note of the things you need to work on. As you learn to cope with one situation, try another that is more difficult.

Anticipate situations in which you find it difficult to assert yourself. You can then prepare for them, scripting what you want to say, rehearsing how you will behave.

Becoming assertive is a gradual process, but having followed this program, you should notice the benefits within a few weeks. But as you become more proficient, remember that just as you have a right to let other people know how you are feeling, others also have the right to be listened to!

'SLOW-DOWN' PROGRAM   P4

The pressures of modern life, whether at work or at home, mean that there is more to do and less time in which to do each thing. This program is designed for those who tend to rush at things, who find it difficult to stop and think things through clearly, or who take on too much. In other words, people who are generally disorganised in their lives. In each case there is a lot of wasted effort and needless wear and tear on yourself. By slowing down you will actually get more done in any given time, simply because you are doing things more efficiently. You will also feel better in yourself having achieved more control over your life and reduced the strain on your mind and emotions.

STEP 1   Relax

Complete the RELAXATION PROGRAM (P10). When you have learned the skills described in P10, make them a regular part of your everyday life. Take several relaxation breaks every working day, even if they are only 5-10 minutes long. Make these a priority and build them into your daily plans (STEP 4).

STEP 2   Decide on Your Goals

Define your life in terms of a series of goals. Make a list under columns that represent the different areas of your life. Everyone will have different goals involving work, accommodation, friends, leisure, skills and relaxation. Make a list of your goals under headings such as Work, House, Family, Social Life; or, Studies, Boyfriend, Finance, Car, Holiday.

In each case they should be –

1. *Realistic* – start with goals that you know you can achieve. Set your sights low to begin with and build up gradually. In this way you can move from success to success, rather than from failure to failure. Accept what cannot be changed, since this will only be a waste of effort, and decide what changes can be made. STEP 4 will help you do this.

2. *Clear* – define your goals in such a way that you can tell when they have been achieved.

3. *Consistent* – your goals should coincide not conflict with each other. Think again if one seems to prevent another, since this will cause frustration and wasted effort. Again, STEP 4 will help you in this.

STEP 3	Learn to Say 'No'

You do not have to agree to do everything you are asked to do. Decide what you *want* to do, what you *can* do, and when you *will* do it. Communicate this clearly. If you experience difficulties in this, consult the ASSERTIVENESS PROGRAM (P3).

STEP 4	Plan Your Time

To achieve these goals you must decide which tasks are necessary to their fulfilment and how and when they are to be carried out. This requires planning. It is possible to plan your life year by year, month by month, week by week, day by day, hour by hour. The more that is planned, the less room is left for uncertainty and stress.

1. *Write your plans down.* Writing things down helps to organise your thoughts, putting less of a burden on your memory. Keep a notebook or a diary rather than scribble on scraps of paper which will get lost. Organise this notebook into clear sections. Your personal schedule should be kept separate from shopping lists, addresses, birthdays. The 'Filofax' files have ready-made sections that you can select accordingly. They are expensive, but you could look at them to get ideas for your own notebook.

2. *Plan in stages.* Whether making long-term or short-term plans, consider all the tasks necessary to achieve your goal. Whether it's a plan for the year or the hour, it can be broken down into stages and so made more manageable.

3. When making your plans consider:

a. *Pace:* What is the best pace for you to work at? Allocate plenty of time to complete the tasks. If you find that you have insufficient time, and are forced to hurry or do sloppy work, reorganise your schedule.

b. *Change:* What rate of change suits you best? Trying to change too many things too quickly means changing nothing satisfactorily. Decide on one thing to change at a time and leave yourself plenty of time to make this change. Only move on to changing the next thing in your life when this is properly completed.

c. *Variety:* How much variety do you want? Too much variety leads to inefficiency, and you are unable to make the most of the experiences that you have. Limit the number of people, places and events to a level that suits you best. You want to achieve a happy medium which avoids both over-stimulation and boredom.

4. When planning your day, *work down from your longer-term goals* and plans. Decide what activities are essential in the coming week and how best they can be arranged. This will mean leaving out less vital items. It may help to go back to the list of goals you made in STEP 2 and place a star beside those that are urgent and postpone the others if necessary.

First thing each day, plan hour-by-hour what you can reasonably manage in the morning. At lunchtime draw up a plan for the afternoon. Strike off the tasks as you complete them.

5. *Allow for periods of free time*. Having regular breaks will enable you stick to your timetable since you will feel fresh, and also you will give yourself a margin in which you can carry over a task which takes a little longer than expected. Incorporate the relaxation skills (P10) into your everyday life.

STEP 5	Making Decisions and Solving Problems

This step will help you to take decisions or solve problems in an orderly fashion. Often people fail to make a decision or solve a problem effectively because they do not have a strategy.

Take a recent situation in your own life – it might be a major decision such as whether you should give up your job, or a minor one such as whether to go away at the weekend. Use this as a test case for the following.

1. Make a detailed statement of the problem.

2. List all the possible solutions and choices that exist. Include 'do nothing' as an option and try to think of unusual options. Regard this as a brainstorming session in which you write everything down, however silly or trivial it may seem.

3. Write down the ideal end result, remembering that you may have to accept a compromise.

4. Consider all the advantages and disadvantages of each option. For example:

OPTION	ADVANTAGES	DISADVANTAGES
1.	a. b. c.	a. b.
2.	a. b.	a.

Weigh up the pros and cons, and select the best (or least bad). Only then take the decision. Gradually your strategy will become second nature and 'snap' decisions a thing of the past. You will see that speed is far from being the most important element in decision making. You will have learned how to 'dictate the pace' rather than being a slave to it.

If your problem is *in*decision – an inability to make a decision or solve a problem, use the same strategy. Ensure you give it enough time to work. Making a decision – even if it is not the best or final one – reduces stress.

1. If, after this, you are no nearer to solving the problem, go back over the options, choose another. Try this one out in practice.

2. If this doesn't work, try seeking someone else's opinion. Even if the problem remains you have achieved the following:

a. You have taken decisions.
b. These were reached through systematic analysis.
c. You have put your decisions into effect.
d. You have shown flexibility in revising your strategy when it didn't work.
e. You have established that this particular situation can't be changed.

3. Discovering what can and can't be done is useful information, since it allows you to work at maximum efficiency. If you find that a goal cannot be achieved, your new goal is to accept this and make the most of it, re-drawing your strategy accordingly. P3 and P10 will help you do this.

HABIT CONTROL PROGRAM   P5

This program allows you to tackle any form of behaviour which has developed into a habit and over which you no longer have control. Typical examples might be smoking, drinking, overeating, overspending, nail biting, laziness. It will also help you with the psychological aspects of addiction. In both cases you will need to know when you drink, smoke, take drugs, who you are with, how you are feeling. Identifying these factors will help you to understand your behaviour and so change it.

STEP 1	What Is the Problem?

1. Describe your problem, using a notebook, and being as specific as possible. For example:

Drinking
— is it troublesome to you or other people?
— do you think that you drink too much, or is it your partner who says so?
— is it the amount of alcohol, or the amount of money, or the amount of time you spend in the pub and not at home?

2. Then record the size of the problem. By each entry note the time of day, who you were with, where you were, what you were doing. Include details specific to your problem. For example:

Drinking — note the number of drinks and/or the amount of time you spend in the pub.

Smoking — note the number of cigarettes you smoke a day.

Overeating — note down every item you eat.

Overspending — note down how often you go to the shops, the amount spent, what you bought, whether it was on cash or credit.

3. Keep your diary for a week. If you have difficulty organising your record, complete Steps 2 to 5 of ANALYSING & MANAGING YOUR PROBLEM (P1).

4. Are you determined to change? If not go to DECIDING TO CHANGE (P9).

STEP 2	Establish a Pattern

Look at your diary. Does there seem to be a pattern to your habit? Consider the following factors:

1. Your habit occurs or is worse in *certain situations*. There are particular places such as clubs or certain pubs where you drink too much. There are particular places you associate with smoking or taking drugs.

2. Is *anxiety or tension* emerging as a key factor?

3. Does your habit occur at *certain times* of the day or week? For example you eat too much in the evening. You overspend in your lunch hour.

4. Does your habit occur *when you are bored*? Often habits build up when there is a lack of other activities to interest us.

5. Does your habit occur when you are on your own or when you are with a particular group of *people*?

6. Does your habit occur when you are doing a *particular task*? This may be a mundane chore that you have always done while smoking. By now you are unaware of how much you smoke as you do the job.

7. Is it that your habit is a major source of *pleasure*?

8. Is your habit connected with a *weight* problem? For example you may feel that smoking will keep your weight down.

9. Does your habit give you a sense of *self-confidence*? For example a cigarette gives you something to do with your hands when you are at a party.

10. Does your habit make you feel *socially acceptable*, *'cool'*, or *'macho'*?

11. Is your habit an *addiction*? Do you crave drink or drugs so much that you will go out late at night to find a bar or shop that is open? Do you consider stealing from friends or family to buy the necessary quantities?

If you have difficulty establishing a pattern, complete Steps 6 and 7 of ANALYSING & MANAGING YOUR PROBLEM (P1).

STEP 3	Alter Your Habits

Having analysed your behaviour, let's decide how to organise change.

Goals – are you going to cut down, change the pattern or cut out the habit completely?

1. A systematic change – this is most satisfactory if you want to reduce your habit rather than give it up completely. Go to STEP 4.

2. The 'Big Bang' method – this is most satisfactory if you want to give up your habit altogether. Go to STEP 5.

Rewards – decide upon a system of rewards. Decide what they should be and when you should enjoy them.

STEP 4	Systematic Reduction

1. You will gradually and systematically introduce control over your habit. First go back over your records in STEP 2 and devise a system of controls that suits your problem.

a. *Certain situations* – work out ways to alter or avoid them: Spend less time at the party, delegate meetings. Substitute orange juice and peanuts for wine and cigarettes. If you usually sit at the bar, move to a table. If you usually buy a round of drinks, now only buy your own. Visit those places where you rarely indulge in your habit. Perhaps the bar at work inhibits your drinking since you have to maintain appearances. If you are with the children at home you may feel less inclined to smoke so much.

b. *Anxiety or tension* – work through STRESS MANAGEMENT (P11) and/or ANXIETY CONTROL (P17).

c. *Certain times* – reorganise your schedules. Replace your empty hours with activities such as a lunchtime exercise class. Deliberately re-arrange your days to avoid temptation.

d. *Boredom* – have you thought about a new hobby, enrolling at evening classes, perhaps? Use your vacant weekday hours for mundane household tasks but give yourself more time at weekends for doing what you really enjoy.

e. *People* – work out why it is worse in the company or absence of certain people. How would everyone react if you said 'No'? Would they applaud or mock your strength of character? Decide whether it is necessary to change your circle of friends.

f. *A particular task* – rehearse this task without your habit as an accompaniment, or consider an alternative accompaniment.

g. *Pleasure* – this will be difficult. Try an alternative form of enjoyment. If the habit is a form of relaxation, work through the RELAXATION PROGRAM (P10).

h. *Weight* – while giving up smoking, people tend to put on weight; but it is unlikely to become a health problem. Take advantage of your healthier body to do some form of exercise – see the FITNESS PROGRAM (P21): Fitness Test 1.

i. *Self-confidence* – your habit allows you to blend in with the crowd. Find an alternative way of fitting in. Work through the SELF-CONFIDENCE PROGRAM (P7).

j. *To be cool* – remember that the majority of people are non-smokers and find the smell of cigarettes unpleasant. Consider whether you need to change your group of friends and work through the ASSERTIVENESS program (P3).

k. *Addiction* – Work through P9 (DECIDING TO CHANGE). If this fails to help, consult Useful Addresses at the back of this book or consult your doctor.

l. Devise *tactical controls* on your particular habit. For example:

Smoking – avoid the first cigarette in bed by leaving the packet downstairs. Delay it more by washing and dressing first.

Drinking – only go to the pub on certain days. Limit the amount of alcohol about the house.

Overeating – buy small amounts of food at a time. Don't buy biscuits or other snack foods.

Overspending – leave your cheque book at home. Take out small amounts of cash.

2. Choose the control idea most suitable to your habit. Introduce it into your daily routine. Don't be tempted to stop recording your behaviour, since this is the only way you will notice when change is effective. Only choose one control idea at a time, otherwise you won't be able to tell what is the cause. Be consistent. Don't let yourself go even one day in the week.

3. Mark the day you employed your control idea in your records and monitor your progress for a week.

a. *If you can see an improvement*, reward yourself. It may be that the control idea has been very effective. To maintain this state, contine to monitor your behaviour, increasing the time between records until you feel able to stop altogether. For example, if the problem seems fairly well under control, keeping a record say one day a week or one week a month will enable you to keep an eye on your performance and feel in control.

b. *If your habit seems to be getting worse*, don't worry. It is common for behaviour to worsen before it improves. *Any* kind of change at this stage is a positive sign. Don't give up. Continue for another week. There should be an improvement. If things really aren't progressing, then select another control idea, it may be more effective.

c. *If you feel that there is still scope for improvement*, add another control idea to your routine. Mark the day you started it in your notebook and monitor your progress. Continue, taking on one control idea at a time until the habit is at a satisfactory level, when you can begin to increase the time between records as in a. above.

STEP 5	The 'Big Bang' Method

While this sounds alarming, it is often much easier than it seems. Most people who successfully give up smoking stop suddenly.

Preparations
— choose the day on which you will start. Avoid times when you know there will be stress. Holidays and weekends may be preferable to weekdays. Starting a diet is easier if you are eating at home.

— tell friends about your intentions, so that they can give you moral support. Ask them not to smoke or drink around you, if this will make things easier.

— list the pros and cons of your habit (see Steps 1 and 2 of DECIDING TO CHANGE — P9). Keep this handy for when you feel weak.

'Big Bang' day
— get rid of cigarettes or bottles so that it is less easy to give in to temptation.

— avoid those situations where, typically, you indulge yourself.

— plan to treat yourself at the end of the week.

— at the end of the day CONGRATULATE YOURSELF — this is your first day of self control.

If it isn't a success, work through P9, then set a new date and try again. Many people have had previous tries before managing the 'Big Bang'.

'PARTNERS' PROGRAM   P6

This program aims to help you through the initial steps of under-standing and confronting a relationship problem.

STEP 1	Define the Problem

First you must clearly define the problem. In a notebook, write down all the things that upset or annoy you about your partner. What, precisely, is it that bothers you? For example:

General	Specific
Doesn't pull his/her weight	Never helps with housework Leaves all decisions to me Leaves all financial worries to me
Doesn't communicate	Spends days without speaking Will not listen to me Avoids attempts to talk
Violent	Verbally abusive Physically abusive
Doesn't seem interested in me	Never asks what I have been doing Never seems pleased to see me
Sexual difficulties	Lacks interest Demands too much Not interested in my satisfaction Orgasm problems Premature ejaculation

Be as specific as you can. Otherwise, when you come to discuss the problem, your partner can claim that you are being vague, and it's your fault. Take several days to compile the list, adding things as you think of them.

STEP 2	The Good and the Bad

On the next page write down all the good things about your partner. Try to be fair, however upset or unhappy you are feeling, or however long it takes you to think of some points. Everyone has something positive about them, even if they don't show this side to you. For example:

– they may be bad at talking to you, but dote on the children.

– aside from their lovemaking, things can be very good.

— they may be permanently aggressive, but also work very hard.

Next, repeat this exercise, but with yourself as the object. List all your good points, and, as far as you can, the bad ones. Try to think how you must appear to your partner. Be as hard on yourself as you can, since you will use this list when negotiating, and need to be as aware of your own faults as possible. It may be that what you take to be a mark of your love is interpreted differently. For example:

— I clean the house all day, but perhaps this is why I never have time for the other things we need to do.

— I devote myself to my work since we'll have more money, but perhaps this is why we never get out together.

STEP 3	Putting the Problem Across

Now you need to discuss the problem with your partner.

1. Before
Go through your lists carefully and highlight the points that you feel are the most important. You may find that it will help to have the lists in front of you while you discuss, or you may choose to memorise the main points.

Choose a convenient time when you are both in a reasonably good mood. Don't pick the exact moment that he/she comes home from work, or when there is something interesting on television. Also make sure that you have privacy and are unlikely to be disturbed.

If your partner is particularly busy, negotiate with him/her a time when the two of you can talk.

2. During
It is important to start off by emphasising your partner's good points and those of your relationship. Remember to thank them for the things that you really appreciate. Introduce the problem gradually, making sure that you indicate the joint aspects. Use 'we' rather than 'you'. At this stage you don't want to sound as if you are making your partner take all the blame.

Maintain a balance. Use the lists you made earlier to acknowledge your own faults and shortcomings. You want to explain the problem fully, without sounding completely negative. Tackling things in an even handed way will make your partner feel less under attack and more receptive and enthusiastic to help with the difficulty.

3. After
According to how your partner responds, you have a series of options.

i) He/she may refuse to listen to you. They may even get up and leave. Go to STEP 4.

ii) He/she may be very receptive and want to help. Go to STEP 5.

iii) He/she may recognise the problem, but refuse to do anything about it, or consider there is no solution. Go to STEP 6.

STEP 4	Your Partner Ignores You

This is the most frustrating outcome, but there are still some options open. You can try again on another occasion, making it clear that you will keep on trying until you have a proper discussion. Alternatively, you can try to get some support from elsewhere. Visit your GP and ask for information about counselling for yourself, either from the local hospital or marriage guidance centre. (Remember, you don't have to be married or heterosexual to consult these people.) This may help you to come to terms with the problem and it may be that your partner will now be prepared to listen and come with you, since your concern is being taken seriously by other people. You can then return to STEP 2.

STEP 5	Your Partner Wants to Help

This is the most encouraging outcome. There are several ways to proceed.

1. *Defining roles* – write down your separate responsibilities. When new things arise, they can be discussed and shared accordingly. Make sure you keep a record, so that both of you stick to the bargain. This is a good way of dealing with a partner who is not pulling their weight.

2. *Making time for each other* – if you find that you spend little time together, try organising a set part of the week to spend together. There may be a particular interest that the two of you would like to follow. If not, a short holiday or weekend together, or a regular evening out, would be a good plan. This is a way to tackle communication problems, or when you seem to have lost interest in each other.

3. *Making time for yourself* – on the other hand, you may be spending too much time together. In which case spend an evening each week with friends, or doing something you want to do alone. This can solve problems of boredom or feeling trapped.

4. *Preventing violence* – try to work out with your partner the situations that lead to violence. Get him/her to warn you when they are becoming aroused. Observe your partner and learn to anticipate anger. You might suggest that they work through the ANGER PROGRAM (P13). If none of these options are successful, visit your GP together and find professional counselling help.

5. *Specific difficulties* – for example sexual problems. Acknowledging a problem is in itself a tremendous step towards solving it. Consider any changes on your lifestyle that might be a cause or a solution. Together, work through a manual designed for this specific problem – there are some very good, cheap manuals available from ordinary book shops and libraries. Alternatively see your GP and obtain professional help.

Notice that in each of the suggestions above, the emphasis is on partnership and sharing. If you are asking your partner to do something for you, offer something in return. If you are suggesting professional help, offer to accompany your partner on the visit. This applies to any problem. You are not trying to attach the blame solely to your partner. Always think of the joint solution. Go on to STEP 7.

STEP 6	Your Partner Refuses to Get Involved

Here, your partner acknowledges the problem but is still not prepared to do anything about it. This can be as frustrating as the situation discussed in STEP 4. You still have some options.

1. You can make a bargain with your partner. If he/she is not prepared to help you, then you are not prepared to do a specific thing for them. Don't give in.

2. You can ask for a regular time to discuss the problem. This is rather different from *doing* something, but you may find that it helps, since your partner may become gradually more available to the idea of change. Then go back through STEP 3.

3. Take the same course of action as STEP 4.

STEP 7	The Future

The most important thing, having decided to tackle the problem, is to keep things going. Don't start off with good intentions and slip back to square one after a couple of weeks.

If you have decided to make specific changes, keep a note of whether you are both fulfilling your share of the responsibilities. If not, point this out.

If you have decided to seek professional help, make sure you go to all the appointments. It is impossible to obtain help if you aren't there. Also don't expect miracles over night – you have to work at this. When things start to improve, show your appreciation. Thank your partner. If he/she is making a special effort, they won't keep it up for long if you don't seem to notice.

Finally, remember that you are a partnership. Try your hardest to work things out *together*.

SELF-CONFIDENCE PROGRAM   P7

This program is for those who lack confidence in what they do; who avoid, rather than tackle, difficult or uncomfortable tasks; or who do not value or respect themselves.

What you think and feel about yourself depends on what you do and the standards you set for yourself. If you have unrealistically high standards, you are more likely to feel unsure of yourself and try to avoid situations in which you feel uncertain. This limits your experience and practice in coping with difficulties, and in turn makes you even more unconfident.

The more you avoid, the less you do, and the less you value and respect yourself. You find it even more difficult to reach the expectations you have of yourself, which makes you ever more unsure and unconfident. This program will help you get out of this downwards spiral by increasing your achievements and self-appreciation.

STEP 1	Make Your Expectations Realistic

Write down a list of standards that you set for yourself at work, at home and with friends. Answer the following questions about each one.

1. Do your standards have to be this high? Could they be lower, at least to begin with?

2. Would you expect other people to perform as well or achieve as much? If not, then lower your standards to what you consider reasonable for others.

3. Do other people really expect you to do things this well? If not, settle for a standard that others will respect.

4. Could you regard the standard as a long-term goal, rather than an immediate expectation? Try and think of steps between your present behaviour and your long-term goal.

Remember that high expectations often lead to poor performance and low self-esteem. Start with moderate expectations and build them up gradually.

Write down a new list of lower standards, based on practicable expectations. For the moment, you must not aim any higher than this.

STEP 2	Confront Difficult Situations

Write down a list of situations in which you feel unconfident or that you avoid altogether, and arrange them in order of difficulty.

Tackle the least difficult first. Often, worrying about it is the worst part. When you are actually *in* the situation you will find it less difficult than you feared. The following programs will help you in different ways. Read through each in turn, looking for the one that is most applicable to your situation. Concentrate on and complete the most relevant one.

ANXIETY CONTROL PROGRAM (P17)
FEAR CONTROL PROGRAM (P16)
SOCIAL SKILLS PROGRAM (P8)
ASSERTIVENESS PROGRAM (P3)

Practise this situation as often as you can. The more you do it, the easier it will be. If after a couple of weeks there is no improvement, go to STEP 3. If there is an improvement, go to STEP 4.

STEP 3	Break Down the Stages

Your lack of progress may be due to your first task being too difficult. Break it down into smaller, easier steps and go to STEP 5. For example:

You have decided to speak out more at meetings.

1. Speak out in smaller groups, during coffee breaks, so that you get used to the sound of your own voice.

2. Write down what you want to say during meetings, so that you get used to ordering your thoughts.

3. Make a small contribution, such as asking a question, or making a brief announcement.

STEP 4	Tackle the Next Problem

When you feel confident in this situation, you are ready to tackle the next one on your list. Remember to reward yourself on your progress. It is you and not the program that has achieved these results.

STEP 5	Value Yourself

The way you think about yourself affects how you feel about yourself. A person who achieves and gives a lot can still think themselves worthless. A person with fewer qualities can hold themselves in high esteem. Also the same person can feel differently about him- or herself at different times, even though *they* haven't changed – only their thoughts!

You are not born respecting yourself, you have to learn it. If you can begin to value yourself, your self-confidence will grow. You will do more, which will add to your self-image. Let's start!

1. List all the good things about yourself. However you feel, there are bound to be some – it's just a question of considering everything and admitting that everything is not bad. At the very least, list your 'least bad' points! Think of all the aspects of your life – at home, at work, when you're with friends, when you're alone – and yourself – your behaviour, your skills, your personality, your feelings, your appearance, your achievements, your aspirations.

2. Remember the last time you did something that you or anyone else considered valuable. Try and recall who and what was involved. This should enhance your previous list.

3. When you thought about your good points, did you find that you were comparing yourself to other people?

NO 〉 Good. You can build your confidence more easily at this stage by comparing yourself with the realistic standards that you have set yourself. Your worth depends upon *you*, not upon other people.

YES 〉 You will always find other people who are better than you, whatever you choose to compare. So if you assess your own worth by comparing yourself with others, you are bound to make yourself less confident. Go back to your list of realistic standards that you set yourself and compare your present behaviour with them.

Can you find good points by doing this?

| YES 〉 | List them and throw your list from STEP 1 away. |

| NO 〉 | Go back to STEP 3 and work at getting nearer the standards you set for yourself. |

4. Congratulate yourself on your good points. You were not born with them, nor were they handed to you on a plate. You have developed these good points and you should give yourself credit for them. Try to keep adding to your list by going through this Section every now and again.

5. You have learnt to think more positively about yourself. You should feel more self-confident. If you can also learn to think more postively about other people and the world in general, you will feel yet more confident. To do this, go to the ASSERTIVENESS PROGRAM (P3).

SOCIAL SKILLS PROGRAM   P8

The days have gone when people lived their lives in the place where they were born and maintained close ties with friends they made as children. Today most of us move around in search of work.

This has meant we have had to learn to make new friends more readily than our ancestors. Making friends is a skill that can be learned. Some people find this very easy; unfortunately, others who do not, can experience loneliness and depression.

This program is for people who find it difficult to make and keep friends. Teaching 'making and keeping friends' as a skill does not in any way belittle friendship, it recognises the realities of modern living, builds confidence in meeting people, and opens the door to friendships which may develop as fully as any that began in the innocence of childhood.

| STEP 1 | Current Social Activities |

Make a list of any and all social situations you find yourself in over the next month. Include *what the event is* (the type of gathering, eg purely social, joint activity, drinks party, coffee morning, function to do with your work, local society or group gathering, etc.), *who is present* (were they friends, mostly strangers, more men/women, mostly older/younger than you, quiet/noisy, with similar/varied interests, smart/casual, etc?), and note *how comfortable you feel* in the situation, using a scale of 0-10 where 0 = very uncomfortable and 10 = very comfortable.

DATE	TYPE OF GATHERING	PEOPLE	REACTION

STEP 2   **What is the Problem?**

It may be that you feel comfortable with people but just don't know how to go about meeting them. Is this the full extent of your problem?

Some people feel naturally at home with others; they seem confident and popular. In fact if you get to know these people, you will discover that some of them are really very shy; their social skills have been learned and practised. This is what you need to do in order to become more confident yourself.

Making reference to your first list, make a second, this time including all the things that seem to be a problem when you are mixing with people. Divide a page into two columns. On one side make a list of things to do with speaking (head it 'Verbal Problems'), and in the other column include anything else under the heading 'Non-verbal Problems'. You should end up with a list that looks something like this:

VERBAL PROBLEMS	NON-VERBAL PROBLEMS
Don't know what to say	My appearance is different
Stammer or stutter	Can't look at people directly
Mind goes blank	Feel panicky
Talk about stupid things	Can't stand still
Seem to bore people	Have funny twitches or mannerisms
Talk too much	Never on time
etc.	

Are your problems more verbal than non-verbal?

It isn't always easy to pinpoint one's own non-verbal problems. For example, your appearance may be more important than you think.

Some situations involve 'appearance' conventions. If an occasion is very formal, you (or others in your presence) may feel uncomfortable if you turn up in jeans. Similarly a formal appearance at an informal gathering can set up barriers to communication. Even if you are against formality (or informality) in itself or simply don't think appearance (or, say, punctuality) should matter, consider their importance to other people when you make your list.

Consider, or if in doubt find out, what conventions are appropriate in advance of any social situation. Forethought of this kind will provide a good platform for communication when you arrive. You will start off 'on the right foot'.

STEP 3	Practise Communicating

Choose a very simple task, eg stopping someone in the street to ask the time. Concentrate on your own behaviour. Look at your list of non-verbal problems and try to overcome each problem one by one. For example:

Suppose you find it difficult to look at someone directly. Try asking someone the time and make a point of looking at the person. Write down whether you succeeded and how comfortable you felt, again using the scale 0-10. Continue doing this exercise several times a day, until the scale shows that you are feeling more comfortable. Then move on to the next problem on your list, and concentrate on that.

DATE	SITUATION	PROBLEM TESTED	REACTION

Once you are feeling more confident about your non-verbal behaviour, alter the exercise, making it more complicated (eg stop someone in the street and ask them directions).

You can go on practising more complicated tasks until you feel you have overcome your difficulties. Remember to keep a careful record of events and how you felt (0-10), so that you know exactly what progress you have made. Then go on to thinking about verbal problems.

STEP 4	Practising Communication

The most common problem people have is entertaining a conversation: knowing what to say, and keeping things going. The best way to learn how to do this, is to listen to other people doing it.

Listen to others' conversations, a good place to do this is on a bus. Sit behind two people who are obviously together. They won't know you are listening. Make a note of any topics you think are particularly good (eg books they have read, holidays they have taken). And notice how the conversation is made up. You will probably find that they ask each other a lot of questions. In other words they demonstrate an interest in the other person, as well as talking about themselves. Notice how these questions are answered. If a person provides a 'closed' answer, it is more difficult for the conversation to be 'picked up' by the other. An 'open' answer makes it a lot easier. Consider the following examples in which you are the person responding to a question:

Q. Have you been here before?

A1. No.

A2. No, what about you?

A3. No, I normally drink at the Red Lion.

Q. Isn't the weather terrible?

A1. Yes.

A2. Yes, do you think it will carry on long?

A3. Yes, but I am lucky, I came by car.

You will see that the first 'closed' answer in each case makes it more difficult for the questioner to respond to you. He or she has to begin all over again. In both cases, the second and third, 'open' answers make it easy for the other person to 'pick up' on what you said and the conversation is under way.

Now try an exercise; try starting a conversation. Pick somewhere – a café or perhaps the bus again – and see how you get on. Pick something natural and relevant so that your interlocutor (the other person) doesn't feel awkward (they may feel more unsure than you!). For instance, ask if they know whether the bus travels the route you want or, in the café, whether they would recommend what they are eating. Avoid beginning a conversation with a stranger by asking anything too personal.

Make sure you keep records of each event and how comfortable you felt, and continue practising until you begin to become more confident.

DATE	SITUATION	WHAT WAS SAID	REACTION

Once your records (on the scale of 0-10) show that you are feeling more confident, practise your skills in a social situation. Continue to watch and listen to other people for clues about your own behaviour. Rather than just hearing yourself when you talk, listen to the other person listening. And continue to keep your records.

STEP 5	Meeting People

Where do people meet? They meet anywhere, but you will generally find that friendships form more easily when you are involved in a shared activity, rather than at clubs simply aimed at introducing people. Another advantage in shared activities is that you automatically know that you have an interest in common with the others. This is important if conversations and friendships are to develop and grow.

Write down a list of your hobbies or talents which may help you to meet others. For example, do you play sport? If not, would you like to learn? Do you play a musical instrument or sing? Now cross out the activities which do not involve social activity (eg the piano is not a particularly social instrument unless you are good enough to participate in a local show, dance class or pantomime; jogging and swimming are not particularly social sports unless you join a club).

If you decide to take up a sport or hobby, go to your local library and ask what clubs and organisations are available in your area. Then all you have to do is make an effort to join! And don't forget that socialising very often goes on after the activity itself, so ensure that you put time aside to go for a drink afterwards, even if you are not thirsty.

What if you don't have any hobbies or interests?

Now is the time to start! Not only will it help you to meet other people, but it will provide topics of conversation with a wider group of people. You can get lists of classes from your local library. Select carefully. Don't choose something that will be too demanding academically, or which frankly doesn't interest you. If you want to meet people of both sexes, photography is more likely to be successful than embroidery or car maintenance.

Don't put off enrolling. Many courses will welcome you at any time of year, not just at the traditional year start in the Autumn.

Once you have begun, keep records of your progress. Make a point of joining other members of the class during a coffee break. For the first week or two, don't be too interrogative (ask too many questions) or self-disclosing (lay yourself too bare) – confine your conversation largely to the topic of your class. As the weeks go by you will find yourself becoming increasingly confident, and may decide to take other classes or to suggest meeting your new friends afterwards for a drink or for supper.

If you do not feel like evening classes, or do not have access to them for some reason, find out what else is going on locally. There may be a local Womens Institute or Round Table. If you have young children there may be Mother and Baby groups or activities linked to local schools or churches.

Don't worry if things don't take off to start with.

Remember that other people may be as shy as you.

Persevere.

STEP 6	Re-cap

Have a good, close look at your records. You are looking for patterns. Which are the situations in which you feel most comfortable now? Underline them in red. Now, what do these situations have in common? Perhaps they involve small groups rather than large, or it may be that you are with people that you know well. Maybe they are joint activities rather than parties (socialising for its own sake). Make a list of these key features.

Can you increase your involvement in the activities you enjoy? For example, if you enjoy being with a particular group of people, what about suggesting some new activities yourself? (Look at STEP 5 for ideas.) You might decide to invite them to your home. This is a good way of increasing involvement because people often invite you back, in return. Don't worry if you cannot cook. Make it a 'take-away' evening.

Choose an activity and organise yourself to do it. Continue keeping records so that you see how much you are going out and how comfortable you feel. Increase the level of social activity until you feel you are doing enough.

What about the situations you still feel uncomfortable in? You may decide simply to opt out of them. Provided you build up the situations you enjoy, there will be no great loss. For example, many people dislike parties where they don't know anybody or where the music is loud and they cannot talk.

What if you feel that you are missing out and would like to enjoy these situations more? In that case, you need to practise by putting yourself in the situation as often as you can.

Make a rule never to refuse an invitation of this kind. Increase your involvement in activities which share similar features (eg if parties remain a problem, try going to a disco once a week). Rate yourself on your scale (0-10) so that you can watch your progress. Gradually you will find yourself becoming more and more comfortable in these situations. (If part of your difficulty lies in doubting your own skills in these situations, work through STEP 2 again, before you start.)

STEP 7	Results

By this point you should have identified some of the difficulties you experience in social situations, and you should have achieved two things:

1. You should have increased your level of social involvement.

2. You should feel more comfortable in the social situations in which you are involved.

If you have achieved these two aims, congratulate yourself. You have made a big effort and have succeeded. You will probably find that having 'started the ball rolling', things will now develop of their own accord. But don't let things slip. It often seems more comfortable to stay in by the fire in winter; make the effort to invite friends in.

Good friends are usually very tolerant. They are prepared to listen to you if you have a problem or feel a bit down. But no one wants to be with someone who is always moaning. If your friends start making excuses about seeing you, ask yourself whether you have been a bit too demanding of the friendship.

Remember that as a friend you must be prepared to give what you expect to get from your friends.

If you have not achieved the two aims above, do not give up. Go back to the beginning of the program and have another try. Remember to be consistent. It is all too easy to do these things in fits and starts. Try to keep up with the program rather than having a week hard at it and then a week off. Your success will be worth all the hard work you put in.

DECIDING TO CHANGE PROGRAM   P9

This program is for those people who are unsure whether they want to change; those who want to change the situation but feel it presents too many difficulties (you may know your situation is stressful, but shy away from changing it because you think it will cause too many upheavals); and it is for those who are finding it difficult to change habits.

STEP 1	Do You Really Want to Change?

Might you be better off staying as you are? Make a list of reasons 'for' and 'against' changing in two columns. For example:

Desired change: 'To be able to get out on my own again'

FOR	AGAINST
I wouldn't sit around the house	I'd be vulnerable outside
I could do my own shopping	The house might be burgled
I'd get some fresh air	I might have a 'turn' in the street
I'd see friends more often	

Look at your two lists. Compare them. Do there seem to be more reasons for changing than not?

NO	YES: STEP 3 ⟩

STEP 2	Consequences of Change

Make a list of the good and bad consequences of change. What events might ensue? What might happen as a result?

GOOD	BAD
I would have a more interesting life	My husband would stop helping
I would feel more normal	I'd have more to do which might
I could go on holiday	be bad for my health
I would see more of the children	

Look at your lists.

Can you think of any more reasons for changing, and good consequences as a result? You might discuss this with a friend to produce more ideas. Add them to your list.

Are all the reasons against changing, and all the bad consequences as real and imposing as they seem? Go back through your lists striking out those reasons that do not seem so real.

If the positive side of your list now exceeds the negative, go to STEP 3.

If there still seem to be more reasons not to change, then try tackling another problem, returning to this one at a later date.

STEP 3	Deciding to Change

You need to find out what might make it difficult to change your behaviour. Having made the decision to change there is always the danger of the 'Yes-Buts'. 'Yes-Buts' are the thoughts, doubts, and attitudes which emerge as soon as we start confronting a problem. It is one thing to say you want to change. It is quite another to do the things necessary to make the change. 'Yes', you hear yourself say, 'I do want to change. But . . .'

Here are a list of 'Yes-Buts'. See if you recognise any as your own.

1. I have tried everything and nothing has worked.
2. I'm just made like that, there's nothing I can do about it.
3. Anyone would have this problem in my situation.
4. It will get better with time, there's no point in doing anything.
5. I need expert help.
6. No matter what I do, it won't last.
7. Other people need to change, not me.
8. The problem is outside my control.
9. If I did change it would hurt X and I'd feel guilty.
10. Change would only produce more problems than it would solve.
11. I won't be able to do what's needed.

Write down the ones that apply to you and any others that have occurred to you in the past. Then go to STEP 4. But if you cannot come up with any 'Yes-Buts' go to STEP 6.

STEP 4	Rate the 'Yes-Buts'

Now that you have identified your 'Yes-Buts', find out how real they are. Sometimes just becoming aware of them makes them seem less real. Beside each 'Yes-But' write a number from 0 to 4 that best describes how far you believe it to be true.

0 = I don't believe it at all
1 = I'm not sure
2 = I believe it slightly
3 = I reckon it's true
4 = I'm absolutely sure

Are all your ratings 0?

NO	YES: STEP 6 ⟩

STEP 5	Removing the 'Yes-Buts'

For each 'Yes-But' apply the following questions and record your answers:

1. What is the evidence for your belief?
   What is the evidence against your belief? (Think carefully about this one.)
2. What alternative views might there be?
   How might someone else view your situation?
3. What is the effect of this belief?
   Does it help or hinder you from getting what you want? How?
   What would be the effect of looking at things less negatively?
4. Is your thinking distorted or misleading?
   Are you exaggerating?
   Are you thinking in all-or-nothing terms?
   Are you remembering only your weaknesses and forgetting your strengths?
   Are you taking the most pessimistic view, expecting the worst?
   Are you predicting the future instead of experimenting with it?
   Are you assuming that things won't work?
   Are you basing your judgement on feelings rather than facts?
   Are you underestimating your control over things?
   Are you only noticing the things that support your beliefs?

Now work through STEP 4 again. If your 'Yes-Buts' are receiving 0 scores, go to STEP 6.

If you are still believing in your 'Yes-Buts', consider the following:

1. Is there anything that can question your belief? If there is, write it down and concentrate upon it. If your belief remains unshaken, answer 2:

2. How can you test this belief? If it were a fact, what would this mean? Set up a situation to see what happens. Does your prediction come true? Try more than once. If your belief remains intact, you will have to try changing with your 'Yes-Buts' in tow. They may not be strong enough to prevent change. Whatever is the case, you have isolated the problems and may be able to change them later on.

STEP 6	Change

1. Draw up a contract in which you promise yourself to act and, if applicable, to carry out a named preventive program within a certain period of time. Decide upon a start date and an estimated completion date. If you ever feel tempted to give up, you have your contract to remind you.

2. Tell your friends about your decision to change. This will help you maintain your resolve. Explain to them how you want to change and how you intend to go about it. Choose people to tell who are likely to be sympathetic and encouraging. You need not say much, just enough to reinforce your commitment.

3. Decide upon a system of rewards. This might be on completion of the entire program, or a certain number of stages. Decide also what your reward will be. The more you achieve, the bigger the treat should be.

Now go ahead! If you are unsure what is keeping your problem going, or which preventive program is applicable to you, try P1 (ANALYSING & MANAGING YOUR PROBLEM) first, and note especially STEP 7.

RELAXATION PROGRAM   P10

Tension wastes energy and it can cause physical pain and emotional distress. If you can learn to relax your body, you can begin to relax your mind.

Relaxation is a skill that has to be learnt. The more you practise, the better you become, until the skill becomes automatic.

If you practise relaxation every day, you will keep your arousal level lower and so cope better with stressful situations. It is like having your car serviced – it is a bit of extra effort that is well worth it, since the car is less likely to break down when put to the test.

This program teaches relaxation by relaxing your muscles, slowing your breathing and calming your mind. By tensing and relaxing different muscle groups one at a time, you will see how your muscles feel when they are properly relaxed. Do not expect to feel the benefits immediately – some people find that they can relax on the first attempt, while others take much longer.

STEP 1	Choose a Time

Decide on your relaxation times. Choose two periods during the day when you can have up to half-an-hour without interruption. (You will find the time needed to relax will decrease as you get more skilled). These times should be when you are least likely to feel pressurised and which fit easily into your daily routine. Also, they should not be straight after a meal. If possible, stick to the same times each day.

STEP 2	Choose a Place

Find the best place to relax. A quiet, dimly lit room that is warm and comfortable is ideal. You can decide whether to relax lying down on a firm bed or carpeted floor, or sitting in a reclining position. All parts of your body should be comfortably supported. If you have a history of low back strain, place a cushion under your knees. Take off shoes and tight clothing. Remove glasses and contact lenses.

STEP 3	Prepare to Relax

Close your eyes. Practise noticing the difference between muscles that are tensed and relaxed. Clench your fist as hard as you can, pushing your fingertips into the palm of your hand. Hold for a few seconds until you feel the muscles become harder. Then relax your hand, letting it go as loose and floppy as possible. Tense and relax suddenly, rather than gradually. Feel the different sensations of warmth and relaxation after the release of tension. Repeat this exercise until you are aware of the difference between your muscles being tensed and relaxed.

Now settle back as comfortably as you can. Take a deep breath and let it out slowly. Then follow the instructions in STEP 4. Have a friend read them to you, or learn them off by heart. Alternatively, record them onto a tape. The instructions should be spoken slowly, in a deep soothing voice. Count up to five at each pause before going on.

STEP 4	Relaxation Instructions

You may find it beneficial to record the following on tape and play back the instructions as you work through them.

Close your eyes and let your body relax. Let it sink back onto the bed and notice how it feels. Now clench your right fist as hard as you can and study the tension as you do so. Keep it clenched and feel the tension in your right fist, hand, forearm (Pause) and now relax. Let the fingers of your right hand become loose, and notice how different they feel than when they were tensed. Try to keep the rest of your body relaxed when tensing a particluar set of muscles.

Now *tense your left fist*, as hard as you can, so that you feel the tension right up your left arm. Notice how uncomfortable the tension feels. Hold the tension, *focus on the tension* (Pause) and *relax*. Let the tension go and notice the feelings of relaxation taking its place.

Now *tense both arms together*, clenching your fists and straightening the arms so that you *feel the tension* from your fingers, along the back of your arms, right up to your shoulders. Hold the tension for several seconds until your muscles begin to ache (Pause) and then release, letting the tension go completely. Let the arms *relax*, further and further, and notice the warm, comfortable feelings of relaxation flowing down your arms, right down to your fingertips.

Now the muscles of your face. *Wrinkle up your forehead* by raising your eyebrows, as tight as you can. *Notice the tension* (Pause) and *relax*. Let the muscles smooth out and unwind (Pause).

Now *frown* and *study the tension* (Pause) and *let it go*, noticing the feelings of relaxation that take its place (Pause).

Now *close your eyes as tight as you can* (Pause) *feel the tension* (Pause) and *relax* your eyes. Keep your eyes closed, gently, comfortably, and notice the relaxation spreading down from your scalp, across your forehead and eyes.

Keeping your forehead and eyes relaxed, *clench your jaw* by biting your teeth together and pulling back the corners of your mouth. At the same time, press your tongue hard against the roof of your mouth. (Pause). Now, *relax*. Let all of the tension go (Pause). Relax your jaw, let your lips part slightly, let your tongue return to a comfortable and relaxed position. Notice the contrast between tension and relaxation. Feel the relaxation all over your face, all over your forehead and scalp, eyes, jaws, lips, tongue and throat. Enjoy the pleasant sensations of relaxation.

Now pay attention to your neck muscles. *Press your head back* as far as it can go and *feel the tension in the neck*. Keeping your face and shoulders relaxed, *press your chin against your chest*, noticing the tension in your neck. *Hold the tension* (Pause) and let your neck go, letting your head return to a comfortable position. Let the muscles in your neck *relax* completely.

Keeping your neck relaxed, *tense your shoulders*, by pushing your shoulder blades together at the back. *Feel the tension* in your shoulders and upper back until they begin to ache (Pause). Then *relax*, letting all the tension go, and letting your shoulders and back sink back into the bed. Let the relaxation spread deep into your . shoulders, right into your back muscles. Feel the warmth of relaxation spreading down your face and neck, across your shoulders and back, and down your arms.

Enjoy those feelings.

Feel the muscles relax and become heavier. Breathe easily and slowly in and out, letting the tension go with each breath. Let everything go, becoming more and more relaxed (Pause).

Now *tighten your stomach* by making it hard. *Hold the tension* (Pause) and *relax*. Let the muscles loosen and notice the contrast. Notice the general well-being that comes with relaxing your stomach. Now *pull your stomach in* and *feel the tension* this way (Pause). Now *relax* again. Let your stomach out and let the tension go as the muscles relax completely. Breathe slowly and gently, letting your chest and stomach relax more and more with each breath. Try and let everything go and relax, deeper and deeper (Pause).

Now your lower back. *Arch your back*, making your lower back quite hollow and *feel the tension*. Hold the tension, notice the tension (Pause) and *relax*, letting your back settle down comfortably into the bed. Relax your lower back completely, letting all the tension go. Notice the pleasant feelings of relaxation, spreading further and further, becoming deeper and deeper – down your face and neck, across your shoulders and down your arms, down your back. Your back should feel quite relaxed, let it sink down into the bed, further and further. Let everything go, becoming more and more relaxed.

Now *tighten your buttocks and thighs* by squeezing them together as hard as you can. *Hold the tension* (Pause) and *relax*. Let all the muscles go and notice the feelings of relaxation.

Tense your legs now, by pushing your heels down and bringing your toes up to point to the ceiling. Straighten your legs, so that you feel the tension from your toes and feet, up your calves and thighs. *Hold that tension* (Pause) and *relax*, letting all the muscles go. Relax your feet and calves and thighs (Pause) keep relaxing for a while.

Now let yourself relax further all over. Feel the heaviness of your lower body and relax still futher. Notice warm waves of relaxation spreading from your feet and ankles, up your legs and hips (Pause). Now spread the relaxation to your stomach, waist, lower back. Let go more and more. Feel the relaxation spread further and deeper (Pause) up your back, chest, shoulders and arms. Keep relaxing more and more deeply. Make sure that no tension has crept into your neck, jaws or face. Keep relaxing your whole body, letting it sink deeper and deeper into the bed (Pause).

Keeping quite relaxed, notice how your body feels. Slowly think about each part, noticing whether any tension still exists. If you find any tension, tense and relax that part again. Focus on your face (Pause) your neck (Pause) your shoulders (Pause) your arms (Pause) your back (Pause) your stomach, buttocks (Pause), your legs.

Let your breathing become slower and deeper. With every out-going breath, let more and more tension go, become more and more relaxed. As you sink further into relaxation, feel your body sinking further and further into the bed. Notice how heavy your body feels, too heavy to move any part of it. Enjoy the warm, comfortable feeling of relaxation, the feeling of calm and peace.

Now, imagine a calm and peaceful scene. Imagine being there, protected from the worries of this world and at peace with yourself. Look carefully at the scene, at yourself enjoying it. You feel at one with the world, totally calm and peaceful. Immerse yourself in this scene, enjoying every detail and moment. Let yourself go completely, feel totally calm and relaxed.

After a few minutes count slowly backwards from 10 to 1. When you reach 1, gradually move your fingers and toes and open your eyes. You will feel alert and refreshed, calm and relaxed, and this feeling will stay with you for a long while. Get up slowly.

STEP 5	Coping with Distractions

At first you may find that thoughts and worries keep interfering with your attempts to relax. Don't be put off – it is quite normal, and should occur less as you become more practised. If thoughts continue to intrude, do not become upset or annoyed. Push them gently to one side and resume the exercise. Remember, there is no correct response to the exercises. You will respond in your own way. Don't try too hard, since relaxation comes at its own speed.

STEP 6	Staying Relaxed

Throughout the day, get into the habit of checking to see whether any of your muscles are tensed unnecessarily. Start relaxing the very moment you notice tension or feel unease. Over time, you will learn to recognise muscle tension earlier and be able to use this as a cue to relax. After you have learnt how to relax using the above exercises, try the next two steps to help you stay relaxed during the day.

STEP 7	Relaxing Automatically

After several weeks of practising relaxation, you will be able to relax without having to tense your muscles. Focus on each muscle group. Examine it for tension. If it is tensed, remember what it feels like when relaxed. The muscles should relax of their own accord.

STEP 8	Relaxation Trigger

After becoming fully relaxed, direct your atention to your breathing. Each time you breathe out, say the word 'RELAX'. Keeping your breathing slow and gentle; repeat this twenty times. This will form a link between the cue word 'RELAX' and the feelings of relaxation. In a few weeks, you will be able to relax yourself at any time simply by closing your eyes, taking a deep breath and saying 'RELAX'.

STRESS MANAGEMENT PROGRAM   P11

This program aims to reduce the symptoms that you have identified as being related to stress and prevent new ones occurring. It will teach you how to find out when you feel most stressed, what makes it worse or better, and what skills are effective in managing stress.

STEP 1	How Do You Experience Stress?

Prompt: think about *physical symptoms* – things happening in your body; *mood* – your emotional state; *behaviour* – 'what you do'; your *thoughts* – what you find yourself thinking.

Copy the chart below into a notebook and describe your experience as precisely as possible.

PHYSICAL SYMPTOMS	MOOD	BEHAVIOUR	THOUGHTS

STEP 2	Select One Problem to Change

If you are not sure which problem to choose, go to Step 1 of the ANALYSING & MANAGING YOUR PROBLEM program (P1).

STEP 3	Decide How to Measure the Problem

Consult Steps 2 and 3 of P1, and see whether the problem you have chosen is best measured by a rating scale or by a frequency count. Draw a sample of your measure into your notebook.

STEP 4	Keep a Record of Your Problem

Keep a record in your notebook for the next 7 days. It should look something like this:

	8am-MIDDAY	MIDDAY-4pm	4pm-8pm	8pm-MIDNIGHT
Monday				
Tuesday				
Wednesday				
Thursday				
Friday				
Saturday				
Sunday				

STEP 5	Draw A Graph

After 7 days consult Step 5 of P1 and convert your records to graphs — one for each daily set of numbers recorded.

STEP 6	How Does the Problem Look?

1. *If the graphs show an improvement*, it may be that keeping systematic records is going to be sufficient.

Keep the records for another 7 days and then return to STEP 5.

2. *If there is little or no change*, go to STEP 7.

3. *If worse*, are you able to see why it has got worse?

NO | **YES: STEP 7**

4. Has it been an unusual 7 days?

NO | **YES: STEP 4**

5. Has the problem been getting worse for a long time?

NO | **YES: STEP 7**

6. Are you prepared to tackle this problem even though it seems to be getting worse?

NO | **YES: STEP 7**

7. Do you think the problem is likely to stabilise soon?

NO | **YES: STEP 7**

You may like to return to this problem later, but for the moment go back to STEP 2, this time choosing a problem you think unlikely to get worse.

STEP 7	Decide How Much You Want to Change

You now have a realistic assessment of the problem. The next step is to decide how much you want to change.

Which of the following statements best describes you now?

1. I am happy with this problem as it is. (Sometimes describing, measuring and recording a stress problem changes it from unacceptable to acceptable.)

NO   Go to Statement 2 below.

YES   Is there anything else related to stress that you would like to change?

YES   Go to STEP 2, using the new problem.

NO   Go through the Symptom Chart before leaving this program.

2. I am not sure whether I want to change.

> YES: P9

3. I would like to change.

> YES: STEP 8

4. I must change.

YES

STEP 8	Analyse the Problem

You are now going to analyse your problem to see what is keeping it going.

Using your problem as the example, work through STEP 6 of P1. Then go to STEP 9 below.

STEP 9	Analysis

Does your problem seem to be big, with hardly any ups and downs?

YES   > NO: STEP 10

After completing the RELAXATION PROGRAM (P10), keep your records for a week. If the problem continues to be big, answer the following question:

Which of these statements is the best description of you and which the least good description of you?

a. I am always in a hurry, trying to get everything done at once with little time for breaks or for enjoying myself.

b. I do not feel able to put forward my point of view, to stand up for myself or to get my own way.

c. I am coping as well as anyone could, but my situation is so bad that anyone would have problems.

d. I worry about things before they happen and think that I am not doing things well and that other people criticise me.

Write all these statements in your notebook, and put a value of '1' beside the statement that is the best description of you, a '2' beside the next description, a '3' beside the next best and a '4' beside the least applicable.

Was a. the best description?

> **YES: P4**

Was b. the best description?

> **YES: P3**

Was c. the best description?

> **YES: P9**

Was d. the best description?

> **YES: P17** and **P7**

After completing the program you have chosen, keep your records for 1 week. If the problem is still big, go to the program recommended by the next best description of you at the moment. Continue until you have worked through all the relevant programs, recording for at least a week between each. If you think one week is not enough time to give the particular program a chance to begin working, record for longer – it may take two or three weeks before you see results, but you will.

If there is no improvement at all after what will be several weeks or months, we suggest that you seek professional advice from your doctor.

STEP 10	Analysis

Does your problem appear to be small, with hardly any 'ups and downs'?

> **NO**

Go to STEP 11.

> **YES**

Has it been an unusual 7 days?

> **YES**

Record for another 7 days and go to STEP 5.

> **NO**

Do you think you're tackling the right problem?

> **NO**

Go to STEP 2, and choose a different one.

YES ⟩ It seems that self-monitoring alone has been effective in your case. Give yourself a pat on the back, but keep recording for another week or two to make sure that the improvement continues.

STEP 11	Establish a Pattern

Did you manage to analyse a pattern in your graph or graphs in STEP 5 and STEP 8 above? (By 'pattern', we mean 'ups and downs' that are not totally random. For example, are they related to time of day, day of the week or weekdays versus weekends?)

NO ⟩ YES: STEP 12 ⟩

Select three time periods when your problem was *biggest* and, in your notebook, complete the following chart:

	PERIOD 1	PERIOD 2	PERIOD 3
Time of day			
Day of week			
What you were doing			
Who was there			
Where you were			
What happened before			
What happened after			

Now complete the same chart for three time periods when your problem was smallest.

If you cannot remember sufficient detail to be precise about what to put in the chart, keep a diary along with your records for one week. Remember to keep a note of the 'who', 'what', 'when', and 'where', before, during and after times when the problem occurs.

Are there noticeable differences about the occasions in your two charts?

NO ⟩ Record your measures (if possible every hour) for one week. Then go to STEP 6. If you have already done this and returned to this point go to the YES section of STEP 9 above.

YES ⟩ Take all your 'big problem periods' and list the problems in your notebook. Go to STEP 12.

STEP 12	Construct your Action Chart

1. Can you spot anything that seems to occur *at the same time as* the stress symptom (whatever it is, we'll refer to it as 'A')?

> **NO**

Go to the next question, 2 below.

> **YES**

Write this down in your notebook plus one way in which you could change it (see STEP 13 for ideas). Now go to the next question:

2. Can you spot something that always happens *before* your symptom (we'll call this 'B')?

> **YES**

Write this down in your workbook plus one way in which you could change it.

> **NO**

Go to the next question, 3 below.

3. Can you spot something that always *follows* the problem (we'll call this 'C' henceforth)?

> **YES**

Write this down in your workbook plus one way in which you could change it. Then go to STEP 13.

> **NO**

If the answer to questions 1 and 2 above was also NO, go to the RELAXATION PROGRAM (P10), then to STEP 13.

STEP 13	Action

How to Change 'A', 'B', or 'C'

* Remove or avoid it.
* Think differently about it (you may find P3 useful).
* Practise relaxation in the presence of it (see P10).
* Involve someone in helping you cope with it.
Referring back to your records made in STEP 12, complete the following 'Action Chart':

	What is happening	Change planned	Details of what to do to bring about change
'A'			
'B'			
'C'			

If you have only filled in one line of the chart, start putting this into practice. If you have completed more than one line, practise changing one thing only. Choose the change that is likely to be the easiest to make and that you think might have the biggest effect.

You need to remind yourself to make the change every time the situation arises. Try placing your Action Chart where you will frequently see it, for example on the fridge, TV, or on the bathroom door. You could also put it in your purse/pocket or in your diary.

STEP 14	Assess Your Success

Keep Action records for one week, then answer the following questions:

1. Did the problem situation occur?

NO 〉 Keep recording for another week and come back to this question.

YES 〉 Go to the next question.

2. Did you stick to your plan of action?

NO: P9 〉

YES 〉 Go to the next question.

3. Can you see any improvement (compare graphs as well as numbers)?

NO 〉 a. Try putting the next line of your Action Chart into practice. Repeat STEP 14.

b. If you have tried all three changes without improvement, go back to STEP 9 – you may need to revise your analysis of the pattern of events which regularly involves your problem.

c. If your problem still does not improve, does 'A' ever occur without being followed by the problem? If so, what did you do that was different in this situation? Do more of it. Repeat STEP 14. If the problem and its antecedent ('A') always occur together, and you still notice no improvement, go to the YES section of STEP 9.

> **YES** WELL DONE! You have discovered what was keeping your problem going and have made some crucial changes. You are learning how to become your own psychologist. Go to STEP 15.

STEP 15	The Future

Keep your records for another week, and then answer the following questions:

1. Has your problem at any time got bigger and then smaller?

> **YES** Good. You have been able to persist with the program in the face of a 'down' and have learnt that such 'hiccups' are temporary.

2. Do you feel confident that your problem is now under control?

> **YES** You have succeeded in using this program. You can stop keeping your records. Give yourself a treat!

> **NO** Repeat STEP 15. Challenge yourself by changing your plan of action so that you make your problem bigger temporarily. This will give you a greater feeling of control over the problem.

PAIN CONTROL PROGRAM   P12

Pain is an unpleasant and complex experience, both physically and emotionally, especially if it is prolonged for many months or years. The fear, anger and anxiety it can engender may worsen the experience, as may lack of sleep or inactivity. Fortunately the reverse can also be true; people often report that enjoyable activity distracts them from pain, sometimes for lengthy periods of time.

Under the right circumstances it seems that people can learn ways of modifying their perception of pain. This in no way suggests that the pain is unreal, simply that a variety of factors are conspiring to make it worse. By identifying some of these factors, you can learn to have some degree of control over pain. This is essential if no treatment is available, as is the case for many people.

It is assumed that if you have had pain for a long time, you will already have consulted your doctor as to its cause. If you have not, you must certainly do so before proceeding with this program.

STEP 1	Preparation

Read DECIDING TO CHANGE (P9) in the context of how pain is influencing your life.

STEP 2	Assessing Improvement

Having made the decision to change the role that pain is playing in your life, consult Step 3 of ANALYSING & MANAGING YOUR PROBLEM (P1). We recommend that you adopt a 5-point rating scale:

0=no pain
1=mild discomfort
2=moderate pain
3=severe pain
4=the worst pain you can imagine

STEP 3	Make a System to Record Improvements

Create a record sheet which will be referred to as your pain diary. The example below is a useful format:

DATE & TIME	RATING 0-5	WHAT YOU WERE DOING	WHO WAS WITH YOU	YOUR THOUGHTS, FEELINGS	WHAT YOU DID TO RELIEVE IT

Rate and record pain levels every morning when you wake up and any changes as they occur; complete every column of the diary on each occasion. Always make your recordings there and then; intensity of pain is notoriously difficult to remember accurately.

If there are few or no changes, still make a diary entry four times a day:

1. First thing in the morning when you wake up.

2. At lunchtime.

3. Early evening (about 6pm).

4. About 10pm or when you're thinking about going to bed.

Keep daily records for two weeks.

STEP 4	Look for Patterns

At the end of two weeks look at what you have recorded. Do you see any pattern emerging? Is your pain worse at certain times of the day than at other times? Is it associated with activity/inactivity? Does it seem to be worse/better in the presence of certain people? Focus particularly on what you were doing and thinking, how you were feeling and, if appropriate, who was there when the pain was lowest according to your ratings.

If you can identify any sort of pattern, go on to STEP 5. If no pattern has emerged, keep further records for two more weeks, and look again for some relationship between your activities and feelings and the intensity and duration of the pain. Don't despair if this takes a further week or two; some sort of pattern WILL emerge, albeit a less obvious one for some people than others.

STEP 5	See the Links

People's pain patterns vary widely, but some examples will help illustrate how you can make use of the information you have gathered.

Examples: When Pain Is Less
– when I am visiting friends or friends are visiting me.
– after a good night's sleep
– when I am physically relaxed.

Examples: When Pain Is More
– when I become angry/tense.
– when I am bored and begin wishing I could be more active.
– when I feel depressed.

Have a look at your own records and see if you can extract information which might lead you to make statements similar to any of the above. Perhaps you notice other links as well, and you can go on to address all of them when you have completed the basic components of this program. Remember, once you begin to appreciate the links between fluctuations in your ratings of pain and what you are doing and feeling, you are already on the way to making changes which will help you have some control over the pain you are experiencing.

STEP 6	Relaxation

When you have been thoroughly investigated by your doctor ask for his or her consent to proceed with this program. Explain that the program will eventually involve building up activities.

As an essential component of learning to control pain, complete the RELAXATION PROGRAM (P10), and develop the skills described there. Most people with chronic pain report that regular relaxation helps enormously. Indeed, relaxation can actually prevent pain.

Once you have learned how to relax properly, record pain ratings before and after relaxation sessions. This will show you how helpful the techniques described in P10 can be. As emphasised in the program, relief is not always immediate. Relaxation is a skill that requires practice but the relief that will certainly follow completely relaxed muscle groups, merits the time allotted to it.

A Word About Pain-Killers
You may have been taking a large amount of medication to relieve pain. There is good evidence to suggest that 'the more you take, the more you will need' and that pain killers can cause undesirable side-effects, such as drowsiness and constipation. Do NOT drop prescribed medication for pain, but talk to your doctor, ask her/his advice and, if appropriate, seek their help to make a systematic reduction of pain medication.

STEP 7	Re-cap

If you have identified that pain is worse when you're bored and inactive, take a few minutes to think about how pain has altered your lifestyle.

Jot down a few lines about how you used to be, before you had a pain problem, and the sort of activities you then undertook regularly.

Next briefly describe what you do now. Don't dwell on this if it seems that the differences are enormous. Now write a few lines on how you would like to be in the future. The chances are that you are far less active currently than you would like to be, and this has probably affected your social life, friends, and your view of yourself – a vicious circle.

Lack of diversion leads to focusing on the pain which in turn heightens the painful experience. Originally, you may have thought that doing less helped relieve pain. But it may actually make it worse. It is time to take action. This involves taking slow, systematic steps towards regaining former levels of activity, with or without accompanying pain. Remember, you need your doctor's consent before proceeding with STEP 8.

STEP 8	Recording Pain and Activity

First, record your current amount of PAIN-FREE activity over a period of three days. It may be that fifteen minutes per day sitting up in a chair is all you can manage before pain forces you to move to another position. Perhaps you can manage a 5-minute walk morning and afternoon, but further activity brings on pain and you have to spend the rest of the day in a chair. Maybe you can read for only half an hour before a headache intervenes. Whatever the case, record the amount of activity, however small, which you can manage without bad pain.

In this context, 'activity' describes anything other than lying in bed, and includes for example sitting, walking, stair-climbing, driving, or riding in the car, recreational exercise and housework. After three days, go to STEP 9.

STEP 9	Increasing Activity

The aim is to increase activity gradually and systematically until you can do what you did before having pain. The secret of success lies in taking very small steps and in rewarding yourself as you go. Decide what you want to work on first and do not try to do too much at once. This will only result in disabling pain which is likely to put you off further attempts.

Let us imagine that you can sit up in a chair comfortably for just half an hour at a time. Make a plan to increase your sitting time by 5 minutes a day in the first week.

By beginning slightly below what you can usually manage you will encourage early success. Build up the length of time by minutes so that if, for example, you can normally manage sitting comfortably for only 25 minutes, by the end of the first week you are spending between 45 minutes and 1 hour per day sitting up.

If you manage this, even with some discomfort, reward yourself. Choose your own small, daily rewards – it might be an extra cup of coffee or a soothing bubble bath. If you meet your target at the end of the week, make yourself a larger reward.

Then plan the following week's activity level based on your success rate in the previous week. You may wish to increase your daily target but REMEMBER it is very important not to do too much too soon or you may discourage yourself.

Similar plans can be made each day for how far you walk, the number of jobs done, minutes spent in recreational exercise, and so on. In the long-term, the benefits will be self-evident and satisfying in themselves, but at the start you will need the regular rewards to encourage your efforts.

Remember, the goal is NOT to be pain-free but to increase activity whilst feeling that pain remains manageable. The pain-reducing and preventive possibilities of the program are enormous but do not expect pain to disappear immediately. It will not. It may be that some pain will always be present but this provides even more reason for getting on and trying to enjoy life to the greatest possible degree.

Record your progress, perhaps on a graph (minutes spent 'doing' your activity on the vertical axis; days on the horizontal axis). Pin the graph on a wall or devise some other way to have a ready reminder of your achievements. (Refer to the ANALYSING & MANAGING YOUR PROBLEM (P1) to remind you how to record your efforts in graphic form.)

It is important to be aware that there may be temporary setbacks; for example, days when you fail to follow the program. Take each day as separate from the one before or after. If the target for a particular day cannot be achieved, don't despair. Resolve to try again tomorrow.

Here are some tips to make this part of the program more effective.

– Have a daily routine and stick to it.

– Make regular plans to do things and see people and never back out, even if the pain seems unbearable.

– Always get dressed in the morning (if you act the invalid, you will become one).

A word about exercise: your doctor may suggest that an exercise schedule might help you, especially if you are committed to increasing your level of activity. While exercise is likely to increase your pain initially, if your doctor recommends it, incorportate it into your daily plan. The long-term benefits will probably be enormous as regular exercise over a period of time has been shown to reduce pain significantly.

STEP 10	Dealing with Other People

If you have reached this stage in the program and are beginning to achieve some progress, you may also be aware of how other people, such as family and friends, respond to your pain and how their well-meant concern can cause you to regress.

If you talk often about your pain and treatments, the chances are that family and friends will feel obliged to ask you about both. Unfortunately this can encourage you to focus on the problem and may well increase your pain as a result. In the long-term, this helps perpetuate the vicious circle.

Equally, some people's family or friends actually begin to avoid them, perhaps because they feel so bad that nothing they do can help.

Consider which, if either, might be true in your case. If you decide that being cast in the 'sick-role' is actually unhelpful to you in any way, here are some suggestions to change how others behave towards you:

1. Don't tell others when you are in pain and don't discuss treatments. Instead, make a special effort to discuss current interests and activities. Focus on what you are doing, as opposed to what you are not doing. It is also very important to talk about what others have been doing.

You will know yourself that there is a natural tendency to become very absorbed in pain, but it is essential for your progress in this program that you maintain an outward-looking attitude.

2. Try not to act as though you are in pain. Many people recognise that they have developed 'pain behaviours', for example frowning, rocking, hugging themselves etc. These rarely relieve pain, but have the effect of making others focus on your pain in sympathy.

Try an experiment.

Act as if you are feeling fine at a time when pain is particularly troublesome. Focus hard on your 'act'; it may help to distract you, and the 'act' itself can also genuinely affect the way you feel.

Remember that you are allowed to rest too, but relate resting to your program by making it a reward. Organise a rest as a break, after some planned activity has been completed.

3. Another barrier to progress can involve the 'trappings' of illness.

Hot-water bottles, special beds, or cushions may be helpful in the short-term, but they are a message to others that there is a problem, and contribute to a perpetuation of the 'sick role'. Get rid of them if possible, or limit them to your bedroom – somewhere where they do not constantly remind others of your pain.

If you have worked through these steps and begun to take some action as a result, congratulate yourself! This program is not easy but you are already beginning to cope with pain by reducing its importance in your life. Tell yourself you are doing very well and keep at it!

ANGER CONTROL PROGRAM   P13

Losing control and behaving angrily is usually unproductive. It hinders solutions and alienates people who might have been helpful in the future.

This program is designed to show people who frequently feel angry how to substitute a rational series of steps in a problem situation.

STEP 1	How Often Do You Feel Angry?

First, record all the occasions when you notice yourself feeling angry. Keep an 'Anger Diary'. Any little notebook will do, and each time specify the situation, recording the following points:

1. The time of day
2. Where you were
3. What you were doing
4. Who or what was the focus of your anger
5. Whether you felt yourself working up to a temper
6. Whether you lost control
7. What the consequences were – did you get your own way?
8. How you felt afterwards (use a scale of 0-10, see STEP 3 of P1).

Keep your records for a month or until you have at least 5-10 events recorded.

STEP 2	What is the Problem?

Looking back through your diary, you should begin to see patterns to your anger.

Is there a daily pattern? Perhaps you get angry towards the end of the day when you are tired. Or maybe it is first thing in the morning that is the bad time.

Is there a monthly pattern? If you are a woman this might coincide with your menstrual cycle. Other things such as rent payments or account deadlines might be to blame.

Does it occur in certain situations? Where are you most vulnerable? At home, in the office, on the bus, in your car?

With certain people? Does a particular person or type of character annoy you?

After drinking alcohol? Can you see a connection with what – and how much – you have been drinking?

Go on to STEP 3 if a clear pattern has emerged. If not, go on to STEP 4.

STEP 3	Altering Anger 'Triggers'

Like a safe driver you must think ahead, spotting dangerous moments to maintain a smooth course. Anticipate high risk situations and so prevent a collision.

Daily pattern – could you reorganise your day, rearrange meetings for those times when you are at your best? Take plenty of exercise such as a walk or squash at lunchtime to keep yourself feeling fresh.

Monthly pattern – plan ahead for those times when you are most vulnerable. Leave these periods for mundane work which is well within your scope. Take things quietly, making sure you get plenty of rest.

People – is it their fault? Try and see things from their point of view. Even if it seems ridiculous, it may give a new aspect to your ideas, and give rise to a possible area of compromise. They will certainly feel happier that you are at least making an effort to understand. Is it their fault? Consider your own reasons for disagreement. Perhaps there is something you are unwilling to see. Are *they* being antagonistic? Learn to keep control of your feelings while still managing to put across your point. (Consult the ASSERTIVENESS PROGRAM (P3).)

Situations – look for opportunities to delegate a task to someone more able to cope. In a group activity, make sure you choose people you enjoy working with. Alternatively, to lessen tension, have a change of place – a sunnier room, a working lunch.

Alcohol – while alcohol may make you feel more at ease, it will also release your inhibitions. You will find it harder to keep control of yourself. (Go to the HABIT CONTROL PROGRAM (P5) if drinking is a problem.)

Make a note of how these changes have altered your behaviour. If they are successful you may find that you can stop keeping records. If you feel that you would like to make changes to your response as well as to the triggers of your anger, go on to STEP 4.

STEP 4	Analysing and Altering Your Response

The door has just slammed. You are left wondering what happened. "What did I do?" you ask yourself. While everything seemed to be over in a minute, there are four main stages in an angry response. These are:

1. The development of angry thoughts
2. The development of physical symptoms
3. The 'confrontation' (or angry behaviour)
4. The consequences

Each of these can be examined closely. In each case the aim is to divert your instinctive reaction into a more controlled, rational form of behaviour.

1. Angry thoughts
Your world is the creation of your thoughts. Your anger speaks of yourself. The key to controlling anger lies in substituting a positive for negative version of events. Rather than interpreting someone's behaviour as a personal slight, try to place it in another light. For example:

Instead of thinking –

Frank hasn't returned my call because he wants to inconvenience me and keep me in suspense.

Decide that –

Frank hasn't had time to return the call. It was a difficult decision. He needs time to think it over.

Instead of thinking –

Frances gave me that poor piece of work because she thought I was stupid and wouldn't notice.

Consider that –

She may have had other projects at the same time and rushed it off to make my deadline. Or perhaps I didn't make it clear what was required.

Look at your notebook and select one occasion when you were angry. Divide a new page into two columns. In the left-hand column record the trigger for your anger and the thoughts you had. Use the right-hand column to record more positive explanations of the conflict.

2. Physical Arousal
Although venting your feelings physically may seem to be a release, it can also serve to increase your anger. Your actions and your thoughts create a vicious circle. Learn to recognise your typical symptoms. These may include:

Becoming tense and agitated
Raising your voice
Your face flushing
Starting to sweat
Starting to breathe quickly

As with your thoughts, the key lies in substituting a different physical response. The most effective response is relaxation since you cannot be physically aroused and relaxed at the same time. For a full description of relaxation skills, consult P10. Make a list of your typical symptoms in the left-hand column and on the right, record some positive ways to lessen the tension. For example:

Muscles tightening	Deliberately stretch your limbs. Relax your shoulders.
Fast breathing	Pause and take a few deep breaths.
Clenched knuckles	Let your hands go, fold your arms, or lay them on the table.

People will be impressed by your ability to maintain composure while appreciating the importance of the issue.

3. The 'Confrontation'

Since this stage cannot occur without the build-up from stages 1 and 2, you should by now have found ways to avoid it. But by recording what actually happened, you can learn to find ways of avoiding a similar occurrence. List in one column what you did, and then, opposite, some more agreeable alternatives. For example:

Paced about the room, waving papers; shouted everyone down.	Sit quietly in your chair. Keep voice down. Throw the matter open to discussion.
Insulted someone.	Deflect it into a joke.

4. Consequences

Where did it get you in the end? Even if you did get your own way, your bullish behaviour has probably jeopardised opportunities in the future. It is not only other people that are affected. You may feel guilty or embarrassed afterwards, and this may create further problems for you.

In one column list the outcome of the confrontation. Next to this, decide upon some suitable solutions that look hopeful. For example:

Conflict unresolved.	It's not so serious. Arrange another meeting, determined to clear the matter up.
Made a fool of myself.	It's over now. Look ahead. Apologise next time and let the strength of your commitment be your excuse.

Go back through your notebook and repeat this exercise for several recent angry episodes. Then collect the most commonly occurring positive statements and go on to STEP 5.

STEP 5	Maintaining Control

By now you will have become quite resourceful at controlling your anger. You have learnt to recognise your symptoms and found ways to redirect your feelings. The important thing is to maintain this improvement. The best way is to have an actual reminder in front of you.

Your Anger Control Sheet

Take a sheet of coloured paper, divide it into two columns as before, and write down the following headings in the left-hand column:

What am I thinking and feeling?
What physical changes are happening to me?
How am I behaving?
What are the consequences?

On the right-hand side record for each section the positive statements that occurred most frequently during the exercise in STEP 4.

This is your anger control sheet. Keep it with you and put it where you can see it. When you feel yourself building up to an angry response, practise your positive statements. After a while, you will have learned them – you may even find that the sight of the paper itself becomes a cue to calm down. Carry on practising the relaxation skills too, so that your general level of arousal is lowered, and you become angry less easily.

Keep on recording each angry incident, and see how you are changing. Don't expect to change overnight; the positive statements and the relaxation skills require practice. And don't give up if you have the odd setback. Two steps forward and one back is still progress!

When you find that the level of your anger falls (as it certainly will), and that the number of angry incidents is less, congratulate yourself. You are making progress.

DEPRESSION CONTROL PROGRAM   P14

Depression can be a very hard problem to understand. In some cases we know what is causing us to feel miserable – a failed relationship, a bereavement, job worries, an illness. But in others it is difficult to find a reason. There may be a general sense of feeling low, having no energy, being indecisive. Depression does not necessarily have any direct bearing on external circumstances: people with the most stable family life and optimistic prospects can still feel terrible inside.

If you already know why you feel depressed, go on to one of the other relevant programs: PARTNERS (P6), STRESS MANAGEMENT (P11), SELF-CONFIDENCE (P7). If not, work through this program step by step. It has been designed for you. Feeling depressed may discourage you and make you feel like giving up the program – this is just a symptom of depression. It is important that you keep to the program. The very fact that you are involving yourself in it shows a will to succeed in it. Keep your records in a notebook so that you can see that you are making progress: a sense of achievement is itself a great help in defeating depression.

STEP 1   **What Is the Problem?**

Feeling 'depressed' covers a range of emotional states. It is necessary to pin down a problem to solve. List all the external symptoms of your depression under the following headings:

WHAT YOU DO
Stay in bed late in the morning
Don't bother about my physical appearance
Don't eat proper meals
Forget to do the housework
Stay at home all day
Watch television all day
Cry a lot

HOW YOUR BODY FEELS
Tired
Aching
Pains with no real cause
Insomnia
Loss of sexual desire
Loss of appetite

HOW YOU THINK AND FEEL
Feeling guilty
Feeling miserable
Thinking depressing thoughts
Feeling irritable
Thinking life is not worth living
Having nothing to look forward to

From the list choose the item which bothers you the most. Turn to STEP 2 of the ANALYSING & MANAGING YOUR PROBLEM PROGRAM (P1) and see how best to record in your notebook how often it occurs or how much time it occupies. Keep a daily record for one week. At the end of the week have a good look at your record. Possibly it occurred less often than you had imagined. In which case choose another. If the problem occurs very often or takes up a lot of time, go to STEP 2.

STEP 2   **Make a Record**

You have discovered that your problem is very time consuming, but what are you doing during the rest of the day? Start a new page in your diary, and write down your activities each hour. Next to each entry write down how you feel using a 0-10 scale. (0 = not depressed, 10 = very depressed.) Keep this diary for one week.

Look at your diary carefully. Are there certain things you do where you tend to feel less depressed? For example, do you tend to feel better when you are doing things outside the house? If so, try to increase the amount of time you spend doing these pleasurable activities. If you normally spend half an hour's pleasurable shopping each day, try to increase this to one hour. This will lessen the time you have free for your problem behaviour.

Similarly, if time of day is a problem (you feel more depressed in the morning), try to alter your timetable so that you do the things you enjoy most in the morning. For example, if you normally watch T.V. all morning, make a plan to go shopping at 11.00 am instead of in the afternoon.

Making sure that you keep a careful record in your diary, try changing your behaviour in one of the ways outlined above. If you find you are successful, try substituting more pleasurable activities for the problem. You may find that it gradually gets squeezed out until it is barely a problem anymore.

When you are satisfied that you have reduced the problem as much as you can this way, go on to Step 3.

STEP 3	Changing Activities

When we have a problem, we often think of *getting rid of it* or *getting it to 'stop'*. An easier way of coping is to work out how to put something else in its place: instead of trying to take something away, we are adding something. For example:

Supposing your problem is not getting up in the morning. It may be that you have a very boring job or no job at all and feel that there is really nothing that is worth getting up for. This is often a problem when you retire, or for women when their children grow older and need them less.

Make a list of all the things that you have always wanted to do but never got around to. If you can't think of anything, go down to your library and get a list of the activities available in your area. If you feel that you want to be doing something for other people, try writing to your local hospital and becoming a volunteer, or contacting other voluntarily run charities. Ask the people who know you well, what *they* think would be a good idea.

Don't go overboard and start lots of new things all at once. Choose one activity that interests you and arrange to do that. (If you are alarmed at the thought of mixing with other people, you may find it useful to work through the SOCIAL SKILLS PROGRAM (P8) first.) Keep your records carefully as you carry on. You will find that as you gradually add new things to your life, the old things that were a problem get squeezed out – and you may find you meet some interesting new friends too. Let's take another example.

Suppose you have small children and are stuck at home with them most days. It may be difficult to think how you can add anything to your life. So, why not visit your local library and find out what is available for small children where you live? It may be that there are centres where you can leave them for a few hours, or organised activities where you will meet other mothers. Choose a day on which you are going to start, and remember to keep recording the number of hours you stay at home each day. It may seem an enormous effort to begin with but things will get easier as you go on, and most people find that getting out of the house and seeing other people makes them feel very much better.

Adding things to your life can apply to *things you think about* as well as *what you do*. If you have a problem with thinking depressing thoughts, go on to STEP 4.

STEP 4	Changing Thoughts

You may be feeling depressed because your mind seems full of depressing ideas and thoughts. Try this exercise:

Make yourself think deliberately of all the depressing things that you can: something happening to members of the family, failing your exams, doing badly at work . . . After a few minutes, think about your mood – you are probably feeling very depressed. Give your mood a number from 0 to 10, where 10 means very depressed.

Now think about something quite different. Either look at a picture and describe the scene to yourself – or look into the street and describe what you can see out there. Now think about your mood. Use the same scale as above to give it a number. Is it lower? Most people find that they feel less depressed after switching their thoughts to a neutral subject.

You can use this exercise to help you on a day-to-day basis. Try to think of a particularly pleasing thought – like being on a hot beach or relaxing in a lovely garden. When you find your mind wandering over the same depressing ground, deliberately substitute your own special thought. This is not as difficult as it sounds, and people are often surprised at how much their mood can change.

Depression often makes you overestimate the unpleasant aspects of life. If your records suggest this, try listing the positive things that you do in your diary. Include things like getting up, getting washed, getting dressed, taking the children to school etc. Try listing three good things that happened yesterday, or write down the things that you know you are doing well at the moment. Try to do this exercise when you find yourself dwelling on your problems. This will help you to focus your attention away from the negative things and on to the positive aspects of your life.

Sometimes adding things to your life can seem just the right solution – but just too big a task when you are feeling depressed. One way round this is to take one task and to tackle it very slowly and systematically.

If you would like to try this, go on to STEP 5.

STEP 5	Good Planning

Choose a task that you would normally do, but haven't been able to face – eg cooking a meal, cutting the grass.

Decide *what* you will do, however unambitious it may be.

Decide *when* you are going to do it, say, Tuesday.

Make sure you have what you need in order to do it. If not, make a list of what you want. Go out to the shop and get just those things.

At this point, you can see how even the things that we think of as very simple have much more to them. Making plans and decisions are very difficult when you feel depressed. If you have made a plan you should congratulate yourself. Don't underestimate the progress you have made so far. Now go on to STEP 6.

If you have not managed to get this far, don't give up. Choose another day and try again. If the task you chose to do was cooking, start with something easier, made from ingredients already in the house, then go on to STEP 6.

STEP 6	Planning a New Activity

Allow yourself plenty of time.

Try to make sure that you are not distracted by other things. (eg, if possible, see that the children are not playing where you want to work.)

Follow the instructions for cooking your meal.

How did you get on? Don't underestimate the achievement. It is easy to say lots of people do that, so it isn't important. It doesn't matter what other people do. You have tackled something that *you* find hard, and that means you should congratulate yourself.

Now decide when you will do it again. You need not start cooking every day to begin with, but try to do two meals, then three and so on.

Carry out the program just as you have done already.

1. Ring the calendar days on which you are going to do it.

2. Choose the menu. Write it down.

3. Buy the food. Try to go on separate trips for each to begin with, so that you don't get muddled.

4. Allow yourself peace and quiet to do the task.

5. Write down what you did in your notebook.

6. Congratulate yourself. Write down, 'I did it!'

Gradually build up so that you are cooking every day, trying more complicated things as you move on.

This principle of starting very simply and building gradually will work for all kinds of difficulties. Perhaps you are unable to concentrate at work. Start, as above, by picking the day on which you are going to tackle a particular piece of work. Aim to spend only half an hour or so on it to begin with. Record the time you spent in your notebook. Congratulate yourself at having started. Gradually build up the time you spend a little each day, keeping a careful record.

STEP 7	The Future

If you have got this far, well done! Most people find that as they start either to achieve more or to give themselves proper credit for what they have done, then they start to feel less worthless and much less miserable. So don't be hard on yourself. Every time you tackle something that you find difficult, you are taking a step towards feeling better. Look at your records. If you are making progress, admit it! Congratulate yourself.

SLEEP MANAGEMENT PROGRAM   P15

Everyone experiences difficulty in sleeping at some stage in their life.
As we grow older we require less sleep. But if you consider that you
have a problem – finding it hard to get to sleep, or re-establishing a
normal sleep pattern after a course of sleeping tablets, or waking and
then being unable to get back to sleep – then this is the program for
you.

STEP 1	Measure and Analyse the Problem

Keep a 'Sleep Diary' for a week, and make an entry each morning
when you get up. Record the total number of hours that you slept and
the times at which you woke up. You will find it helpful to have a clock
or watch with luminous hands so that you can check the time during
the night. If you catnap during the day, write down how often and
how long each spell lasted. Your aim is to get as clear a picture as
possible of when and for how long you were asleep during each
24-hour period.

If your problem is falling asleep, make a note of how tense you feel on
each occasion. Use a scale of 0 to 10, where 0=relaxed, and 10=very
tense.

Your aim is to have a detailed picture of when and for how long you
were asleep during each 24-hour period. Keep your Sleep Diary for a
week. Consult STEPS 2 to 5 of ANALYSING AND MANAGING YOUR
PROBLEM (P1), if you have difficulty in devising an effective
monitoring system.

Now look at your records. You may find that the total number of hours
that you are asleep are more than you thought. It is easy to think of the
problem as occurring most nights when in fact it is only once or twice a
week.

If your Sleep Diary indicates that there a problem only once or twice a
week, extend the Diary for another three weeks just to be sure. At the
end of one month add up the disrupted nights. If there doesn't seem to
be a significant number, then insomnia is not really a problem for you.
If there still seems to be difficulty, then go to STEP 2.

STEP 2	Environmental Problems

Write down factors in your environment which might be interfering
with your sleep. The examples may seem simplistic but are also ones
that are frequently overlooked:

Noise
– baby crying
– noisy neighbours
– partner snoring
– general activity, if you sleep in a ward or dormitory
– traffic outside in the street

Light
– you sleep during the day
– sun early in the morning in the summer

Discomfort
– uncomfortable bed
– too hot or too cold
– partner restless

Diet
– drinking tea, coffee, Coca Cola
– eating too late
– drinking too much, have to get up to go to the toilet

Here are some simple ways to counteract these sleep-related problems:

– Talk to your partner, or your neighbours. Negotiate with them to reduce the noise.
– Try using earplugs. They are very effective once you get used to them.
– Get thicker curtains or blinds to reduce light and sound.
– Wear an eyemask to reduce light.
– Reorganise your bedding with more or fewer bedclothes, as appropriate. Wear thicker or thinner nightclothes.
– No fluids, particularly those containing caffeine after 6.00 pm.

If the problem remains, go to STEP 3.

STEP 3	Is There a Pattern to Your Insomnia?

Do you sleep during the day at inappropriate times?

YES: STEP 5 ⟩

Do you regularly wake up during the night and then fail to get back to sleep?

YES: STEP 6 ⟩

Do you sleep badly the night before an important day at work?

| YES: STEP 4 ⟩

Are you in pain?

| YES: P12 ⟩

Is your sleep disrupted at certain stages of your menstrual cycle?

| YES: STEP 7 ⟩

Is your sleep affected by changeovers in shiftwork?

| YES: STEP 8 ⟩

Do you lie in bed worrying?

| YES: STEP 9 ⟩

Have you recently broken a drugs or alcohol habit?

| YES: STEP 4 ⟩

| STEP 4   **Planning Bedtime Activities** |

You may be able to help solve your problem by relaxing yourself in the hours that lead up to bedtime.

First, work through the RELAXATION PROGRAM (P10).
Then go through the following steps:

1. Sleep can be a particular problem during exams or other times of high tension. Draw up a timetable. Leave at least two hours before your last piece of work and going to bed. If you are preparing for an exam or important day at work, do so as fully as you can, but allow yourself the two hours – you can only absorb so much information, and sleeping will make you more efficient the next day.

2. In those two hours you might try:

– doing relaxation techniques
– watching television
– playing some sport
– taking a brisk walk
– listening to music, particularly a piece you find relaxing

– some light reading
– taking a long bath
– having a milky drink

3. Once in bed do your relaxation exercises. You may find it helpful to record these on a cassette which you play to yourself.

Try to clear your mind. Think of something calming such as lying on a beach or sitting in a garden.

Remember that rest can be as useful as sleep.

Above all, persevere, and keep records in your Sleep Diary. You may not get instant results, but if you follow these guidelines, you will sleep in the end.

STEP 5	Deciding When To Sleep

You sleep at inappropriate times. Sometimes the sleep cycle seems to reverse itself so that you sleep little at night but catnap through the day. The total number of hours is the same, but the timing is inconvenient.

Decide whether it is wise to sleep when you do. It may be that it suits you to work at night and sleep during the day. But if it doesn't you will have to cut out your daytime sleeping, no matter how tired you feel. Decide upon a series of preventive tactics. For example:

– Avoid sitting in a comfortable chair.

– Organise activities for the 'danger periods' when you are likely to feel drowsy.

– Take exercise instead of sleeping; it can be as refreshing. Consult the FITNESS PROGRAM (P21): Fitness Test 1.

– Get up at a reasonable time, even if it feels as if you have just dropped off. Work back gradually, hour by hour, until you are in a normal routine.

Once you have restored yourself to a routine, sleeping at night may follow automatically. If not, follow the advice in STEP 4 above.

STEP 6	Waking In The Night

If you wake in the night it is tempting to lie there, getting more and more frustrated by your inability to sleep.

– Get up. Establish the idea that your bed is for sleeping, not lying awake in.
– Plan activities for this time, a particular book, tidying your room.
– Try the tips in STEP 4 above.

STEP 7	Sleeping Badly due to Your Menstrual Cycle

Knowing when to expect poor sleep allows you to plan ahead so that it doesn't coincide with your busiest times at work. You will also benefit from the tips in STEP 4 above.

STEP 8	Sleeping Badly due to Shiftwork

If you can, keep shift changes to a minimum. You might suggest working for a month rather than a week on each shift. Plan your busiest times so that they do not coincide with change. Use the tips in STEP 4 above.

STEP 9	Sleeping Badly due to Worry

Remember that everyone has periods of sleeplessness which come and go. If you are worrying over general matters, work through the ANXIETY PROGRAM (P17). Then go to STEP 4.

STEP 10	Reassessing

Look back through your Sleep Diary. How have things changed? Consider whether your sleeplessness is completely solved. If it is, well done. If not, perhaps you have cured one of the problems only to have triggered another. Go back to STEP 3.

FEAR CONTROL PROGRAM   P 16

This program is for people who are frightened of specific things (eg animals, public speaking, travelling, heights), rather than for people who are just generally anxious. Such fears can result in two things:

1. You try to cope with the subject of your fears, but you experience considerable distress.

2. You avoid situations that have frightened you in the past or that you think may frighten you now or in the future.

STEP 1	Consult the Fears & Phobias Scan, 1

If your score is above 2 for question 1 (p 91), complete P17, but for 'anxiety' read 'fear', for 'anxious' read 'frightened' etc.

After completing P17, return to STEP 2 of this program. If your score is below 3 for question 1 of the Fears and Phobias scan, go to STEP 2.

STEP 2	Consult the Fears & Phobias Scan, 2

If your score for question 2 of the Fears and Phobias scan is below 3, practise and learn the techniques of relaxation and 'graded exposure' to difficult situations outlined in P17. If your score is above 2, go to P7.

ANXIETY CONTROL PROGRAM   P17

This program shows you how to manage a general, recurring sense of anxiety that does not seem to be related to anything in particular. Other programs will be helpful for other kinds of anxiety:

STEP 1	Which Program for You?

1. If you are frightened of particular things or situations, go to the FEARS AND PHOBIAS PROGRAM (P16).

2. If, in your anxiety, you are responding normally to an extremely stressful situation, go to the STRESS PROGRAM (P11).

3. If you lack confidence or cope by avoiding things, go to the SELF-CONFIDENCE PROGRAM (P7).

4. If you are always rushing around, go to the SLOW-DOWN PROGRAM (P4).

5. If you lack confidence in meeting or dealing with people, go to the SOCIAL SKILLS PROGRAM (P8) or the ASSERTIVENESS PROGRAM (P3).

If none of these categories apply, or you have completed another program and still feel anxious, work through the following steps.

STEP 2	Learning to Relax

Before you begin to deal with your anxiety, practise the relaxation skills in the RELAXATION PROGRAM (P10) for several weeks.

STEP 3	Recognising the Signs of Anxiety

Although this program will not rid you of stress, it will give you techniques to cope with it and change how you respond to stressful situations. First you must learn to recognise the 'early warning signs' of anxiety. Think back to a situation in which you felt especially anxious. Recreate it in detail – the place, what you were doing and thinking. Try to pinpoint the feelings of anxiety you experienced. Write them down under three headings, as in the following examples:

Physical
— rapid breathing
— sweaty hands
— tense muscles
— pounding heart
— butterflies in the stomach
— nausea

Mental
— fears about being unable to cope
— racing thoughts
— thoughts about how dreadful it is to feel anxious

Emotional
— apprehension
— depression
— terror

Look at your early warning signs carefully. Once you recognise them for what they are, you will be in a position to intervene with special anxiety control techniques before they build up into an anxiety attack. Carry the list around with you. During the day watch out for them. If you don't notice them occurring, refer to your piece of paper to remind yourself of what you are looking for.

STEP 4	Anxiety Control Techniques

You can learn to control your anxiety by means of a combination of regular exercise and distraction techniques. Brisk walking, swimming, cycling, gardening, all help to reduce your level of arousal in a manner similar to that of relaxation techniques. Work through the FITNESS PROGRAM (P21), beginning with Fitness Test 1.

The moment you notice your early warning signs, employ the following techniques to distract yourself:

1. Concentrate on your surroundings. Devote your attention to the clothes people are wearing, passing cars, advertisements, the sky above. Describe them to yourself in as much detail as possible.

2. Engage in some mental activity, such as reciting from memory a poem or your favourite song, doing mental arithmetic or going over a pleasant visual memory in as much detail as you can.

3. Do *something* – count your footsteps, compile a shopping list – anything, however humdrum, that will divert your attention.

Use these techniques as often as possible (preferably several times a day) and whenever you notice the early warning signs. Do so for at least two weeks.

At the end of this period, ask yourself whether your anxiety is more under control. If so, good – keep the exercise and distraction techniques going even when you are not experiencing anxiety. This will make you suffer anxiety less often as well as making you more able to deal with it if it does occur.

If these techniques do not work for you, you may be doing the wrong program for your kind of anxiety. Go back to STEP 1, and if necessary the Symptom Chart.

STEP 5	Make a Hierarchy

Make a priority list of some six to ten situations that cause you anxiety. Arrange the list to begin with the situation that bothers you *least*. For example:

1. Walking out on my own
2. Going into a small local shop
3. Travelling by bus
4. Shopping in a large, uncrowded supermarket
5. Travelling on a tube train with someone I know
6. Travelling by tube on my own
7. Going to a large, crowded supermarket at peak shopping time
8. Travelling on the tube at rush hour

STEP 6	Use the Imagination

Relax yourself, using the skills you have learnt from P10. Now, picture the first anxiety-provoking scene (1) in your hierarchy. Create it in your imagination as vividly as you can, so that it seems as real as possible. Watch out for your early warning signs.

When you notice one, use it as a sign to relax. Switch your mind to a calm, peaceful scene which you have used successfully in the relaxation program. Say the word RELAX to yourself, and let your body relax completely. If you notice any tension, use your skills to relax that part of the body. Enjoy the feelings of relaxation for a few moments.

When you have mastered this, repeat it. But this time, when you notice the early signs of anxiety, keep picturing the anxiety-provoking scene. Keep it firmly in your mind's eye. Use the word RELAX and the relaxation exercises if necessary, but keep yourself in the stressful scene. Try imagining yourself behaving in a calm and confident manner in the stressful situation, and coping well with it.

Over time your anxiety will reduce. You will have learned to cope with anxiety while staying in the stressful situation. You no longer need to escape from it. If this doesn't happen on the first attempt, do not give up. If you keep practising, eventually it will come.

Repeat the exercise for each situation in your hierarchy, working up to the most stressful situation. Having tackled these situations in your imagination and learnt how to stay relaxed while picturing them, go on to tackle them (one by one) in real life.

STEP 7	Managing in Real Life

Begin by putting yourself in Scene 1 in your hierarchy. Relax yourself before you set out, and if you notice any early warning signs, use your techniques (breathing, the word 'relax', muscle relaxation, imagining a peaceful scene).

When you have successfully tackled siutation 1, tackle situation 2. If you get stuck on any situation, go back to imagining it and managing your anxiety within it. Then try it again for real. The secret is to go over the situation again and again. Eventually, you will find that your anxiety reduces.

When you have successfully managed your anxiety in all the siuations on your list, try to predict new ones. Prepare for them by rehearsing them in your imagination and then confront them in the real world.

MEMORY MANAGEMENT PROGRAM   P18

Forgetting is a common cause of worry and distress. Most forgetfulness is normal and does not imply that anything is wrong with a person's brain. Even so, everyone would like to make fewer mistakes and have a more reliable memory. There is, unfortunately, no way as yet of developing extra memory capacity. The training methods sometimes offered in newspaper advertisements are unable to help with everyday kinds of forgetfulness.

The following program is designed to increase the efficiency with which a forgetful person carries out tasks: it will help you remember better, but only with some effort on your part.

STEP 1	Analyse

Describe on paper a recent example where failing to remember something caused difficulties or was an embarrassment to you. Was it leaving something behind, forgetting an important piece of shopping, failing to keep an appointment?

Analyse and record why it happened. Some common reasons why we forget things are listed below. But think carefully what contributed in this case.

1. Failing to pay sufficient attention when information was proferred.

2. Failing to recall information at the right time (for example, the time of an appointment).

3. Being distracted by something.

4. Following an established habit instead of recalling a necessary change in normal routine.

5. Being tired, stressed, overloaded with things to do.

 Does the same reason serve to explain any other examples of your forgetfulness?

Is there a common factor in the kinds of information which you do not remember, or to the situations in which forgetfulness often occurs?

Is there a certain time of day when your attention begins to wander?

Recognising a pattern is a useful start to finding a way out of your difficulties, because it makes forgetfulness easier to predict and, therefore, to manage.

STEP 2	Stop Worrying!

Worrying about memory is self-defeating. Stress and anxiety cause most normal loss of memory. We all make mistakes: when they occur, they should be accepted for what they are, dealt with promptly and realistically, and not brooded over.

Use the programs in this book designed to reduce worry, manage stressful or anxiety-provoking situations and increase relaxation and tranquility (for example, P10, P11 and P17).

1. Our attention to the external world (what we are seeing, hearing, and otherwise experiencing) automatically increases as inner tensions are reduced.

2. When memory is called upon, it works more efficiently when there are fewer distractions from internal problems.

STEP 3	Understand the Problem

It is quite possible to control undue anxiety and stress and yet suffer a poor memory. What do memory mistakes mean? Do their increase as we get older indicate a growing physical malaise, or that our mental capacity is becoming increasingly limited?

Happily, most people do not develop a cerebral illness or disorder of the brain as they grow older. The brain is the body's most privileged organ, liberally supplied with oxygen and nutrients from the blood. It has and retains enormous power, much of which is under-used. The following steps of the program are designed to switch on more of the existing power at the right times.

STEP 4	Boost Initial Learning

In order to remember something, first pay attention to it.
A common cause of failing to remember is that something was not taken in properly in the first place. Someone new is introduced to you and you want to remember their name. Try the following:

— Speak their name out loud while saying hello.

— Repeat it to yourself under your breath a few times during the conversation.

— When you say goodbye, check that you still remember the name and use it again. If it has gone, ask to be reminded of it.

— Think about the person immediately afterwards. Devise a link between a distinguishing characteristic they have and their name, or think of someone else with the same name whom you know well.

— If remembering a name is very important, get into the habit of carrying a small notepad and write the name down.

— If remembering information is important, make an association with the sound of its name or with something similar in a context which is different but familiar to you.

STEP 5	**Get Organised and Plan Ahead**

Your memory is like a filing system; the better organised it is, the easier it is to operate and the less information goes astray. Writing down information may be sufficient to trigger your memory at a later date: the act of writing makes you organise your thinking in a more definite way.

1. Put aside a time each week (or each day if necessary) to check what has been done and what has not been done, and to bring calendars, diaries or lists up-to-date. Do not think of this as wasted effort, because it will save you time and energy in the future.

2. Avoid keeping the information on scraps of paper all about the house; they'll only get muddled up or lost. (If this is a particular difficulty of yours, there are various Home Organiser or Office packs available which will help keep your system tidy and under control; make a small investment in folders or boxfiles if need be.) At first you may find it tedious to keep well-organised records – until you begin to reap the results.

3. Each time you make an arrangement for the future, think what you are likely to be doing or where you are likely to be just before you need to remember it, and try to fix up a reminder.

If being distracted by subsequent matters is the common reason for your forgetting something, then planning ahead may be the key to improving your performance. In the here-and-now it may strike you as impossible that you will forget something so important to you, but as soon as the next significant thing occurs it may 'blot out' what has gone before.

Memory works best when provided with clues and prompts, so arrange for reminders to occur at the right moment. A reminder may be something mechanical which rings an alarm after a set time, or these days an electronic alarm on a watch or other device. It may be an entry in a diary or a calendar, anywhere that is likely to be consulted regularly. It might be another person, especially if they are involved in the event or if the event is in some other way important for them.

Check that no usual habit or routine might get in the way of the event. If you make an arrangement to see a friend, ask yourself whether the arrangement coincides with a time when you habitually do something else? If so, make allowance for the fact that the previous habit will probably assert itself in your memory. Consider what extra reminder might prevent this happening. Think of a reminder which can be built into the way the appointed day is likely to be run.

Be ingenious with your reminders. The more imagination you put into setting them up, the more likely you are to remember the event when it is due.

STEP 6   Develop Routines

Develop routines to manage your memory. Consider the following example. Many people have a problem remembering to take the right things with them when they leave home in the mornings. Develop a routine to get these things ready the evening before. Put them somewhere obvious so that they will be seen as you leave. It may even be necessary to put them where they will be tripped over in order to catch attention! If one routine does not work, try another until you find the right one for the way your life works.

STEP 7   Situation Problems

Occasionally, forgetfulness is associated with being with a particular person or group of people. In such a case, it might be worth considering in what way you are receiving the information 'message'. Perhaps it has a low priority for you, or you dislike or feel burdened by these people's business. Take account of such thoughts before you promise to do things in the future!

STEP 8   Remember

'Forgetting' is a normal part of everybody's life, and cannot be justified as either a source of distress or embarrassment.

Recommended reading for the general reader and for those with special problems:

1. 'Your Memory: A User's Guide', by Alan Baddeley, pub. by Penguin Books 1982 (for all readers).

2. 'Clinical Management of Memory Problems', by Barbara Wilson and Nick Moffat, pub. by Croom Helm 1984 (of interest to specialists and those who care for elderly sick or neurologically impaired people).

WEIGHT REDUCTION PROGRAM   P19

The first thing you need to do is set a target weight. If you have a lot of weight to lose — ie you are in the very overweight or obese category (p 22), set your initial goal within the next weight-grade down. Having achieved this initial target, set yourself a second goal and so on, until you have reached an acceptable weight for your height.

It is best to lose weight at a rate of about 1kg (2lbs) a week. Losing weight faster than this may be satisfying, but the weight loss is unlikely to be permanent. The process of losing weight involves learning new eating patterns and habits which will remain with you forever. See P5 if you have trouble breaking a habit.

When you are trying to lose weight it is also a very good time to make your diet healthier. They amount to much the same thing: less fat and sugar and more fibre will help you lose weight and make you generally healthier. Additionally, high fibre foods are filling, and so cushion the effect of cutting out calorie-high sugar and fat.

STEP 1	Calorie Counting

To lose **2lbs** a week you need to cut your calorie need by **1,000** calories per day. To lose **1lb** a week you need to eat **500** calories less than you need each day. What is your 'calorie need'? Needs (or metabolic rates) vary greatly from one person to another and depend on a person's sex, age, weight and activity level, but you can use the following table as a rough guide.

MEN/AGE	ACTIVITY LEVEL	CALORIES TO MAINTAIN WEIGHT
18-34	Sedentary	2510
	Moderately active	2900
	Very active	2350
35-64	Sedentary	2400
	Moderately active	2750
	Very active	3350
65-74		2400
75+		2150
WOMEN/AGE		
18-54	Most occupations	2150
	Very active	2500
55-74		1900
75+		1680

STEP 2	Set Your Goal

Decide whether you want to lose 1lb or 2lbs a week, and select the appropriate calorie-intake goal. It may also help to set yourself rough goals for each meal. You could assign one third of your calorie-intake to each meal (breakfast, lunch and supper), or you may prefer to assign only a quarter of your allowance to each meal and leave a quarter for in-between snacks (healthy, slimming type snacks, like fruit and low-fat yoghurts and cereals). See also point 2 of General Guidelines below. Do not cut back below 1,000 calories per day.

STEP 3	Select Your Foods

In order to combine your reduction program with healthier eating, refer to the tables in the FAT REDUCTION (P22/1), SUGAR REDUCTION (P22/3) and FIBRE INTAKE (P22/2) programs (and read the General Guidelines in each) in order to select your menus.

Note: In order to work out how many grams of fat to eat to satisfy your new calorie-intake level, multiply the calories you have selected by 35 and divide the answer by 9.

Note: The fibre goal of 30g detailed in P22/2 is likely to be a bit high for a diet that's set at 1,500 calories, or less. For a diet that's set between 1,000 and 1,500 calories, try to aim for between 15 and 20 grams of fibre a day.

STEP 4	The Slimming Process

1. Select D Day – day one of the process. First weigh yourself and make a record of your weight, the time of day and the sort of clothes you were wearing. You should now start a written record with the details of your diet program on it – how much you weigh, how much you want to lose, what your expected rate of weight loss is (one or two pounds a week), your calorie allowance for each day and maybe for each meal.

2. Count the number of calories you are eating. At first, this will involve weighing all the food you are eating, and using the calorie tables (provided below) to calculate roughly how many calories you are consuming. There is no need to be too meticulous, a few calories here and there won't make that much difference. Because of this, we have rounded all the figures to the nearest five calories.

Once you have weighed the food you are eating for a few days you should begin to get an idea of what a standard portion of each sort of food looks like. After a while, instead of weighing, you should be able to calculate the number of calories in what is your average portion of each food. Column **A** shows the number of Calories in 100 grams of food unless otherwise stated.

Calorie Table
This table shows many common foods but there is not space to produce an exhaustive list; buy a calorie counter if you need to be meticulous.

MEAT	A	BISCUITS/CAKES	A
Grilled bacon	390	Cakes	300-500
Beef	230	Sweet biscuits	450-530
Lamb	270	Rye crispbread	320
Pork	330	Water biscuits	440
Chicken, no skin	150	Oatcakes	440
Ham	170	Cream crackers	440
Pate	350		
Beef sausages	270	CEREALS	
		All-bran	280
FISH		Cornflakes	370
Grilled white	80	Muesli	370
Fried white	240	Sugar Puffs	350
Mackerel	280	Weetabix	340
Herrings	250	Rice Krispies	370
Sardines in oil	220		
Tuna in oil	290	BREAD	
Prawns	110	Wholemeal/brown	220
		White	230
EGGS			
Boiled	150	FLOUR	
Fried	230	White	340
		Wholemeal	310
FATS	A		
Butter	740	RICE/PASTA	
Low-fat spread	370	White/brown rice	360
Margarine	730	Egg/wholewheat pasta	380
Oils	900		
		PRESERVES/SWEETS	
DAIRY FOODS		Honey	300
Low-fat natural yoghurt	70	Jam/marmalade	260
Single cream	200	Sugar	390
Double cream	400	Milk chocolate	530
Cheddar cheese	470		
Cottage cheese	100	SAUCES/PICKLES	
Cheese spread	290	Sweet pickle	140
Brie	300	French dressing	660
Edam	310	Tomato ketchup	100
Blue	360	Mayonnaise	720
Full-fat milk (½ pint)	190	Salad cream	310
Skimmed milk (½ pint)	60		

SOUPS (per 100 ml)

Creamed	50
Consommé/broth/clear	30
Lentil	110
Minestrone	30

DRINKS

Orange juice (140ml)	60
Tomato juice (140ml)	30
Lemonade (160ml)	30
Cola (1 can)	130
Beer (½ pint)	110
Dry cider (½ pint)	110
Sherry (50ml)	70
Spirits (25ml)	60
Wine 120ml	80

PULSES

Baked beans	80
Kidney/soya beans	95
Lentils	100

VEGETABLES

Courgettes/spinach	30
Peas	70
Sweetcorn	90
Boiled/baked/mashed potatoes	80
Chips	230
Oven chips	160
Roast potatoes	150

VEGETABLES (per 110g)

Cauliflower	20
Turnips	20
Sprouts	10
Cabbage	10

VEGETABLES (per 110g)

Carrots	10
Green beans	10

VEGETABLES (per 60g)

Celery	20
Cucumber	20
Mushrooms	20
Peppers	20
Tomatoes	20

VEGETABLES (per 30g)

Onions	10

VEGETABLES (per 30g)

Lettuce	20

DRIED FRUIT — A

Dates/figs/raisins/sultanas	250

NUTS

Almonds/peanuts etc.	570

FRUIT

Bananas	80
Berries/currants/plums	30
Grapes	60

FRUIT (per 110g)

Apples/pears/pineapple	40-50
Cherries/oranges	40-50

FRUIT (per 170g)

Grapefruit	20

FRUIT (per 140g)

Melon	20

General Guidelines

1. Don't miss meals altogether: resultant hunger will threaten the success of the slimming process.

2. Eat more of your food allowance earlier in the day; have breakfast and a reasonably big lunch, but only a light evening meal.

3. Have healthy snack foods around the house – low fat yoghurts, fresh fruits, raw vegetables cut into strips, low-fat milk to make fresh fruit milkshakes, etc.

4. Remove any temptations from the house.

5. Experiment with some new recipes, interesting salads or vegetarian casseroles and bakes. Make slimming an opportunity to become more adventurous in the kitchen.

6. Eat slowly and take a minute or two's break before helping yourself to more or going on to the next course – it takes a while before food reaches your stomach and only then does it give that feeling of fullness.

7. Use a slightly smaller plate than usual and don't pile the food up on it. Generally have smaller portions than usual.

STEP 5	One Week Later

Wait a week before you check your progress by weighing in. If you check your weight too regularly, you'll find the results very disappointing. One week from the starting date, weigh yourself again, at the same time of day and wearing roughly the same clothes as on the last occasion. Record your new weight and compare it with your goals and targets.

In this first week you might very well have lost more than your target of 1 or 2lbs because when you begin slimming you often lose a few extra pounds in body fluid.

1. If you have lost at least your goal weight, carry on with your slimming program, checking your weight loss each week, until you reach your target weight. You may find that after several weeks of slimming your weight loss begins to slow down. If this happens it is because your body has got used to having fewer calories to run on. If you want to continue to lose weight at roughly the same rate as before you will need to cut your calorie intake by slightly more. But **don't cut back below 1,000 calories a day** – you need to eat at least this much to get the various nutrients your body needs to keep well.

2. If you don't achieve your target weight loss in the first week there are several possible explanations.

a. You've been cheating, deliberately or not. You may not have been keeping a sufficiently accurate record of what you have been eating, or you may have been underestimating the size or your portions. If this sounds likely, then you'll need to begin again, but this time be very meticulous about keeping a record of what you eat and how much it weighs.

b. The original estimate of your calorie needs was too high. Reduce your daily calorie limit by 500 calories for one week, and note your progress. Do not on any account reduce your calorie intake to a figure below 1,000 calories a day.

If the problem persists you may need the assistance of a doctor or nutritionist who can monitor and advise you on your specific requirements.

AIDS/HIV PROGRAM   P20

AIDS (which stands for the Acquired Immune Deficiency Syndrome) results from infection with HIV (Human Immunodeficiency Virus). It has been described as one of the most pressing medical problems of the 20th Century. Both having AIDS/HIV or worrying that one might be or become infected can severely disrupt one's everyday life.

1. Those who have AIDS may fear suffering a painful death.

2. Those who have HIV and who show no symptoms of illness may become overwhelmed by the uncertainty that surrounds their medical condition.

3. Lastly, there are those who may not yet be infected with HIV but who fear that they may become infected which may, in turn, interfere with their ability to form and maintain relationships.

This program is designed to help people in all of these groups to make some initial decisions about their health care. This may lead to their being able to live better with AIDS/HIV.

STEP 1	How to Protect Yourself from AIDS/HIV

Follow 'safer sex' guidelines in order to protect yourself and your partners. The following activities are considered safe:

– mutual masturbation
– hugging and body rubbing
– massage
– dry kissing
– sex toys used only on yourself

In addition, you should:

1. Choose sexual activities that prevent semen, blood (including menstrual blood), or vaginal secretions from other people entering your mouth, vagina or anus.

2. Use condoms if you have penetrative sex. Only water-based lubricants, such as KY Jelly should be used. Vaseline and spit are not recommended.

3. Nonoxynol-9 spermicide with a condom may provide added protection (available at chemists and supermarkets alongside other family planning products).

If you think you are at risk for AIDS/HIV, go to STEP 2.

STEP 2	The HIV Antibody Test

AIDS and HIV infection are medical conditions. Only a doctor can diagnose AIDS or test for HIV. For this reason a link with a medical practitioner is essential. General Practitioners and specialists in Sexually Transmitted Diseases Clinics (Special Clinics) are usually experienced in doing this. They will be able to advise you about the implications of the test and current treatments that are available. They will also be able to discuss with you personal strategies for preventing the spread of HIV. The doctor will be able to refer you to other specialists if necessary.

The HIV antibody test is a simple blood test. The result will indicate whether you have been infected with HIV in the past. It is not a test for AIDS. Recent exposure to HIV (within the last three months) may not be detected by this test. For this reason, if the activity that has put you at risk for HIV has been very recent, you might be advised to return to have the test in several weeks. Results usually take about a week to come back to the doctor.

STEP 3	Before Having the Test

You should *insist* on being counselled before having the test. Counselling can help you to prepare for the result and make better adjustments. The doctor, or a counsellor, would need to discuss with you the meaning of the test, the implications of the result (personally, socially, medically), and the implications of being tested (for example, how this might affect your ability to obtain life insurance, how you might cope with a positive result and who you might tell, among many other issues). You will need to consider the potential effect of a positive result on your job, colleagues, friends and family. You would also need to discuss safer sex practices and methods of preventing the spread of HIV and how you might form and maintain sexual relationships in the future.

When you get your result, you should again receive counselling. The meaning of the result should be clearly explained and its implications gone over again. Remember, it is not a test for AIDS.

The following flow-chart should be used for making decisions about being tested for HIV.

You have a worry you may have AIDS/HIV.

Consider what has put you at risk for HIV eg:
1. Sexual activities
2. Blood or blood product's received before 1985
3. Needles shared with other drug users

Was the risk in the last 3 months? If yes, delay having the test until 3 months after potential exposure.

Think about the impact of knowing your HIV status on yourself and others. Adopt 'safer sex' practices.

Make a decision about having the test.

If you decide not to take the test, avoid future risk.

If you decide to take the test, arrange for counselling through:
1. General Practitioner
2. Special Clinic in your local hospital
3. Voluntary agencies

Blood sample taken. Arrange for follow-up.

Result given. Post-test counselling.

If negative, are you reassured? If not, discuss with doctor or counsellor.

If positive, arrange for medical follow-ups and further counselling. Ask to be put in touch with various support groups.

STEP 4	How to Adjust to a Positive Result

First, it is sometimes reassuring to know that there are many people who are in a similar position. Furthermore, advances are being made in the treatment of symptoms even though there is no cure. Trials are currently underway to evaluate the effectiveness of certain drugs in preventing infections in infected people. There are a number of things that you can do to help you live better with AIDS/HIV. Some may even help you to stay well.

1. Coping with distress

Any illness can lead to emotional distress. This may be a direct result of the illness or it may be secondary to it. Living with a life-threatening illness can be stressful. Symptoms of distress include: anxiety, sleep disturbance, feeling moody, loss of interest in sex, poor concentration, hyperventilation, depression, bouts of crying, poor appetite.

Some strategies for coping with distress are outlined in other programs. You should follow the guidelines as appropriate: relax (P10), build up your self-confidence (P7), reduce your fear (P16), manage anxiety (P17), stress (P11) and pain (P12), and improve your memory (P18) and sleep (P15).

It has been found that emotional distress can also be reduced when people find a way of talking to their friends, family and relatives about their concerns. This may present problems for some who may then face discrimination or ostracism. A counsellor who has experience in helping others in a similar predicament would be a useful person to consult over relationship problems.

2. Staying healthy

There is evidence to suggest that certain activities can help people to stay healthy or at least to feel better in themselves. The contribution of each activity alone is probably very modest. However, in combination, some people report that paying attention to health-maintaining behaviours helps them to feel that they have some control over their illness. These activities include:

a. *Exercise* – in moderation exercise makes one feel good and can even stimulate the immune system in a small way.

b. *Sleep* – get enough sleep and take rest when necessary.

c. *Food* – although there is no conclusive proof that some diets are better than others, it makes sense to eat enough of the right food (P22/5).

d. *Reducing stress* – take on what you can realistically manage and find time to relax.

e. *Having fun* – you may not feel up to it sometimes, but there is no reason why you should not carry on going out with friends, visit pubs and clubs, go to the cinema or theatre, or enjoy yourself in the ways you may have done previously.

f. *Safer sex* – for a while, many people who have AIDS/HIV do not feel like having sex. In time, this may change. Safer sex is as important for those who have AIDS/HIV as it is for those who do not. Not only can it help to control the spread of HIV, but it can also prevent you from acquiring any new infection, such as a venereal disease. New infections can further damage your immune system.

3. Living with uncertainty
Much remains unknown about AIDS/HIV. People who are infected, and their friends and family, have to live with much uncertainty. This can be quite stressful at times. Here are some strategies for coping with this.

a. *Talk about uncertainty* – this may help to reduce your fears and feelings of isolation. If a friend or lover cannot help, talk to your doctor or counsellor. Although they may not have answers to many questions, they may be able to give you a new perspective about your situation. This in turn may help you to live better with some uncertainty.

b. *Join a support group* – there are now many support groups for people who have AIDS/HIV. Support ranges from emotional comfort to practical support in the form of friends who can help with shopping and transport.

c. *Keep a perspective on what you can manage* – only undertake tasks and activities that you can realistically manage. Achieving your goals helps you feel that you are accomplishing something. Avoid trying to tackle everything at once. If your worries become overwhelming choose one issue that concerns you most, and plan how you are going to deal with it.

d. *Keep your affairs in order* – it is always helpful to plan ahead of events. Considerable additional stress may result from not having legal and personal affairs in order should you face illness. This may include: drawing up a will, nominating a next-of-kin, providing for one's children, setting aside money, and other activities. These affairs should be kept in order irrespective of whether or not you have AIDS/HIV.

FITNESS PROGRAM   P21

	Stamina	Suppleness	Strength
Aerobic Dance (1)	★★★	★★★	★★
Badminton	★★	★★	★★
Canadian Airforce (XBX)	★★★	★★★	★★★
Cricket	★	★★	★
Cycling (hard)	★★★	★	★★
Ballroom Dancing	★	★★	★
Disco Dancing	★★	★★	★
Football	★★	★★	★★
Golf	★	★★	★
Hill Walking	★★	★	★★
Jogging	★★★	★	★
Judo	★	★★	★★
Keep Fit Classes (1)	★★★	★★★	★★
Rowing	★★★	★	★★★
Sailing	★	★★	★★
Cross Country Skiing	★★★	★★	★★★
Down Hill Skiing	★★	★★	★★
Squash	★★	★★★	★★
Swimming (hard)	★★★	★★★	★★★
Tennis	★★	★★	★★
Walking (briskly)	★★	★	★
Weightlifting	★	★	★★★
Yoga	★	★★★	★
EVERYDAY ACTIVITIES			
Climbing stairs	★★	★	★★
Digging garden	★	★	★★★
Housework (moderate)	★	★★	★
Mowing Lawn (with hand mower)	★	★	★★

(1) These will only be so highly rated if a well-balanced schedule has been developed.

Key: ★ – little, if any, effect; ★★ – moderate effect; ★★★ – very good effect.
Adapted from 'International Guide to Fitness and Health' Larson and Michelman, Crown, 1973.

1. Are you over 60?

2. Have you or any close relative had diabetes?

3. Do you smoke?

4. Have you ever been told that you are hypertensive?

5. Have you ever had chest pain, tightness, discomfort, breathlessness or palpitations?

6. Do you have a family history of heart attacks?

If YES to any of these, consult your doctor before embarking upon this exercise program. If you wish to give up smoking, consult P5.

You have to be realistic about the amount of physical prowess you can expect from your body. If it's too late to be a gold medal athlete — don't pretend, choose a more sedate form of exercise.

STEP 1	Which Exercise for You?

Do You Enjoy Competition?
Competitive games are probably the least relaxing form of exercise, so have a good think about your daily life before embarking on competitive exercise. Competitive sport can help reduce aggression, but if your work is highly competitive you would almost certainly benefit from a form of exercise with an element of relaxation to it, for example, yoga.

How Much Money Do You Have?
Exercise can be either cheap or expensive. Work out the costs of classes, facilities (courts etc) and necessary transport, before you become too heavily committed. Proper running shoes are a 'must' for jogging. Home-based exercise or walking are probably the cheapest options, swimming and running are pretty good seconds.

Do You Get Bored Easily?
If so, you will probably find that a standard set of exercises (whether at home or at a keep-fit class) will eventually pall. Consider a team activity, or something that takes you outside with an opportunity to explore new places and keep your mind occupied.

How Much Time Do You Have for Exercise?
If not much, then there is no point in planning regular squash tournaments with friends. It would be much better to pick a form of exercise that can be done anywhere and almost any time, such as an

individual exercise schedule that can be done in twenty-minute bouts.

How Much Self-Discipline Do You Have?
If your self-discipline is poor, consider activities which involve other people: choose activities which require a partner, or commit yourself to offering a friend a regular lift to an exercise class.

Do You Want to Meet People through Exercise?
If part of the benefit of exercise is social, investigate local sports centre facilities. Choose an activity that involves other people, team games for instance, classes or a club activity. On the other hand, if you are worried about making a fool of yourself, being awkward, or 'looking fat', don't make life difficult for yourself. Begin a 'shape-up' program at home and 'go public' when you become more confident.

Are You Pregnant?
Swimming is a useful aerobic exercise now, but consult your ante-natal clinic and follow their advice about ante-natal exercises.

The chart on p 254 suggests ideas for different exercises and tells you what sort of contribution each type of exercise makes to overall fitness.

Whichever form of exercise you choose, don't start too suddenly. Some sports are very demanding physically – you need to be pretty fit to play them in the first place. And always remember to warm up properly before you do anything strenuous – the 'Getting Fit to Get Fit' program (suppleness and strength exercises) are a good warm-up routine.

STEP 2	Fitness Test One

Complete this stage if you scored 9 or more in the Exercise scan, or have been directed to it in any other scan. Otherwise turn to Fitness Test 2, STEP 3 below.

This test is designed to discover whether or not you are fit enough to start a reasonably strenuous exercise schedule, and if not, which aspects of fitness you should concentrate on improving before embarking upon one.

Stamina
Walk up and down a flight of 15 steps three times, you should be able to carry on a normal conversation throughout this exercise and afterwards – you shouldn't be breathless. If you are, you need some stamina training. See STEP 4.

Suppleness
Try and touch your toes with your knees straight, you can do this from standing – feet together, or sitting on the floor – legs straight out in front of you, whichever you find more comfortable.

You can touch your toes – there's nothing to worry about here.

You're about 5ins away – you need some suppleness training. See STEP 4.

You're 5-10ins away – you're in urgent need of some suppleness training. See STEP 4.

Strength
Lie on the floor, with your knees slightly bent and your hands behind your head. Using your tummy muscles, raise your trunk about 8ins from the floor and lower without touching the ground, repeat this exercise as many times as is comfortble, up to 20.

You manage less than 5 – you are badly in need of some strength training. See STEP 4.

You manage 6-15 – you need some strength training. See STEP 4.

You manage 15 or more – you don't need to pay special attention to strength exercises in your exercise routine.

Result
If you passed Fitness Test 1 in every respect, select an exercise program (see STEP 1), and read Fitness Test 2.

If you failed Fitness Test 1 in one or more respects, select an exercise program (see STEP 1) and go to STEP 4 and STEP 5.

STEP 3	Fitness Test Two

This test is for people who scored between 1 and 8 in the Exercise scan or who have passed Fitness Test 1 and want to take up a vigorous exercise schedule, eg squash, football.

Try running a mile. Men should be able to do this in 10-13 minutes, women in 12-15 minutes. If you fail, you need to develop your fitness a bit more before you are ready to begin a vigorous activity. Use the 'Getting Fit to Get Fit' program, but begin with at least five of each suppleness exercises, commencing with stage b. of exercise 5, and stage c. of each of the strength exercises, and engage in a reasonably demanding bout of stamina training. See STEP 4.

STEP 4	Getting Fit to Get Fit

If you did particularly badly with any of the stamina, suppleness or strength sections of Fitness Test 1, spend a little more time doing the exercises in the appropriate section of this program.

Suppleness
Each exercise should be repeated twice. Gradually increase the number of repetitions as your suppleness improves, to a total of ten rotations. The schedule should be followed once a day.

1. Stand with your feet hip-distance apart, tummy pulled in and hands on your hips. Moving only your head and neck, tip your head forward (looking at the floor), turn your head to the right (looking over your right shoulder), tip your head backwards (looking at the ceiling), to the left (looking over your left shoulder). Bring your head back to the forward position. Repeat this circular motion in the opposite direction – forwards, to the left, backwards to the right, and back to the forward position.

2. Stand in the same starting position, with your arms at your sides. Moving only your arms, bring them straight out in front of you, up and over your head (past your ears) and backwards down to your sides again – a circular motion. Repeat the same exercise in an opposite circular motion, swinging your arms backwards from the relaxed position, up past your ears, and so on.

3. Stand in the same starting position with your arms at your sides. Keeping your face forwards and your hips quite still, bend at the waist to the right, reaching down the outside of your right leg with your right arm. Return to the upright position, then bend to the left side, this time reaching down the outside of your left leg with your left arm. Be careful not to swing your hips out to help you bend further.

4. Stand in the same starting position, with your arms straight out in front of you at shoulder height, keeping your hips still, facing the front and looking at your right hand, twist your top half (including your arms) to the right. Turn your head as you twist, following your right hand with your eyes. Return to the centre and repeat the action to the left.

5a. Stand with your feet hip-distance apart, your arms slightly bent and your hands resting on the back of a chair. Raise your right knee and bring your head toward your raised knee, trying to touch it with your forehead. If you find it helps, your left leg can be slightly bent. Return to upright and repeat the exercise, this time raising your left knee. Once you can manage ten examples of this exercise on several consecutive days, move on to level b.

5b. Do the same exercise, but this time don't rest your hands on the back of a chair. Instead, use your hands to grasp your rising knee and gently pull it towards your forehead. Once you have achieved ten examples of this exercise on consecutive days without discomfort, move to level c.

5c. Stand with your feet hip-distance apart, and bend forwards, moving your hands down the front of your legs, towards the floor. Try to touch the floor with your fingers while keeping your knees as straight as possible. If you suffer from mid-back pain, no matter how mild, you shouldn't try to reach below knee level. If you experience balancing problems, or find that putting your head down to the floor makes you feel dizzy, adopt a sitting position for this exercise – legs straight out in front of you.

Strength
There are four stages to each of these exercises. Aim to repeat exercises 1a, 2a and 3a ten times. You may only manage one or two repetitions to begin with, but if you do the exercise regularly, you will gradually find that you increase your performance and achieve your aim. Build up the number of repetitions until you can do 20 comfortably. Once this is reasonably easy, move on to level b of the appropriate group. Again gradually build up the number of repetitions, building up to 20, then move up to level c and finally level d. These exercises should be done at least every other day.

1a. Stand facing a wall, with your palms resting against it, shoulder distance apart, feet together. Stand on tiptoes. Keeping a straight back, bend your elbows so that your chest and chin move toward the wall and touch it. Straighten your arms and so push yourself back to a standing position.

1b. This time put your hands on the edge of a steady table, with your feet about 4-5 feet away, with your back straight, bend your elbows and allow your chin to move toward the table top – keep your head up. Straighten your arms and push back up to standing position.

1c. This time repeat the exercise resting your hands on a well-secured chair seat. As your arms bend, your chest will move towards the chair edge, and away again as your arms straighten.

1d. Now lie on your front on the floor with your hands in press-up position (palms on the floor at shoulder level). Keeping your lower leg (ie knee and below) on the floor, push the rest of your body up and down slowly (stretching and bending your arms), using your knees as pivot; keep your back straight and eyes looking forward at all times, and never let your chest collapse onto the floor. Once this form of press-up is comfortable, you can have a go at the real thing, pushing your entire body up and down, with only your toes and hands resting on the floor. Keep your back straight.

When you have finished a round of any of 1a-1d, swing your arms gently to release any tension in the muscles.

2a. Sit towards the front edge of a chair seat, with your legs straight out in front of you, heels on the floor, arms slightly bent. Grip the sides of the chair seat, pull in your tummy muscles and keep them taut throughout the exercise. Keeping your upper body steady, bend your knees and bring them up towads your chest. Return to the starting position.

2b. Sit on the floor with your knees bent and feet on the floor hip-distance apart. Roll gradually backwards, unwrapping your spine as you go, until you are lying flat on your back. Holding your arms straight out in front of you, and pulling your tummy muscles in tight, pull your upper body off the floor, until your outstretched hands touch your knees. Move back down toward the floor, but don't touch it with your back.

2c. Repeat the exercise above, but this time pull up until your hands reach past your knees and your head is nearly touching them.

2d. Lie down on the floor as before, but this time put your hands behind your head, elbows out to the side. Put your right leg straight out and raise it slightly off the floor, bend your left knee up toward your chest keeping your tummy muscles tight and trying not to use your arms to pull you up; pull your upper body up from the floor, twisting slightly as you do so, so that your right elbow touches your left knee. Lower your upper body, but don't touch the floor. Repeat the exercise but this time bend your right knee into your chest and twist as you raise your upper body so that your left elbow touches your bent right knee.

After completing every session of 2a-d, lie on your back and curl up, pulling your knees in to your chest for a count of 20. Then lying on your back, knees bent and feet on the floor, arms straight up in the air, push your knees down toward the floor on your right and twist your upper body and arms to the floor on your left. Return to the starting position, and repeat in the other direction. These exercises help to relax your tummy muscles after exercising them.

3a. Stand with your feet together, back straight and hands resting on the back of a chair. Bend your knees, and keeping your back straight squat down with your heels off the floor. Return to standing.

3b. Repeat the exercise, but this time with your hands on your hips, instead of on the chair back.

3c. Repeat the exercise, but put a bit more life into it: as you push yourself up from squatting, jump into the air. Bend your knees as you land on the floor, and return to the squatting position.

3d. This time push up from the squatting position and really jump up into a full blown star jump. Return to squatting position.

Whenever you complete these exercises, shake your legs out to relax the muscles you have been using.

Stamina
You have a choice of walking and jogging, swimming or cycling as your stamina exercise. Swimming is a particularly good form of exercise, because the water holds you up and takes the strain off your joints. This is helpful for people who are overweight, especially those lacking in suppleness or who have joint and/or back problems.

Cycling also takes the weight off your legs and is a useful stamina exercise for people with problematic leg joints or feet.

Walking and jogging appeal to people who enjoy getting out into the air. If you find exercising outside in cold weather too daunting, you may substitute any of the following: running on the spot, stepping up and down (on to something that is about the height of two stairs – 18ins or so), or skipping.

Stamina exercises should be done at least three times a week. Before you start, always warm up by doing some suppleness and strength exercises even when you are super-fit. Before you start jogging you should:

1. Buy some proper running shoes with cushioned soles to stop your calf muscles getting bruised.

2. Wear cotton clothes to soak up sweat and stop chafing.

Walking/Jogging: Stage 1
Walk as briskly as possible for as long as possible, up to 30 minutes.
Gradually build up the length of time from 10 minutes: 5 in one
direction and 5 back home.

Stage 2
Start to mix jogging and walking. begin with say 5 minutes brisk
walking, followed by 20 seconds jogging and 30 seconds walking
(repeated 3 times), 5 minutes walking, 30 seconds jogging and 30
seconds walking (3 times) and ending with 5 minutes walking.

Stage 3
Gradually increase the periods of time spent jogging and reduce the
number of periods of walking. Reduce the centre period of walking and
finally cut it out altogether, until finally you are jogging for 20 minutes
with a 2 to 3 minute walk at each end. The walking at the beginning and
at the end is important for warming up and cooling down; starting or
stopping too quickly can cause damage to your muscles.

Swimming: Stage 1
Begin by swimming widths of the pool, resting when you get puffed,
after each width if need be. Carry on swimming and resting for about 30
minutes, but aim for 20 minutes non-stop width swimming.

Stage 2
Start swimming lengths as in Stage 1. Aim to do 20 minutes non-stop
length swimming. Try to vary your swimming stroke as much as possible
because each stroke exercises different sets of muscles.

Stage 3
Gradually increase the number of lengths you do in your 20-minute
stint, as you increase the speed of your swimming.

Cycling
Start by cycling for about five minutes gently. Gradually increase the
length of time for which you are cycling and then increase your speed,
so that you cover more ground in the same period of time. You should
aim for a 30-minute period of fairly intensive cycling.

Exercise Cycling: Stage 1
Cycle for three minutes at the minimum tension setting (about 15 miles
an hour or 50 revolutions per minute). Increase the tension slightly
(without stopping the cycling action) and cycle for a further 2 minutes.
Reduce the tension again for a further minute and raise higher than
before for 3 more minutes. Back down to mid-tension setting for 2 more
minutes and then 1 minute at the minimum setting. Try to keep the
speed constant throughout the exercise period.

Stage 2
Stick to the same basic pattern of raising and lowering the tension (3 minutes at the minimum, 2 minutes at a mid-point, 1 at minimum, 3 minutes at a high level, 2 at the mid-point and then 3 at the minimum). Gradually increase the tension setting for both the mid-point and the high setting.

STEP 4	Moving On from the 'Getting Fit' Program

Once you have done two to three weeks of the 'Getting Fit to Get Fit' program, return to Fitness Test 1.

1. If you fail – carry on with the 'Getting Fit' program and try the test again in about two to three weeks.

2. If you pass and you decide to take up a gentle form of exercise, such as golf or a beginners' class in keep-fit, continue with the program for a total of three months, or until you have completed suppleness exercises and reached stage c in the strength exercises, whichever takes longer.

3. If you pass and you decide to take up swimming, jogging or cycling as your long-term exercise schedule, just keep on developing the stamina aspect of the 'Getting Fit' program, gradually increasing the intensity of the workout and always doing your strength and suppleness exercises before starting your chosen stamina exercise.

4. If you pass Fitness Test 1, and you decide to take up a vigorous exercise such as squash or football, carry on with the fitness exercises until you have reached the maximum stage in the Suppleness, Strength and Stamina sections. Now try Fitness Test 2. If you pass, you are ready to start your chosen activity, if not, just carry on with your schedule of suppleness, strength and stamina exercises until you can pass Fitness Test 2. Test yourself every three to four weeks.

FAT REDUCTION PROGRAM   P22/1

The calories, or energy, that you get from food are provided by the fat, protein and carbohydrate in your diet. The problem for most people is that they are getting too many calories from fat and too few from carbohydrate – it is this balance that needs to be changed.

On average we get over 40% of our calories from fat, but we should get only abut 35% or so. Cutting back on fatty foods isn't particularly difficult, but you need to be sensible so that you don't imbalance your diet by cutting out important foods altogether.

WOMEN/AGE	ACTIVITY LEVEL	MAX GRAMS/DAY
15-17	Average	80g
18-54	Average	80g
18-54	Very active	100g
55-74	Average	70g
75+	Average	65g
Any age	If pregnant	90g
Any age	If breastfeeding	110g
MEN/AGE	**ACTIVITY LEVEL**	**MAX GRAMS/DAY**
15-17	Average	110g
18-34	Sedentary	100g
18-34	Moderately active	110g
18-34	Very active	130g
35-64	Sedentary	90g
35-64	Moderately active	110g
35-64	Very active	130g
65-74	Average	90g
75+	Average	80g

Where the Fat Comes From

Most of the fat we eat comes from one of three sources: dairy foods, meat and meat products (such as pies and patés) and fats and oils. On average we get 30% of our fat from dairy foods – 12% milk, 11% butter, 7% cheese; 27% from meat and meat products; 26% from oils and fats – 13% oils, 13% margarine and spreads; and 6% from cakes, pastries and biscuits. The remaining 11% represents a little fat in each of a wide variety of foods.

How Much Fat Are You Eating?

Make a record of how many portions of each of the foods listed in the fat table you eat each day, and add up the fat totals for each section, and then for each day. Do this for about 5-7 days. Add the daily figures together and divide by the number of days, to give a rough guide to your average fat intake.

Cutting Back

Below, we give you some general guidelines for cutting back on fat, but you don't need to follow them all, only those that are appropriate to your diet and which seem easiest to accommodate in your lifestyle. You can use the fat tables to help you identify lower fat alternatives to higher fat foods, and to calculate roughly your fat intake as you try and reduce it. Column A = grams of fat per 100 grams of food; Column B = grams of fat per average portion, unless otherwise stated.

Fat Goals

The goal for fat in your diet depends on your calorie intake, which in turn depends on your sex, age and activity level. Select the appropriate goal from below.

Fat Table

CHEESE	A	B		MEAT	A	B
Cheddar-type	33.5	17		Roast chicken, meat & skin	13	15
Cheddar/low-fat	15-16	8				
Stilton	40	20		Roast chicken, meat only	5.5	6
Danish blue-type	29	15				
Parmesan	29.5	15		MEAT PRODUCTS		
Cream cheese	47.5	24		Corned beef	11	4
Edam	23	11		Ham	11	4
Camembert/brie	23	12		Salami	45	18
Processed cheese	25	12		Pate	32	13
Cheese spread	23	11		Beef sausage	17.5	20
Feta	20	10		Pork sausage	24.5	26
Cottage or curd	4	2		Fried beefburgers	17.5	20
				Steak & kidney pie	17	39
CREAM/YOGHURT						
Double cream	48	14		FISH		
Single cream	24	7		Baked/poached/ steamed/grilled white fish	1	1.3
Low-fat yoghurt	1	2				
Full-fat yoghurt	12	18				
Evaporated/ condensed milk	10	3		Fried cod in batter	14.5	24
Dairy ice cream	6.5	3		Fried plaice in breadcrumbs	13.5	23
Non-dairy ice cream	8	4				
				Fried whole herrings	20.5	29
MILK (per ½ pint)				Whole mackerel	33	32
Full-fat milk	11			Pilchards in sauce	5.5	6
Semi-skimmed	5.5			Canned salmon	8	9
Skimmed	0.3			Sardines in oil	18.5	20
				Tuna in oil	22	24
MEAT				Boiled prawns	22.5	14
Grilled lean bacon	19	15		Grilled trout	4.5	6
Fried lean bacon	22	17.5		Fried fish fingers	12.5	11
Stewed minced beef	15	18				
Stewing steak	11	13		FATS AND OILS		
Roast beef, lean & fat	21	25		Lard/dripping	100	30
Roast beef, lean only	9	11		Butter/margarines	80	6
Roast lamb, lean & fat	18	22		Low-fat spreads	40	3
Roast lamb, lean only	8	4		Deep-fried chips	10	14
Stewed lamb, scrag/neck, lean & fat	21	25		Oven chips	4	6
				Roast Potatoes	4.5	5
Stewed lamb, scrag/neck, lean only	15.5	19		Boiled/baked potatoes	0.1	0.1
Roast pork, lean & fat	20	24		Oils	100	28
Roast pork, lean only	7	8				
Pork chop	24	44				

NUTS	A	B
Almonds	53.5	27
Peanuts	49	25
CAKES/BISCUITS/PASTRIES		
Digestive biscuits	21	6
Chocolate cake + butter icing	31	26
Currant buns	75	3

CAKES/PASTRIES	A	B
Fruit cake	12.5	11
Jam tarts	13	5
Madeira cake	17	14
Apple pie	15.5	26
Cheesecake	10.5	12
Crisps	36	9

General Guidelines
For reducing the amount of fat gained from dairy products:

1. Use low-fat spreads in place of butter and margarine.

2. Use yoghurt in place of cream on puddings and in cooking sauces etc.

3. Use skimmed or semi-skimmed milk in place of full-fat milk, at least when preparing sauces and puddings. You can use full-fat milk in tea, coffee and on cereal, if you find you prefer the taste.

4. Buy lower fat cheeses or stronger tasting ones – you can use less when cooking and still get the flavour you like.

5. For reducing the amount of fat gained from meat and meat products:

   – Eat less meat, especially red meat, and more fish and poultry.

   – Buy leaner cuts of meat: you will be able to get by with using less, and you can increase the overall quantity by adding some extra vegetable or pulses (dried beans and peas).

   – Skim the fat off meat juices by using a double-spouted gravy boat, or by leaving the cooking juices to cool and taking off the fat that will settle on the surface.

   – Fry less, and braise, stew, steam, grill and bake more with no added fat.

   – Cut down on meat products generally.

For reducing the amount of fat gained from oil and fats:

1. Generally use oils and fats less – less frying in particular.

2. Cook vegetables in a tiny bit of water instead of frying, or use a non-stick pan for sweating onion etc.

3. Make lemon and yoghurt dressings for salads in place of oil-based ones.

For reducing the amount of fat gained from cakes and pastries:

Reduce the amount of cakes, biscuits, pasties and pastry that you eat, especially the manufactured types.

For reducing the amount of fat gained from saturates:

1. When cutting back on fats, it is also a good idea to reduce the amount of saturated fat you eat and increase the amount of polyunsaturated fat. Most of the fat found in dairy products, meat (especially red meat) and meat products and most margarines (unless labelled 'high in polyunsaturates') is saturated. Saturated fat is generally solid at room temperature. Polyunsaturated fats are found in vegetable oils, fish (especially oily fish) most nuts and a little in wholegrain cereals. In order to achieve a shift from saturated to polyunsaturted fats it is a good idea to eat more fish and poultry in place of red meat use a high-in-polyunsaturate margarine when baking use a high-in-polyunsaturate vegetable oil in salad dressing and in cooking.

2. Reduce your intake of processed high-fat foods such as cakes and biscuits. Manufacturers tend to use fats that are high-in-saturates.

3. Cut down on dairy products or use lower fat equivalents.

Reducing the Calories
Finally, if you successfully reduce your fat intake, you will also be reducing your calorie intake. Unless you need to lose weight (and no one can afford to do this indefinitely), you will need to replace those calories with other foods, and the best way to do that is with an increase in high-carbohydrate foods. Consult the FIBRE PROGRAM (P22/2).

FIBRE INTAKE PROGRAM   P22/2

It is estimated that on average British adults eat about 20 grams of fibre a day, but experts think we ought to be eating about 30 grams a day. Fibre is found in fruit and vegetables, beans, peas, lentils and cereals (for example, wheat, corn, rye, rice and all the products they are used to make, from flour and bread to breakfast cereals).

Fibre is a form of carbohydrate (the other types of carbohydrate are starch and sugar). Eating more fibre will necessarily mean eating more carbohydrate, if you want to increase your fibre intake, the first thing you need to do is forget all those old fashioned ideas about carbohydrate and starchy foods making you fat. To eat more fibre, you will need to eat more bread and potatoes.

The more unprocessed a food is, the nearer the original cereal grain, fruit or vegetable is the product, and the more fibre it will contain. So, for example, wholemeal bread and flour is less refined, and so contains more fibre than white bread and flour, as brown rice, wholemeal pasta and whole fruit and vegetables (as opposed to fruit juices and purées).

The fibre tables below give you fibre in grams for each 100 grams of a variety of foods, and for an average portion of each food. Use these tables to help you work out approximately how much fibre you are eating. Keep a record of how many portions of each food you have each day for about 5 to 7 days, add up the daily totals and then average them out. Then use the tables to work out how to adjust your fibre intake to meet your target of 30 grams a day. The middle column (**A**) shows grams of fibre per 100 grams of the food listed in the left-hand column; the right-hand column (**B**) shows grams of fibre in an average portion of the same food.

CEREALS	A	B
Bran-based cereals	25	10.5
All-bran	26	11
Puffed Wheat	15.4	6.5
Wheat Flakes	12	5
Muesli	7.4	5
Porridge Oats	7.7	5.5
Shredded Wheat	11.2	4.5
Ready Brek	7.6	3
Weetabix	9.3	4
Grapenuts	7	5
Rice Krispies	6	1.5
Special K	5.5	1.5
Sugar Puffs	6.1	1.5
Cornflakes	7	2

BREAD	A	B
White bread	4.1	1
Brown bread	6.4	2
Wholemeal and rye bread	8.5	2.5
Wholemeal flour	8.1	2.5
White flour	4	1

RICE/PASTA	A	B
Brown rice	4.5	2.5
White rice	2.5	0.5
Pasta	3	2
Wholewheat pasta	10	6

FRUIT	A	B
Apples and Pears	2	3.5
Bananas	2.4	6
Oranges/Tangerines	2	3.5
Blackberries	3	8
Cherries	1.7	2
Blackcurrants	8.7	10
Gooseberries	3.2	3.5
Grapes	0.4	0.5
Peaches	1.4	1.5
Plums	2.1	1.5
Raspberries	7.4	8.5
Strawberries	2.2	2.5
Rhubarb	2.6	3
Melon	1	1.5
Raisins/Sultanas	6.8	3.5
Dates	8.7	5
Prunes	16.1	9

NUTS		
Hazel Nuts	6.1	3
Peanuts	8.1	4
Almonds	14.3	7
Walnuts	5.2	2.5

VEGETABLES		
Broccoli	3	3.5
Spinach	6.3	7
Cabbage	3.4	3.5
Sprouts and runner beans	2.9	4
Cauliflower	1.8	2
Peas	5.2	4.7
Sweetcorn kernals	6	6.5
Most root vegetables	3	3.5
Carrots	2.9	3
Leeks	3.1	1
Onions	2.5	1
Lettuce	1.5	0.5
Tomatoes	1.5	1
Beansprouts	3	2
Cucumber	0.4	0.1

VEGETABLES	A	B
Mushrooms	2.5	1.5
Potatoes (baked with skin)	2	4
Chips	1	1.5
Potatoes (boiled or mashed)	1	1
Lentils	3.7	4
Baked beans	7.3	10
Kidney beans	8	9
Broad beans	4.2	4.5
Butter beans	5.1	5.5
Chick peas	6.0	6.5

BISCUITS/CAKES		
Digestive biscuits	5.1	1.5
Rich Tea biscuits	2.3	0.5
Crispbread	11.7	3.5
Ginger biscuits	2.0	0.5
Oatcakes	4.0	1
Water biscuits/crackers	3.0	1
Sponge cake	1.0	0.5
Fruit cake	2.8	2

General Guidelines

1. *Bread* – eat more of it, especially wholemeal bread. Have thinner slices, but don't use this as an excuse to eat more high-calorie, high-fat toppings and fillings for sandwiches.

2. *Breakfast cereals* – choose a high fibre variety of cereal and no sugar toppings. Cereals make a good snack food – they certainly don't have to be reserved for the breakfast table.

3. *Fruit* – use fruit as a snack food, instead of sugary, salty and fatty snacks such as chocolate biscuits, peanuts and crisps. Make fruit based puddings, using dried fruit as a sweetener, in place of sugar.

4. *Vegetables* – eat more vegetables, preferably fresh, and only lightly cooked, in their skins where appropriate. Steaming vegetables leaves more flavour and they remain crisp and usually nicer for it. Ring the changes by using herbs and spices in your vegetable cooking. Chopped fresh herbs served on top of potatoes and green vegetables, for example. Baked potatoes in their jackets are a good way to increase your fibre intake.

5. *Rice* – use the brown variety, not just with a hot main meal, but also in salads and rice puddings.

6. *Pasta* – wholewheat pastas with sauces, but again also in salads.

7. *Flour* – use wholemeal flour in baking and cooking, even in sauce thickening, in place of white flour.

8. *Beans, peas and lentils* – add them to stews and soups in place of some of the meat that you might normally use. They are also good for salads.

9. *Vegetarian cooking* – buy a new cookery book and experiment; a vegetarian book should give you some new ideas about preparing high-fibre foods.

SUGAR REDUCTION PROGRAM   P22/3

Amazingly, very little is known about how much sugar we eat and which foods it comes from. The best estimates are that about a third comes from packet sugar (used in tea, coffee and home baking), probably up to a half comes in processed foods of one sort or another (such as jams, soft drinks, ice creams and biscuits) and the remainder is found naturally in fruit, vegetables and dairy foods (milk contains natural sugar).

Perhaps the most difficult thing in cutting back is the thought of acclimatising your palate to less sweet tastes; tea and coffee on their own, for example, can taste very bitter if you are used to taking them sweetened. But if you persevere, you will find that your taste preference changes after a few weeks.

Because much of the sugar we eat comes from processed foods (and there aren't always accurate figures for the sugar content of these), it is difficult to provide a table that will inform you accurately about how much sugar you are eating. However, the table below shows which foods contain a lot of sugar and which don't. The middle column **A** shows grams of sugar per 100 grams of the food listed in the left-hand column; the right-hand column **B** shows grams of sugar in an average portion of the same food.

Sugar Table

CEREALS	A	B		A	B
All Bran	15.4	7	Shredded Wheat	0.4	-
Cornflakes	7.4	2	Special K	9.6	3
Muesli	26.2	18	Sugar Puffs	56.5	16
Puffed Wheat	1.5	1	Weetabix	6.1	3
Rice Krispies	9	3			

BISCUITS/CAKES		
Coated biscuits	43.4	12
Digestive biscuits	16.4	5
Choc digestive biscuits	28.5	8
Ginger biscuits	35.8	10
Sandwich biscuits	30.2	8
Wafer biscuits	44.7	13
Shortbread	17.2	5
Fruit cake	54.2	47
Sponge cake	30.5	15
Doughnuts	15	5
Jam tarts	37.5	15
Puddings	10-30	17-51
Apple crumble	23.8	32
Fruit pie	30.9	53
Ice cream	22.6	11
Plain yoghurt	6.2	9
Fruit yoghurt	17.9	27

FRUIT		
Apples	11.8	20
Bananas	16.2	28
Dried apricots	43.4	24
Apricots canned in syrup	27.7	31
Cherries	11.9	13
Dates	63.9	36
Fruit salad canned in syrup	25	28
Grapes	15.5	18
Melon	5.3	7
Nectarines	12.4	14
Oranges	8.5	14
Peaches	9.1	10
Peaches canned in syrup	22.9	26
Pineapple	11.6	20
Pineapple canned in syrup	20.2	34
Plums	9.6	11
Prunes	40.3	23

FRUIT	A	B
Raisins	64.4	36
Sultanas	64.7	36

SWEETS/PRESERVES		
Sugar	100	5
Golden syrup	79	8
Honey	76.4	8
Jam/marmalade	69	7
Chocolate	56-60	28-30
Chocolate filled sweets	65.8	20
Liquorice/toffee, etc	60-70	18-21

DRINKS		
Drinking chocolate	73.8	9
Cola	10.5	35
Lemonade	5.6	10
Juice/orange/grapefruit	8	12
Tonic water	8.5	14.2
Ribena, diluted	1.4	26
Orange drink, diluted	1.4	30
Beer	1.5-3	4-9
Dry wine	2	2
Medium dry wine	5.8	7
Sweet white wine	9.2	11
Port	12	6
Dry sherry	1.5	1
Sweet sherry	7	4
Liqueurs	28-32	7-8

SAUCES/PICKLES		
Chutney	40-50	8-10
Ketchup	22.9	4
Brown sauce	23.1	4

PROCESSED FOODS		
Baked Beans	5.8	8
Tomato Soup	2.6	6

General Guidelines

1. Concentrate on reducing the amount of processed foods and packet sugar in your diet, rather than cutting back on fruit, vegetables and dairy foods, which contain only natural sugars — there is so much other nutrititional value to be gained from these.

2. *Tea and coffee* — cut out or reduce sugar in these drinks. If you really need to replace the sweetness with something try an artificial sweetener, but have a go with nothing at all for a couple of weeks.

3. *Soft drinks* – reduce your consumption of drinks such as squash and lemonade, tonic water and cola drinks. Drink low-calorie versions instead, and switch to calorie-free mineral waters, or fruit juice let down with water.

4. *Sweets and chocolates* – cut these out altogether for preference. If you like them too much to cut them right out, begin by reducing your intake. Set a limit of say three chocolate bars in a week. If you do eat sweets, it is better for your teeth to do so after a meal, rather than between meals. Eat fresh fruit and/or raw vegetables as nibbles between meals, in place of sweets, chocolates, cakes and biscuits. See P5 if you need to break a habit.

5. *Processed foods* – cut down on high sugar processed foods like cakes and biscuits, sugary puddings and ice cream. Look for low-sugar alternatives such as low-sugar jams, fruit canned in its own juice (instead of syrup) and baked beans without sugar.

6. *Cooking* – you can often reduce the amount of sugar suggested in recipes, unless the action of the sugar is essential to the recipe itself (for example when making caramel). In cakes and biscuits, home-made ice creams and other puddings, you can probably use about half the sugar that's suggested. When sweetness is esential (for example, when stewing cooking apples), try using dried fruit or honey as a sweetening agent, instead of packet sugar.

SALT REDUCTION PROGRAM   P22/4

The potentially harmful ingredient in salt is sodium. Some sodium is assimilated into our bodies from sources other than salt, for example monosodium glutamate.

There is very little sodium naturally present in food; most sodium that we eat is added in the food manufacturing process. It is estimated that only about 12% of the salt we eat is added by way of seasoning. These factors make cutting back our intake of salt a bit tricky – because it necessarily involves eating less of the processed, more convenient foods on which many people depend.

It is estimated that of the salt we eat: 12% is added in cooking at home and at the table; 36% comes from cereal products – bread and breakfast cereals, for example; 24% from meat and eggs – mostly from meat products and cured and smoked meats; 14% from cheese, cream and fats, mostly in cheese production, and from salt added to butter and margarine; 6% from milk – there is naturally very little in milk, but we drink quite a lot of it; 6% from vegetables – mostly added in the processing; and 2% from fish – mostly from smoked fish and shellfish.

Accurate figures for the salt content of processed foods are not available. Since these foods contribute such a large proportion of salt to the average diet, it is difficult to work out how much salt one is consuming. Nevertheless the tables below should help to give you some comparison of the salt content of different foods – which are higher and which are lower in salt content. The tables give the sodium content of foods. Column **A** shows mg of sodium per 100 grams of food; Column **B**, mg per average unless otherwise stated. The sodium content of the 7-10 grams of salt which, on average, we eat each day, is about 3,400 milligrams. It is generally thought that it would be a good idea to reduce this amount by at least 1,000 mg – a greater reduction would probably no bad thing. The general guidelines given below will help you to reduce your own salt intake.

Salt Table

CEREALS	A	B
All-bran	1670	700
Cornflakes	1160	325
Muesli	180	125
Rice Krispies	1110	30
Special K	880	245
Weetabix	360	150

BREAD		
White/brown/ wholemeal	525-560	165

BISCUITS	A	B
Digestive/plain/ chocolate	440	125
Semi-sweet	410	115
Fully coated chocolate	160	45
Cream crackers	610	170
Rye crispbread	220	60
Oatcakes	1230	345
Water biscuits	470	132

CAKES	A	B
Butter iced chocolate	440	375
Fruit cake	170	145
Madeira	380	325

MEAT PRODUCTS		
Grilled bacon	2404	1925

MEAT PRODUCTS	A	B
Individual pork pie	720	935
Sausages	1085	1195
Ham	1405	560
Paté	762	305
Salami	1850	740
Beefburgers	880	970
Sausage roll	550	330

DAIRY PRODUCTS		
Salted butter	780	55
Unsalted butter	12	1
Margarine	800	55
Low-fat spread	690	50
Brie/Camembert	1410	705
Cheddar-type	610	305
Danish Blue	1420	710
Edam	980	490
Stilton	1150	575
Cottage cheese	450	225
Processed	1360	680
Cheese spread	1170	585
Feta	1260	630
Milk (per ½ pint)	140	

VEGETABLES	A	B
Canned sweetcorn	270	300
Baked beans	480	670
Tomato soup	460	1105
Canned peas	380	340

FISH	A	B	SNACKS	A	B
Smoked haddock	1220	1710	Salted peanuts	440	220
Fish fingers	320	270	Salted crisps	550	140
Tinned pilchards	370	405			
Sardines in oil	650	715	SAUCES/PICKLES		
Tuna in oil	420	460	Tomato ketchup	1120	190
Prawns	1590	955	Sweet pickle	1700	340

Unprocessed flours and cereals contain only a trace of sodium. Vegetables, meat, fish and eggs in themselves contain virtually no sodium.

General Guidelines

1. *Tinned foods* – eat less or select low-salt versions such as tinned vegetables with no added salt, fish in oil instead of brine.

2. *Snack foods* – reduce the quantity of salty snack foods you eat, such as peanuts and crisps. Most of these foods are also high in fat. They can be replaced with higher fibre snacks like raw fruit and vegetables.

3. *Smoked and pickled foods* – eat less of these. Use just for flavour rather than as a main item in a meal. Buy unsmoked bacon and ham.

4. *Biscuits and cereals* – select low-salt versions.

5. *Cooking* – don't add salt to vegetable cooking water. Steam vegetables to maximise the flavour and keep crisp. Use herbs and spices to flavour meals instead of salt.

6. *Eating* – take the salt cellar off the table, or buy one with very small holes in it. Never add salt until you have tasted your food.

7. Cutting back on salt could make your food taste bland, at least for the first few weeks, but your palate will soon adjust to a lower sodium diet.

VITAMIN AND MINERAL INTAKE PROGRAM   P22/5

Vitamin A
This vitamin is found in carrots, dark green or yellow and orange fruit and vegetables (although not in oranges), margarine and butter, animal and fish liver and kidneys, eggs, and fish liver oils.

Your body can store Vitamin A from one week to the next, so it isn't necessary to eat your daily allowance each day. A daily allowance of 750-1,500mcg is variously recommended in different countries. 750mcg can be achieved by eating one portion of cheese, two portions of green vegetables, one portion of fruit and three portions of butter or margarine. In addition one portion of liver will give you the equivalent of 29 days supply of Vitamin A, and a portion of carrots gives three days supply. Column **A** shows mcg of Vitamin A per 100 grams of food; column **B**, mcg per average portion.

VITAMIN A TABLE	A	B
Cheddar cheese	363	180
Eggs	190	114 (1 egg)
Lambs liver	19900	21890
Pigs kidney	160	175
Mackerel	45	65
Butter	985	70
Margarine	800	55
Cabbage	50	55
Spinach	1000	1100
Peas	50	45
Watercress	500	150
Carrots	2000	2200
Tomatoes	100	60
Dried apricots	600	335
Peaches	500	550
Full-fat milk (per ½ pint)	155	

Vitamin B1 – Thiamin

Good sources of this vitamin are milk, liver and kidneys, pork, eggs, vegetables, fruit, wholegrain breakfast cereals (some have B1 added in the processing). But this vitamin is easily lost in cooking, so the contribution that foods such as cooked fruit and vegetables make to the average diet is fairly small.

A generally accepted daily allowance is about 1-1.5mg a day (depending on calorie intake). Your body can't store this vitamin, so you need to establish a reasonable intake each day.

1.2mg can be found in the following foods: three portions of wholemeal bread, one portion of cereal, one piece of raw fruit, one portion of milk, two portions of vegetables. But since this vitamin is easily lost in cooking, you would need to cook very carefully or eat more than this amount to ensure 1.2mg or more was available to your body. Vitamin B1 is lost to vegetables in the boiling process (so steaming helps to maximise the vitamin content). Meat juices also contain a lot of B1, as do the liquids in which foods are canned. To maximise B1 intake, these fluids should be used in the cooking process. Column **A** shows mg of Vitamin B, per 100 grams of food; column **B**, mg per average portion.

VITAMIN B1 TABLE	A	B
Bacon	0.45	0.36
Beef	0.6	0.07
Chicken	0.11	0.13
Pork	0.57	0.69
Peas	0.32	0.29
Potatoes	0.2	0.24
Kidney beans	0.54	0.59
Oranges	0.1	0.17
Peanuts	0.23	0.12
White bread	0.21	0.06
Wholemeal bread	0.34	0.1
Cornflakes (added vitamins)	1.8	0.5
Rice	0.41	0.25
Muesli	0.33	0.23
Milk (per ½ pint)	0.14	

Vitamin B2 – Riboflavin

Good sources of this vitamin are milk, meat, dairy foods, eggs and cereals, including fortified breakfast cereals.

A daily allowance of 1.3 to 1.8mg will be sufficient, but it needs to be a daily allowance, because your body can't store this vitamin. 1.2mg of this vitamin is given in the followimg combination of foods: one portion of milk, one portion of meat, three portions of wholemeal bread, one portion of cereal, one portion of cheese.

Vitamin B2 is lost in water and in light, so foods should be stored in the dark and liquids produced by processing or cooking should be used in other cooking, eg in sauces. Column **A** shows mg of Vitamin B2 per 100 grams of food;   column **B**, mg per average portion.

VITAMIN B2 TABLE	A	B
Cheddar cheese	0.5	0.25
Beef	0.23	0.28
Chicken	0.13	0.16
Lambs liver	4.64	5.1
Eggs	0.47	0.28
Potatoes	0.02	
White bread	0.06	0.02
Wholemeal bread	0.08	0.02
Cabbage	0.03	0.03
Carrots	0.05	0.06
Muesli	0.33	0.23
Cereals (added vitamins)	1.6	0.45
Milk (per ½ pint)	0.47	

Niacin
Good sources are meat, cereals (including fortified breakfast cereals), and bread.

The suggested daily intake of this vitamin is between 15 and 20mg. 18mg of niacin is contained in the following foods: one portion of milk, one portion of cheese, one portion of potatoes, one portion of vegetables, three portions of wholemeal bread and one portion of meat, fish or pulses. Column **A** shows mg of niacin per 100 grams of food; column **B**, mg per average portion.

NIACIN TABLE	A	B
Cheddar cheese	6.2	3.1
Beef	8.5	8.6
Pork	7.2	13
Chicken	9.6	11.5
Fish	6	8.4
Eggs	3.7	2.2
Kidney beans	5.5	6.1
Peas	2.6	2.3
Potatoes	1.5	1.8
White bread	2.3	0.7
Wholemeal bread	1.8	0.5
Milk (per ½ pint)	2.5	

Vitamin B6
Good sources are liver, meat, fish, eggs, cereals, pulses and poultry. A generally accepted daily allowance for this vitamin is 2mg. 1.1mg can be found in the following foods: one portion of milk, one portion of vegetables, one portion of potatoes, one portion of fruit and three portions of wholemeal bread. **Women taking the contraceptive pill** may need more than the generally accepted intake and may find it difficult to get enough B6 from dietary sources. Vitamin pills containing B6 may in this case be a useful addition to dietary sources. Column **A** shows mg of Vitamin B6 per 100 grams of food; column **B**, mg per average portion.

VITAMIN B6 TABLE	A	B
Beef	0.27	0.3
Chicken	0.29	0.3
Turkey	0.44	0.5
Fish	0.29	0.4
Kidney beans	0.44	0.5
Peas	0.1	0.09
Potatoes	0.25	0.3
Oranges	0.06	0.1
Bananas	0.51	0.87
White bread	0.07	0.02
Wholemeal bread	0.12	0.04
Milk (per ½ pint)	0.17	

Vitamin B12

This vitamin is found only in animal products. The generally accepted requirement is set at 3mcg a day. 4.25mcg can be found in the following: one portion of milk, one portion of cheese, one portion of meat. So it is easy enough for meat eaters to maintain the required level. But, **vegetarians** need to pay particular attention to their intakes of this vitamin because it is only available from animal food sources. **Vegans** are likely to be deficient unless they take vitamin B12 supplements. Column **A** shows mcg of Vitamin B12 per 100 grams of food; column **B**, mcg per average portion.

VITAMIN B12 TABLE	A	B
Cheddar cheese	1.5	0.75
Eggs	1.7	1.0
Meat	2.02.4	
Fish	2.0	2.8
Cereals (added vitamins)	1.7	0.5
Milk (per ½ pint)	1.1	

Folic Acid

Folic acid is not found in great quantities in any foods, but most foods contain a little. In particular this is found in offal, green leafy vegetables, most fruit and vegetables, meat and dairy products. A recommended daily allowance for folic acid was set by the British Government at 300mcg a day, but it has since been declared too high. In other countries a level of 400mcg has been set. Very little is known either about our requirements for this vitamin or the content of folic acid in foods. The figures given below are based on the total amount of folic acid found in these foods, but it is thought that some of this may not be usable by our bodies. 285mcg of folic acid can be found in two portions of green vegetables, one portion of potatoes, one portion of fruit and three portions of wholemeal bread, but whether our bodies can utilise all this folic acid is not clear. What's more, folic acid is easily lost in cooking, especially in boiling vegetables. Steaming, using only small quantities of water and re-using the liquid in a sauce of some description, will help to maximise intakes of this vitamin. Column **A** shows mcg of folic acid per 100 grams of food; column **B**, mcg per average portion.

FOLIC ACID TABLE	A	B
Liver	240	264
Cabbage	50	55
Peas	78	70
Peanuts	110	66
Oranges	37	63
Potatoes	10	11
White bread	27	8
Wholemeal bread	39	12
Sprouts	110	121
Broccoli	110	121

Vitamin C

Vitamin C is found most concentrated in fruit, vegetables and milk.

The British recommended daily allowance for this vitamin is 30mg a day per person. But in other countries the recommended level is set at anything up to twice this amount. 30mg can be found in a combination of the following food: one portion of potatoes, one portion of green vegetables, one piece of fruit and a glass of orange juice.

Vitamin C is lost in cooking and it is also lost when food is stored in the light. New potatoes eaten soon after digging, contain up to three times the vitamin C content of old potatoes that have been stored for six months or so. To maximise the Vitamin C content of fruit and vegetables, store them in the dark and for as short a time as possible; when cooking, steam them (using the resulting liquids for cooking sauces etc); prepare fruit and vegetables just before cooking and don't soak in water to cleanse. Column **A** shows mg of Vitamin C per 100 grams of food; column **B**, mg per average portion.

VITAMIN C TABLE	A	B
Sprouts	40*	44*
Cabbage	20*	22*
Cauliflower	20*	22*
Lettuce	15	2
Peppers	100	30
Potatoes	5-9*	6-11*
Tomatoes	20	12
Apples	5	8.5
Bananas	10	17
Blackcurrants	200	170
Grapefruit	40	68
Oranges	50	85
Orange juice	35+	50+

*indicates cooked state

Vitamin E

This vitamin is found in vegetable oils, wholegrain cereals, eggs and meat.

The generally accepted recommended daily allowance is 10-12mg. You would get this amount by using at least some vegetable oil, and since the vitamin can be stored in your body from one week to the next, you don't need to eat the recommended amount each day. Column **A** shows mg of Vitamin E per 100 grams of food; column **B**, mg per average portion.

VITAMIN E TABLE	A	B
Wholemeal bread	0.2	0.06
Cornflakes	0.4	0.1
Muesli	3.2	2.2
Rice	0.3	0.2
Eggs	1.6	1
Beef	0.31	0.4
Pork	0.03	0.04
Chicken	0.11	0.13
Polyunsaturate vegetable oils (2 tblspns)	15.5	

Iron

Iron is found in meat, poultry, cereals, bread, seafood, kidneys, liver, vegetables and potatoes in usefully large amounts. A daily allowance of 10-15mg should be enough. **Women during menstruation** require an intake at the higher end of the scale. But you don't need to eat this amount every day, because your body stores iron. Around 10mg iron can be found in the following combinations of foods: three portions of wholemeal bread, one portion of cereal, one portion of fish or meat, one portion of milk, two portions of vegetables and one portion of potatoes. But iron can be difficult for the body to absorb, so you need to eat more than the amount shown to provide your body with 10mg of iron that is available for use. Column **A** shows mg of iron per 100 grams of food; column **B**, mg per average portion.

IRON TABLE	A	B
Eggs	2	1.2
Beef	1.9	2.3
Chicken	0.7	0.8
Pigs kidney	6.4	7
Lambs liver	7.5	8.3
White fish	0.5	0.7
Oily fish	1	1.4
Cabbage	0.6	0.7
Potatoes	0.4	0.5
Dried apricots	4.1	2.5
White bread	1.6	0.5
Wholemeal bread	2.7	0.8
Cornflakes (added vitamins)	6.7	1.9
Kidney beans	6.7	7.4
Peas	1.2	1.1
Peanuts	2	1
Muesli	4.6	3.2
Milk (per ½ pint)	0.3	

Calcium

Calcium is found in reasonably large amounts in dairy products and bread (to which, in Britain, it is added to meet the requirements of regulations).

In Britain the recommended daily allowance is 300mg, but other authorities recommend up to about 500mg a day. **Pregnant and lactating women** need more, about 1,200mg a day.

One portion of milk, full fat or skimmed, gives 300mg calcium. Add a portion of any other dairy product and you will reach 500mg. Pregnant women may need to take calcium supplements to reach their required levels, or drink a lot of milk. Column **A** shows mg of calcium per 100 grams of food; column **B**, mg per average portion.

CALCIUM TABLE	A	B
Yoghurt	200	300
Cheddar cheese	800	400
Eggs	52	30
White fish	22	30
Sardines in oil	550	605
White bread	105	45
Wholemeal bread	54	15
Milk (per ½ pint)	285	

Phosphorus

This mineral is available in all foods and a deficiency is unknown.

Potassium

This mineral is found particularly in green vegetables, fruit, nuts, seafood and meat. There is no generally accepted recommended daily allowance for this mineral, but deficiency is unknown.

POTASSIUM TABLE	A	B
Cheddar cheese	120	60
Eggs	136	80
Beef	330	395
Pork	360	610
Chicken	290	430
White fish	300	420
Potatoes	360	430
Cauliflower	300	330
Peas	100	90
Tomatoes	290	175
Oranges	180	305
White bread	110	35
Wholemeal bread	230	70
Milk (per ½ pint)	385	

Magnesium
This mineral is plentiful in most foods, especially vegetables and cereals. Deficiency is very rare indeed, and only occurs when someone has had very acute diarrhoea for an extended period of time, in which case your doctor should advise you to take some sort of supplement.

Zinc
This mineral is found in reasonably large amount in meat, dairy products and cereals. In addition there is a little zinc in a large range of other foods.

A generally accepted daily allowance of this mineral is 15mg. One portion of milk, one portion of cheese, one portion of meat or fish, one portion of potatoes, three portions of wholemeal bread, one portion of cereal and two portions of green vegetables will give you 8.5mg. Quantities of zinc, found in small amounts in a wide range of other foods will boost this figure, but this is one mineral where taking supplements in the form of tablets may be useful. Column **A** shows mg of zinc per 100 grams of food; column **B**, mg per average portion.

ZINC TABLE	A	B
Cheddar cheese	4	2
Beef	3.8	4.6
Chicken	1.1	1.3
White fish	0.4	0.6
Eggs	1.5	0.9
Potatoes	0.3	0.4
White bread	0.6	0.2
Wholemeal bread	1.8	0.5
Sardines	3	3.3
Peanuts	3	1.5
Cornflakes	0.3	0.8
Muesli	2.2	1.5
Kidney beans	2.8	3.1
Carrots	0.4	0.4
Peas	0.7	0.6
Cabbage	0.2	0.2
Milk (per ½ pint)	1.1	

USEFUL ADDRESSES

AIDS

The Terrence Higgins Trust
BM AIDS, London. WC1N 3XX
Telephone: 01 242 1010 (Helpline) 15.00 – 22.00 every day

AIDS Information Service
(D.H.S.S.)
Telephone: 01 407 5522 or 0800 535535 (Freephone 24 hours)

Body Positive
C/o Terrence Higgins Trust, BM AIDS, London. WC1N 3XX.
Telephone: 01 831 0330
Support for people who are HIV antibody positive and their partners and friends.

Gay Bereavement Project
Telephone: 01 837 7324

London Lighthouse
178 Lancaster Road, London, W11 1QU.
Telephone: 01-221 6513.

National Advisory Service on AIDS
Telephone: 0800 567123: 10.00 – 22.00 seven days a week.

ALCOHOL

Al-Anon Family Groups UK and Eire
61 Great Dover Street, London SE1 4YF
Telephone: 01 403 0888
A fellowship of relatives and close friends of alcoholics who share their experience in an attempt to solve the problems of living with a problem drinker.

Alcoholics Anonymous
P.O. Box 514, 11 Redcliffe Gardens, London SW10 9BQ
Telephone: 01 352 9779
A fellowship of men and women who share their experience, strength and hope with each other, to solve their common problem and help others to recover from Alcoholism.

ALLERGY

AAA (Action Against Allergy)
43 The Downs, London SW20 8HG
Telephone: 01 947 5082
Provides advice and information and refers to doctors.

British Migraine Association
178A High Road, Byfleet, Weybridge, Surrey. KT14 7ED
Telephone: 91 52468
Campaigns and provides a line of communication between Migraine sufferers
and the world of medicine and research.

National Eczema Society
Tavistock House North, Tavistock Square, London WC1H 9SR
Telephone: 01 388 4097
For people with Eczema and their relatives. Also local groups.

Asthma Society and Friends of Asthma Research Council
300 Upper Street, London N1 2XX
Telephone: 01 226 2260

ANOREXIA

Anorexic Aid
The Priory Centre, 11 Priory Road, High Wycombe, Bucks, HP13 6SL
Telephone: 0494 21431
Support and information to sufferers from Anorexia and Bulimia Nervosa and
their families through self-help groups organised regionally by 'contacts'.

Anorexia Anonymous
45A Castlenau, Barnes, London SW13
Telephone: 01 748 4587/3994
Advice for treatment of Anorexia and Bulimia Nervosa.

National Information Centre for Anorexic Family Aid
Sackville Place, 44/8 Magdalen Street, Norwich NR3 1JP
Telephone: 0603 621414
Help and information.

ANXIETY AND DEPRESSION

Depressives Anonymous
36 Chestnut Avenue, Beverley, North Humberside HU17 9QU
Mutual aid national organisation for those with Depression, or who have
experienced Depression.

Friends by Post
6 Bollin Court, Macclesfield Road, Wilmslow, Cheshire
SK9 2AP
Fights loneliness by linking like-minded people of similar age and
background.

Open Door Association
447 Pensby Road, Heswall, Wirral, Merseyside L61 9PQ
Advice and information for sufferers from Anxiety and Agoraphobia.
Postal contact only, please enclose s.a.e.

Samaritans
17 Uxbridge Road, Slough SL1 1SN
Exists to help the suicidal and despairing. Branches all over the country
advertise a telephone number, most telephones being manned 24 hours a
day, 7 days a week. Callers may also visit practically every branch any day or
evening of the week. The service is free and completely confidential.

TRANX (Tranquillizer Recovery and New Existence)
25A Masons Avenue, Harrow, Middlesex
Telephone: 01 427 2065
Support and advice for people wishing to come off medically prescribed minor
tranquillizers and sleeping pills.

ARTHRITIS AND RHEUMATISM

Arthritis Care
6 Grosvenor Crescent, London, SW1X 7ER
Telephone: 01 235 0902/5
Provides information, advice and financial grants, holiday centres, self-
catering units, a visiting service for the housebound and over 340 branches
throughout the UK.

BEREAVEMENT

Compassionate Friends
6 Denmark Street, Bristol BS1 5DQ
Telephone: 0272 292778
Self-help group of bereaved parents who, by visiting, writing and holding
area gatherings attempt to help newly-bereaved parents to come to terms
with their situation.

Cruse (National Organisation for the Widowed and their Children)
Cruse House, 126 Sheen Road, Richmond, Surrey, TW9 1UR
Telephone: 01 940 4818/9047
Counselling service.

DIABETES

British Diabetic Association
10 Queen Anne Street, London W1M OBD
Telephone: 01 323 1531
Information and welfare service and a wide range of literature on all aspects
of diabetes. Runs educational and activity holidays for children and adults and
holds teach-in weekends for diabetic children and their families. Over 300
local branches and groups throughout the U.K.

DISABILITY AND HANDICAP

Disabled Living Foundation
380-384 Harrow Road, London W9 2HU
Telephone: 01 289 6111
Answers enquiries on the daily living problems of disabled people.

Disablement Income Group
Attlee House, 28 Commercial Street, London E1 6LR
Telephone 01 247 2128/6877
Promotes economic and general welfare of all disabled people.

Disability Advice Centre (North Tyneside)
17 Wellington Street, North Shields, Tyne and Wear
NE29 6PS

DRUGS

Narcotics Anonymous
P.O. Box 246, London SW10 ODP
Telephone: 01 351 6794/6066/6067
A fellowship of men and women who meet regularly to help each other stay
clear from mood-altering chemicals.

Release
347A Upper Street, London N1 OPD
Telephone: 01 837 5602 (office hours)
          01 603 8654 (emergency 24-hour service)
Provides advice, information and referral to those with problems (including
legal difficulties) related to drug-taking or dependence. Runs a 24-hour
emergency legal service.

South Wales Association for the Prevention of Addiction
111 Cowbridge Road East, Cardiff, CF1 9AG
Telephone: 0222 26113
24-hour counselling, advice and information service.

Turning Point
CAP House, 9-12 Long Lane, London EC1A
Telephone: 01 906 3947
Counselling, rehabilitation centres. Also for alcohol abuse.

FEMALE DISORDERS AND PROBLEMS

National Association for Premenstrual Syndrome
25 Market Street, Guildford, Surrey
Telephone: 0483 572715 (Daytime Helpline: 0483 572806)

Understanding Women
6 Hillside Cottages, Leverstock Green, Hemel Hempstead, Herts.
Telephone: 0442 63289
Offers understanding and support to PMT sufferers.

Pre-Menstrual Tension Advisory Service
P.O. Box 268, Hove, East Sussex
Telephone: 0273 771366

Women's Health Concern
WHC Flat, 17 Earls Terrace, London W8 6LP
Telephone: 01 602 6669
Provides advice to women on how to seek treatment and other help for their gynaecological and obstetric disorders.

Women's Health Information Centre
52/54 Featherstone Street, London EC1Y 8RT
Telephone: 01 251 6580
National information and resource centre on women's health.

Mastectomy Association
26 Harrison Street, Gray's Inn Road, King's Cross, London WC1H 8JG
Non-medical advice and support to women who are about to have or have had a mastectomy.

HERPES

Herpes Association
41 North Road, London N7 9DP
Telephone: 01 609 9061
Information and advice. Telephone Help-line (number as above). Strictly confidential service.

INFERTILITY

CHILD
'Farthings', Gaunts Road, Pawlett, Nr Bridgwater, Somerset
Telephone: 0278 683595
Assists those with infertility problems.

National Association for the Childless
Birmingham Settlement, 318 Summer Lane, Birmingham, B19 3RL
Telephone: 021 359 4887
Support and information.

KIDNEY DISEASE

British Kidney Patient Association
B.K.P.A. Bordon, Hampshire
Telephone: 042 03 2021/2
Deals with material and physical needs of patients and their relatives. Lobbies for more facilities so that all patients requiring treatment can receive it. Provides holiday dialysis facilities both here and abroad.

MOTHERHOOD

National Childbirth Trust
9 Queensborough Terrace, London W2 3TB
Telephone: 01 221 3833
Ante-natal preparation and classes. Breastfeeding counselling and post-natal
support.

MAMA (Meet-A-Mum Association)
3 Woodside Avenue,
London SE25 5DW
Telephone 01 654 3137

Hyperactive Children's Support Group
59 Meadowside, Angmering, Nr Littlehampton, West Sussex
To help parents cope with their hyperactive child.

Association for Post-Natal Illness
7 Gowan Avenue, Fulham, London SW6 6RH
Puts depressed mothers into contact by telephone with women who have
suffered and recovered from the illness.

Miscarriage Association
18 Stoneybrook Close, West Bretton, Wakefield, Yorkshire WF4 4TP
Telephone: 092 485 515
Support, help and information.

SANDS (Stillbirth and Neonatal Death Society)
28 Portland Place, London W1N 3DE
Telephone: 01 436 5881
Aims: to co-ordinate a national network of befriending parents.

MYALGIC ENCEPHALOMYELITIS

ME
Sue Finley
P.O. Box 1, Carnwath, Lanark ML11 8NH

SEXUAL PROBLEMS

Albany Trust
24 Chester Square, London SW1W 9HS
Telephone: 01 730 5871
Counsels people with sexual and relationship problems.

SPINAL/BACK PROBLEMS

Back Problems
20 Redhill Drive, Fishponds, Bristol BS1 2AQ
Collects useful information from patients to be shared for all to benefit.